D1714575

# Navigation by Judgment

# Navigation by Judgment

*Why and When Top-Down Management
of Foreign Aid Doesn't Work*

DAN HONIG

OXFORD
UNIVERSITY PRESS

# OXFORD
UNIVERSITY PRESS

Oxford University Press is a department of the University of Oxford. It furthers
the University's objective of excellence in research, scholarship, and education
by publishing worldwide. Oxford is a registered trade mark of Oxford University
Press in the UK and certain other countries.

Published in the United States of America by Oxford University Press
198 Madison Avenue, New York, NY 10016, United States of America.

Library of Congress Cataloging-in-Publication Data
Names: Honig, Dan, 1981– author.
Title: Navigation by judgment : why and when top down management of
foreign aid doesn't work / Dan Honig.
Description: New York, NY : Oxford University Press, [2018] | Includes bibliographical references.
Identifiers: LCCN 2017040300 | ISBN 9780190672454 (hardcover) | ISBN 9780190672478 (epub)
Subjects: LCSH: Economic assistance—Developing countries. | Economic development projects—
Developing countries—Management.
Classification: LCC HC60 .H6664 2018 | DDC 338.9109172/4—dc23
LC record available at https://lccn.loc.gov/2017040300

1 3 5 7 9 8 6 4 2

Printed by Sheridan Books, Inc., United States of America

Cover photo is courtesy of Marty Luster, who in sending the photo wrote
"Please include the usual photo credit in any commercial use"

*For Vivian Esther Sloan Honig,*
*who taught me to ask "Why?"*

CONTENTS

# PREFACE

Friedrich Hayek and James Scott are not often seen as kindred intellectual spirits. Hayek, often associated with the Chicago school of economics , is one of the intellectual fonts of modern libertarianism; Jim Scott is an anthropologist and political scientist recently described as a "Marxist (of the American academic type)."[1] Hayek and Scott share at least one intellectual position, however. Both Scott and Hayek agree that top-down control is unlikely to produce the best outcomes, particularly when the individuals at the top do not have all the relevant information.[2]

Conventional wisdom is that when it comes to economic markets (following Hayek) and the design of social interventions (following Scott), tight top-down control often causes more problems than it solves. When we shift our gaze toward the internal organization of firms in public and private sectors, however, conventional wisdom often reverses. We see malfeasance and bad behavior by employees, and we debate not strategy -*whether* to use tools of control (rules, performance targets, and so on) to prevent agents from behaving in undesired ways, but rather tactics - *how* these tools might best be deployed to prevent bad acts . But what if here, too, top-down controls sometimes induce more difficulties than they resolve?

I suspect many of us can recall examples where rules or instructions that came from above seemed counterproductive to our organization's performance. We often believe it better that our organizations put more power in our hands; that we are in the best position to make decisions about the work we do. We might be wrong, of course; perhaps our unconstrained actions would carry the organization in the wrong direction. Alternately, perhaps the policy against which we chafe is generally beneficial even if it constrains us. But perhaps we are right. Perhaps our organization would be better off not trying to control things from above but rather letting our judgment and that of our colleagues "in the trenches" drive what the organization does. Maybe the "red tape" that so many of us complain about actually is indeed sometimes counterproductive.

This is a question I've been mulling over for some time. The seed of this book began in an almost painfully clichéd development-worker moment: I was on the back of a motorcycle in rural East Timor being pounded by stinging monsoon rains. Vicente Brito—my colleague at our small nongovernmental organization (NGO) focused on youth agriculture—was in front, piloting our motorcycle as we tried to navigate our way down the side of a mountain. That morning, as we headed up the mountain to a community meeting in Darulete, the "road" had been dry and passable, if not much more than a rough track. Now we drove over what looked to me like a shallow stream, indistinguishable from many other streams flowing downhill under the heavy rain.

We paused to discuss our options; the rain was loud enough that we had to half-yell to be heard. I wanted to stop for the night, thinking that as painful as the night might be we would live to tell the tale, and in morning's light we could find our way down the mountain. Vicente disagreed. In Tetun (East Timor's lingua franca), he argued that he "knew" the road. I said once again that it was better to live for tomorrow than risk the way down. "You're the boss," he said.

I looked at Vicente—or toward Vicente, as amid the rain and darkness I couldn't make him out clearly, though he was no more than three feet away. And I thought about what he meant by "knowing" the road. So much of our NGO's work came down to what each of us "knew" in a difficult-to-articulate way. Knowing when to push a group of young people to do more, and when to offer a sympathetic ear. Knowing which local leaders to put faith in, and which to keep at arm's length. And now Vicente—who grew up just a few kilometers from where we were—was telling me he "knew" the road. "OK," I said, "let's go." We picked our way slowly down the mountain, the thin beam from the headlight of our Honda Win motorcycle sometimes not strong enough to see anything beyond the rain. Vicente navigated by feel, by memory, guided first and foremost by his own informed judgment as we muddled through. And then we reached the bottom. Vicente lifted his visor and turned back to me as if to say, "I told you I could do this." And off we went back to our office in Dili, East Timor's capital.

That stream-masquerading-as-a-road has come to feel to me like a kind of object lesson. There is often tension between relying on educated yet ultimately fallible judgment on the one hand and management by rule or instruction from the top on the other. There are many reasons not to Navigate by Judgment. Agents may not have the same goals at their bosses or they may lack the skills, knowledge, or ability to execute properly despite the best intentions. Our judgments are often flawed. On the other hand, there can also be bad or inappropriate rules; even the best-designed, most logical controls may sometimes preclude good action in their desire to avoid bad action.

In my relatively short working life I have had the great fortune to be exposed to a wide variety of occupational settings. I have managed apartment maintenance crews. I have helped run a government ministry as special assistant, then aid management adviser, to the Liberian minister of finance. I have worried about employee motivation and its interaction with potential fraud in supervisory roles at a Timorese NGO. I have worried about the same things while managing the gift shop of a Detroit inner-city hospital. I have been judged by performance measures I sometimes felt inexact by my bosses at the *Princeton Review* when I was teaching SAT preparation courses. I have evaluated Thai grantees based on their ability to deliver on stated objectives for the international NGO Ashoka. I've needed to read people on the fly, using intuition and judgment, when serving drinks at a comedy club. The same needs came up when I was part of a team negotiating Liberia's debt relief under the Heavily Indebted Poor Country (HIPC) Initiative. My view is that from a judgment-versus-control standpoint there is more that is similar among these contexts than different. In each role, I have sometimes felt controls prevented me from taking actions in the organization's interest. And in each supervisory role, I have wrestled with whether and how to implement control systems without suggesting to those I supervised that I did not trust their motives and judgment, which in turn would undermine performance. There is a persistent tension between when to use rules, standards, and objective performance measures and when to put faith in the uncodifiable judgments of those operating at the coalface, at the front lines of delivery.

In the past decade (in Liberia, and recently more briefly in South Sudan and Somalia), my working life has led me to sit across the table, figuratively and quite often literally, from foreign aid donors whose stated goal is national development. In my growing sample of experiences, it has often seemed to me that the donor agents who were most interested in contributing to national development trajectories, public goods, and citizens' welfare often seemed to spend much of their time in conflict with their own organizations over procedures and process. The organizations' missions were all laudable, and on those occasions when I have met senior leadership of donor agencies I have invariably walked away impressed by the earnestness and genuineness of their desire to forward positive change. I have begun to wonder if systems of control within donor agencies preclude actions that are actually in agencies' best interest.

Foreign aid organizations present a fertile and relatively unique data-generating environment. Aid agencies are rare examples of organizations that keep systematic (if far from perfect) data on their own performance and are involved in an almost dizzying array of different tasks ranging from dam construction to judicial reform. These firms also attempt to deliver interventions in a wide range of environments from South Sudan to South Africa, China to the Central African Republic. What's more, these firms largely continue to be present irrespective of their performance, as the empirics will show; failure to perform does not lead foreign aid agencies to exit a country.

The data aid organizations generate, then, can speak to the more general tension between agent judgment and top-down control. Public schools must balance standardization and central control against allowing teachers to respond dynamically to what they judge appropriate for particular classes and students. Multinational organizations increasingly need to adapt to unfamiliar and unpredictable contexts where both process controls and performance measures are unavailable, such as when entering new markets. A senior official at a major financial-sector firm recently estimated to me that no more than 40 percent of the units in his organization generated a quarterly measure (such as profit) of adequate quality to allow pay-for-performance schemes to operate. When and how to navigate when clear rules are not practical and good performance measures are hard to come by is a critical, and quite general, question.

All that said, this book is first and foremost an attempt to make headway on a problem that has long puzzled me and one that I have come to believe consequential for the conduct of foreign aid. It is an attempt to figure out whether all those complaints about red tape and hitting prespecified numeric targets I've heard over the years in the aid business are justified— whether and when these mechanisms do seem to systematically harm aid agencies' performance.

My intuition from the outset was that it was likely these complaints were sometimes, though not always, well founded. The errors that stem from too little control—malfeasance (in U.S. government parlance, "waste, fraud, and abuse") or simply mistaken judgments—are visible to organizations and those that provide them funds and authority to act. On the other hand, the errors that stem from too much control—forgone positive action—are frequently unobserved. I suspected development organizations would be inclined to focus on the problems they could see at the expense of those they could not and thus might engage in more control than necessary.

Throughout my analysis of these data I have fought what I know to be my own bias in favor of human agency and our species' capacity to hold subtle and difficult-to-articulate wisdom. As Michael Polanyi put it, my view is that "we know more than we can tell."[3] I have attempted to fight my bias on this front, focusing on objective tests and highlighting where judgment fails. I leave it to the reader to use their judgment in determining whether I have succeeded in remaining data-driven and even-handed in my analysis.

The great economist Albert Hirschman once described the implementation of international development projects as "in fact a long voyage of discovery in the most varied domains, from technology to politics."[4] My intellectual travels in trying to understand that "long voyage of discovery" have taken me to places, methods, and perhaps insights I did not anticipate at the outset. I hope that this work might contribute something to others attempting to navigate development's often unpredictable waters.

# ACKNOWLEDGMENTS

A book seems to me—on this first experience of writing one—an attempt to fit a linear narrative to a complex web of data, theory, and personal perspective. Just as there are many possible paths through the material, there are many truths about where the germ of the idea that grew to fill these pages came from.

In some sense this book comes from Vicente Brito, my Timorese colleague discussed in the preface, and a rainy night in Liquiçá. In another it comes from Bob Keohane and Anne-Marie Slaughter's class at Princeton's Woodrow Wilson School on Designing International Institutions, which both alerted me to the importance of organization and inspired me to pursue a PhD by demonstrating some of the possibilities academic study of these issues offered. In yet another sense, it comes from my late mother, to whom this book is dedicated, who taught me to scratch the itch of intellectual curiosity and stubbornly persist until satisfied.

The framing of *Navigation by Judgment* owes substantial debt to a great man I barely knew. I had, by somewhat random chance, the opportunity to spend an afternoon walking the bluffs of seaside Gloucester, Massachusetts with the late Peter Bell just as I began the research that ultimately led to this book. Peter was a veteran development hand—he'd previously been president of the international NGO CARE in addition to working for the Ford Foundation in Latin America and for the Carter administration. As I explained my hypotheses regarding field agent versus central control, Peter said something like, "Yes, that's right. Not that different than the fishermen who have sailed these choppy waters for generations, guided by their wits." This book's cover art (courtesy of Marty Lustig) depicts the Gloucester Fisherman's Memorial, known locally as "Man at the Wheel." It seems appropriate inasmuch as it honors those sailors who have lost their lives at sea, suggesting that Navigation by Judgment often fails—but is for some contexts nonetheless better than any alternative.

I learned I was admitted into a PhD program in perhaps an unusual fashion. In early 2009, in my capacity as the Liberian minister of finance's aid management advisor, I was having lunch with a visiting delegation from the European Commission in a Monrovia restaurant. My phone kept ringing with the same unknown U.S. phone number, so eventually I excused myself and answered the phone. When I returned to the table I apologized, and shared that I'd just been called by a Harvard Kennedy School professor presumably to be offered PhD admission, though I would call back later to confirm. Tentative congratulations were roundly offered. Then one of the delegation members remarked that they hoped I continued to have a substantive positive impact on the world, as they felt I had in my position in Liberia. I smiled and looked at one of the team members whom I had come to admire for her desire to prioritize development outcomes over bureaucratic process, Erica Gerretsen.

Erica was one of the many truly exceptional people I have had the good fortune to meet via my connection to development assistance. Erica, Randolph Augustine, Sinee Chakthranont, Monique Cooper, Fiona Davies, Bronte Flecker, Chris Gabelle, Garth Glentworth, Ellen Goldstein, Brian Hanley, Drayton Hinneh, Bettina Horstmann, Jacob Hughes, Yea Yea Johnson, S. M. Kumar, Augustine Ngafuan, Talik Reis, Gama Roberts, Jordan Ryan, Carlos Santiso, Antoinette Sayeh, Tove Strauss, Michael Tharkur, Amitabh Tripathi, and Pam White are but a few of the many individuals whom I have seen point themselves toward political or management headwinds when they believed it was the right thing to do. Some of these individuals ran organizations or served as ministers; others were more junior. Some were advisers with outside options; some were career civil servants. But while their scope of action might have varied greatly, their common commitment to the most productive thing to do as they defined it led me to question our standard assumptions about what truly drives those "at the wheel". I thank all these individuals for their inspiration and commitment, and hope this book can help to support their work.

If this book is my intellectual offspring, it truly has taken a village of wise, generous souls to raise it. Peter Hall stands out in my nascent academic career for his wisdom and support. Steve Radelet has served as a mentor and guide through the world of development practice and scholarship, an object lesson in how to use serious scholarship in policy-relevant ways. Tony Bertelli, Sarah Bush, Dan Nielson, and Dr. James Raymond Vreeland very kindly participated in a book conference, offering generous and constructive feedback that helped in vastly improving the pages that follow. Dedi Felman was incredibly generous with her time and wisdom in helping me better understand how to begin writing in a way that others might want to read. Matt Andrews, Sam Asher, Nancy Birdsall, Paul Brest, Mark Buntaine, Peter Ehrenkranz, Jeff Friedman, Andreas Fuchs, Tarek Ghani, Anand Giridharadas, Ron Honig, Dan Hymowitz, Judith

Kelley, Graham Kelly, Bob Keohane, Chris Kilby, Steve Knack, Aart Kraay, Horacio Larreguy, Jane Mansbridge, Sheila Page, Mitch Pollack, Woody Powell, Lant Pritchett, Simon Quinn, Biju Rao, Tristan Reed, Alasdair Roberts, Dan Rogger, Bill Savedoff, Evan Schofer, Ryan Sheely, Chuck Shipan, Beth Simmons, Paul Skidmore, Ben Spatz, Vivek Srivastava, Jonny Steinberg, Martin Steinwand, Mike Tierney, Dustin Tingley, Rachel Tronstein, Jeremy Weinstein, Eric Werker, Michael Woolcock, anonymous reviewers for Oxford University Press, and many others have provided comments and suggestions that have strengthened this book.

I thank the National Science Foundation Graduate Research Fellowship for its support under grant #DGE-1144152. Many thanks to Yi Yan, Smriti Sakhamuri, and a number of individuals contracted via the online job hire plat-form Odesk for their research assistance. I thank the European Commission, the United Kingdom's Department for International Development, the Asian Development Bank, the Global Fund for AIDS, Tuberculosis, and Malaria, and the German Development Bank for providing project outcome data used in this project. Inasmuch as the World Bank data employed here are—uniquely among the nine organizations whose data form the basis for this book's quantitative analysis—publicly available and easily downloadable, the World Bank deserves perhaps the greatest thanks. I also thank the World Bank Archives staff, and particularly Sherrine Thompson, for all of their research assistance. I thank USAID and DFID staff for their responses to Freedom of Information requests. Grace Chao has been exemplary in her assistance in preparing this manuscript. The case studies would not have been possible without the hundreds of hours spent by a diverse group of interviewees listed in Appendix I talking to me, and answering odd questions, for which I am very grateful.

Last and not least—rather, most—I am grateful to my wife Özsel and our son Dylan. Özsel's wise comments and weekends watching Dylan both shaped and enabled my work. As critical as those interventions were, they are but the tip of the iceberg. Without Dylan and Özsel I wouldn't be the person who writes these words but rather some other, different and lesser, version of myself. I feel so incredibly lucky to be on the voyage of life in their company.

# LIST OF ACRONYMS

| | |
|---|---|
| A-Plan | (Accelerated Plan for PMTCT), a DFID South Africa health project |
| AsDB | (Asian Development Bank) |
| ASI | (Adam Smith International) |
| BRDG | (Building Reform and Recovery through Democratic Governance), USAID's capacity building project in Liberia |
| CDC | (Centers for Disease Control) of the United States |
| CDI | (Commitment to Development Index) |
| CISCAB | (Civil Service Capacity Building), DFID's civil service reform project in Liberia |
| CMTP | (Consolidated Municipal Transformation Programme), DFID's municipal governance project in South Africa |
| COIN | (U.S. government counterinsurgency) |
| DBSA | (Development Bank of Southern Africa) |
| DDD | ("Doing Development Differently") |
| DFID | (Department for International Development) |
| DPLG | (Department of Provincial and Local Government) |
| EC | (European Commission) |
| FARA | (Fixed Amount Reimbursement Agreement), a USAID financing mechanism used in the Liberian health sector |
| GFATM | (Global Fund to Fight AIDS, Tuberculosis, and Malaria) |
| GIZ/GiZ/GTZ | (German Society for International Cooperation) |
| GM | (General Motors) |
| GPRA | (U.S. Government Performance and Results Act) |
| IDOs | (international development organizations) |
| IFAD | (International Fund for Agricultural Development) |
| IMF | (International Monetary Fund) |
| IR | (international relations) |

| | |
|---|---|
| ISF | (Integrated Service Facilitator), DFID's municipal governance advisors under CMTP |
| JICA | (Japan International Cooperation Agency) |
| KfW | (German Development Bank) |
| LGSP | (Local Governance Support Program), USAID's municipal governance project in South Africa |
| MCC | (Millennium Challenge Corporation) |
| MFMA | (Municipal Finance Management Act) of South Africa |
| MFMTAP | (Municipal Finance Management and Technical Assistance Programme) of South Africa |
| MSP | (AIDS Multisectoral Program), a DFID health sector project in South Africa |
| NGOs | (nongovernmental organizations) |
| NUMMI | (Toyota-GM automotive plant) |
| ODA | (official development assistance) |
| OECD | (Organization for Economic Cooperation and Development) |
| OFDA | (Office of Foreign Disaster Assistance), a unit of USAID |
| OTI | (Office of Transitional Initiatives), a unit of USAID |
| PDIA | ("Problem Driven Iterative Adaptation") |
| PEPFAR | (President's Emergency Plan for AIDS Relief) of the United States |
| PMTCT | (Prevention of Mother to Child Transmission) |
| PPD | (Project Performance Database) |
| QuODA | (Quality of Official Development Assistance) |
| RBHS | (Rebuilding Basic Health Services), a USAID health sector project in Liberia |
| RRHF | (Rapid Results Health Fund), a DFID health project in South Africa |
| RTI | (Research Triangle Institute) |
| SARRAH | (Strengthening South Africa's Revitalized Response to AIDS and Health), a DFID health project in South Africa |
| SFI | (State Fragility Index) |
| TAC | (Treatment Action Campaign) of South Africa |
| U.K. | (United Kingdom) |
| U.S. | (United States) |
| UN | (United Nations) |
| UNAIDS | (Joint United Nations Programme on HIV/ AIDS) |
| UNHCR | (Office of the United Nations High Commissioner for Refugees) |
| UNICEF | (United Nations Childrens' Fund) |
| USAID | (United States Agency for International Development) |
| WB | (World Bank) |

# PART I

# THE WHAT, WHY, AND WHEN
# OF NAVIGATION BY JUDGMENT

# 1

# Introduction

## *The Management of Foreign Aid*

A foreign aid agency wanted to help East Timorese farmers improve their agricultural practices. The agency's plan was to train government agricultural extension workers to deliver much-needed support to farmers regarding agricultural methods and inputs (e.g., fertilizer). However, as the project was implemented, a funny thing kept happening. Virtually every government extension worker who received training promptly left government employment shortly thereafter, getting higher-wage jobs elsewhere. The vast majority of these jobs had nothing to do with the agricultural practices of rural Timorese. In building the skills of government extension workers, the agency was not in fact strengthening the government's ability to deliver or improve the lives of rural Timorese farmers. It was instead providing government agricultural extension staff with marketable job skills and better job prospects.[1]

Employees of a contractor implemented this training project on the aid agency's behalf; these employees felt a change in the project's strategy was warranted. These employees wanted to shift to delivering training directly to farmers, who could then teach one another. This change would, in these employees' judgment, allow the project to improve the lives of farmers rather than soon-to-be-former government bureaucrats, and it would also strengthen farmers' peer networks in the process. The aid agency representatives based in East Timor agreed this strategy would likely work better—the existing plan was clearly not delivering on the project's development goals. Nonetheless the aid agency's representatives faced a difficult choice. As it stood, the key metric on which the project reported to headquarters was the successful training of government agricultural agents. By this measure the project currently appeared quite successful, despite the fact that the project was failing to serve its original aim of helping farmers. Changing the project strategy would require securing high-level approvals from staff at the aid agency's headquarters. The very act of asking superiors to approve a revision would make it clear that the project was not serving its development goals, something agency managers, and certainly the politicians to whom the agency reported, would otherwise be unlikely to realize. Failures had to be explained to senior agency officials and sometimes to politicians. The aid agency's field agents in the country would have to take a career risk to improve the project.

No change was asked for, or occurred. Unfortunately, the existing strategy remained in place despite the fact that all the actors who were actually in East Timor believed a change would be beneficial. The project ultimately trained many government agricultural extension workers but had little discernible impact on farmers.

## Foreign Aid: A History of Mixed Performance

Foreign aid, or official development assistance (ODA), has as its primary objective "the economic development and welfare of developing countries."[2] Despite this laudable goal, foreign aid does not always have the desired impact. A number of wise thinkers, including Angus Deaton, the winner of the 2015 Nobel Prize for Economics, believe the challenges so insurmountable that we ought to stop giving foreign aid entirely.[3] Nonetheless, international development organizations (IDOs) such as the United States Agency for International Development (USAID) and the World Bank continue to deliver foreign aid to developing countries. Sometimes the work of IDOs has clear, demonstrable success.[4] Often, however, the picture is mixed; while the world is richer, healthier, and more educated than ever, aid is but one possible cause of these massive improvements.[5] It is also undeniable that many aid interventions fail.[6]

International development organizations and scholars alike have spent a great deal of energy trying to make foreign aid more effective.[7] Universal success may not be an achievable goal, given the variety and complexity of the challenge the development industry sets for itself. That said, with global aid flows of well over USD$200 billion annually, even small improvements in aid effectiveness have the potential to impact many lives for the better.[8]

## Two Types of Errors: Too Little
## Control ... and Too Much?

This book focuses on the internal organization of IDOs, focusing on the management processes by which IDOs seek to translate resources into results. International development organizations themselves have begun to change the way they go about delivering development assistance, seeing management practice as an important avenue for increasing aid effectiveness.[9] Occasionally these solutions involve putting more substantive control in the hands of IDO field agents.[10] More often the push for effectiveness has led IDOs and the politicians to whom they are ultimately accountable to seek measurable results, to drive better performance via setting quantitative targets, and to ask agents to report against these targets.[11]

I think the challenges that IDOs encounter exemplify a more general class of problems known as "principal-agent problems." Employees of IDOs working in a given developing country are ultimately agents of their bosses at headquarters; that is, their principal. Principal–agent relationships can be applied at multiple levels; a country's foreign aid agency as a whole is an agent of its principal, the donor-country legislature that controls its budget. This legislature is in turn the agent of the citizens who elect representatives.

One of the key features of principal-agent relationships in general is that the principal needs the agent to perform work on the principal's behalf. However, the agent knows more about what's happening "on the ground" than the principal, and it is hard for the principal to fully observe the agent. This is what gives rise to the "problem" in "principal-agent problems". The principal's interests are affected by the agent's actions, even when the principal doesn't in fact know precisely what the agent is doing.

While principal-agent problems can be found in a wide variety of settings, IDOs face a relatively (though not uniquely) difficult strain. Ben Ramalingam refers to international development as a field with "wicked problems" that are hard to simplify into clear tasks with predictable implementation schedules.[12] This "wickedness" makes it even harder for the principal to know what the "right" action is at any given time. International development organizations often operate in contexts that are very difficult to monitor, and they deal with problems for which there are frequently no complete preexisting solutions that allow for easy monitoring.

The risk of too little control for principals is clear. Letting "the chickens run the henhouse" can yield dysfunctional, inadequately supervised development projects.[13] Conventional solutions to principal-agent problems, then, focus on strengthening principal control. Controls allow those in charge to better guide interventions, preventing agents who may not share the organization's best interests from distorting projects or simply failing to put effort toward an organization's goals. Organizations seeking tight principal control can invest in costly monitoring technology. Organizations can also induce agents to do what the principal wants by tying compensation, success, promotion, and the renewal of contracts to outcomes the principal can observe. Inasmuch as IDOs work in settings where direct observation of agent action is often difficult, IDOs often choose to orient agents toward quantifiable performance targets. Performance targets can orient field staff action and give principals a way of holding staff accountable if targets are not reached.

There is also a risk of too much control, a risk I believe is often overlooked. There are underappreciated costs to either a monitoring or an incentivizing strategy beyond the actual resources spent on monitoring or performance pay.[14] Attempts at control inevitably produce rules, targets, and other accountability measures that constrain agents. This constraint is not a side effect of control; rather, it is control's primary purpose. But the very constraint that precludes bad behavior by agents may also unintentionally preclude behaviors that *are* in service of an organization's mission. It is also possible for constraints—particularly when they take the form of output targets against which agents must deliver—to induce behaviors that appear to forward an organization's goals but in fact do not. Strengthening principal control risks undermining, rather than enhancing, organizational performance.

This book is an exploration of the costs and benefits of top-down control as compared to relying on the judgment of field agents. I will argue that just as there can be too little control, there can also be too much.[15] In doing so, I echo the view of no less an authority than former USAID administrator Andrew Natsios, who has argued that the IDO he used to run suffers from "Obsessive Measurement Disorder (OMD), an intellectual dysfunction rooted in the notion that counting everything in government programs . . . will produce better policy choices and improve management."[16]

## Navigation Strategies as an Organizing Image

In a recent book focused on working in developing countries, Matt Andrews, Lant Pritchett, and Michael Woolcock use the metaphor of an overland journey from St. Louis to Oregon.[17] Today Google Maps and clear highway signage make this journey a logistical challenge that can be managed using top-down controls and measurement. Trucking companies hauling freight do just this; trucks have GPS trackers, so headquarters can track their location and speed and computers can determine optimal routes.[18] Engine electronic control modules can record and transmit speed and engine wear data; US regulators have proposed incorporating speed regulators into these modules, to prevent drivers from exceeding the speed limit.[19] Truck drivers have little discretion or opportunity to use judgment; trucking companies manage by Navigation from the Top. Minimizing the scope of agent judgment and maximizing top-down measurement and control clearly serves trucking companies well.

Trucking companies' modern management techniques require not just modern technology but also known, dependable, and predictable roads. In 1804, when U.S. explorers Lewis and Clark undertook their journey from St. Louis to Oregon, there were no maps; the explorers had to rely primarily on their own judgment (i.e., Navigation by Judgment). Lewis and Clark made many mistakes, of course. They took wrong turns on their journey and were nowhere near as efficient as a trip enabled by Google Maps and tightly monitored from a trucking company's headquarters would be today. That Lewis and Clark's Navigation by Judgment would not be a good strategy in 2015 does not mean it was not the right choice in 1804. The "best" management strategy depends on the available alternatives, which in turn depend on how well understood and predictable the environment is.

Andrews, Pritchett, and Woolcock describe development problems as involving a blend of 2015 and 1804 challenges. An IDO's purpose is to address, or to help others address, a series of challenges that vary in the extent to which the road to a solution is known. For some tasks and environments the image of Lewis and Clark's traversing of unknown lands is apt; others have more in common with the challenges I would face in attempting a similar journey in my Chevy Traverse today.[20] For all the sophisticated models, frameworks, and rhetoric, the nature of an IDO's mission means it must sometimes navigate in only dimly known seas.

Critically for the empirical strategy of this book, those dimly known seas are both *differentially* dimly known and dimly knowable. Exploiting these differences, I compare the performance of a navigation strategy based around targets, controls, and monitoring to one where primary control and decision making is in the field. When IDOs rely on the judgments of field agents to guide the strategic direction of development projects, I consider these IDOs to be using Navigation by Judgment. Chapter 2 will explore what Navigation by Judgment is and why it is sometimes critical to IDO success.

Navigation by Judgment, and the Navigation from the Top with which I contrast it, are stylized ideal types. IDO navigation strategies differ from one another in degree, not kind; no IDOs are able to, or should, live at either pole. Neither is one ideal type navigation strategy "right" and the other "wrong". This book is an argument for nuance in organizational approaches—matching a navigation strategy to the nature of the context and activities that IDOs are undertaking.

## Development Projects: The Basic Functional Unit of Foreign Aid Delivery

In implementing their work, IDOs structure their activities through projects. A "project," as defined by USAID (and typical of the term's use more broadly by IDOs), is "a set of complementary activities, over an established timeline and budget, intended to achieve a discrete development result."[21] A given project contains discrete, time- and place-bound activities implemented after careful planning and preparation. Projects can vary widely in location, sector, and purpose. World Bank projects approved by its executive board in April 2017 include projects in the Dominican Republic focused on the quality of educational statistics, in Bosnia on public health behavior, in Benin on enhancing agricultural productivity, and in India on state-level urban development.[22]

There is much wise scholarship focused on changing the goals of IDOs. This book focuses on the extent to which a given project successfully achieves its stated development goals, whatever they may be; as such, it asks a fundamentally instrumental question. Taking an IDO's project goals as fixed, what management practices facilitate achievement of those goals? A project's goals, as I (and projects themselves) use the term, are broader than a project's immediate output (e.g., nurses trained) but narrower than, say, national economic transformation. By way of illustration, project goals discussed in Part II of this book include improving the financial management capacity of South African municipalities and improving the health outcomes of South Africans suffering from HIV/AIDS.

Development projects vary on many dimensions. This book will focus on two of these dimensions. Table 1.1 illustrates these dimensions with hypothetical IDO projects. First, I will consider *project external verifiability*. Project verifiability is about the tightness of the link between the best possible quantifiable output and project goals. Sometimes a focus on measurable and verifiable targets will be an excellent management strategy. Road construction and HIV/AIDS drug delivery are project types where outputs—the actual laying of tarmac or delivery of pills to infected patients—are likely to drive projects toward their broader development goals. In other projects, relying on what can be counted and reported will lead to production of outputs but not progress toward development goals. The East Timor agricultural example that opened this chapter is an apparent case in point. Counting the number of extension workers trained relied on externally verifiable data, but this did not make the project itself

*Table 1.1* **Project Verifiability and Environmental Predictability. Different kinds of projects, and different environments, may require different management strategies**

|  | *High Project Verifiability* | *Low Project Verifiability* |
|---|---|---|
| **High Environmental Predictability** | New Road Construction in China | Health Systems Strengthening in Malaysia |
| **Low Environmental Predictability** | New Road Construction in Haiti | Health Systems Strengthening in Papua New Guinea |

verifiable. Counting the number of extension agents trained is an output much less tightly linked to farmers' outcomes than the extent to which the distribution of appropriate antiretroviral drugs is tightly linked to HIV+ patients' outcomes. The less verifiable a project, the greater the possibility that project outputs will become unmoored from project goals, as indeed occurred in the case of the East Timor example above.

Second, I will focus on the *environmental predictability* of the developing country environment in which the project takes place. Predictability captures the extent to which the project environment is one in which there are "unknown unknowns," where even the best contingency planning is likely to be incomplete. Predictability is closely linked with legibility, the extent to which those outside a context can make sense of what is going on and respond accordingly. Chapter 2 will further develop task verifiability and environmental unpredictability.

## The Central Argument

It is harder for all IDOs to realize successful projects in more unpredictable environments and when projects are less verifiable. However, IDO navigation strategy plays an important role in mediating how these features of the project type and environment translate into development project success. Top-down control is likely an appropriate management strategy for building a road in China; there is a clear technical plan to follow, clear intermediate steps to measure, and a predictable environment. On the other hand, I expect IDO project navigation led primarily by the judgments and perceptions of field staff to be the superior strategy when trying to strengthen the health system of Papua New Guinea; such a project requires more 1804 navigation, less 2015. Simply put, different kinds of projects and environments require different management strategies. Figure 1.1 depicts the basic predictions.

The claim is not, then, that Navigation by Judgment is always superior; nor is it that Navigation by Judgment allows IDOs to improve their absolute level of performance as environments become less predictable or projects less verifiable. It is simply that Navigation by Judgment is sometimes a good idea, particularly as contexts become harder to navigate using top-down controls and measurement.

Using Navigation by Judgment requires relying on agent judgment, and even the best agents will sometimes make mistakes. Navigation by Judgment is a second-best strategy—a strategy to employ when it is less bad than the distortions and constraints of top-down control. The need to appear successful to the politicians to whom IDOs report plays an important role in driving IDO management to control their field agents. For agencies that face insecure political authorizing environments, tight control will minimize the chance of agents' inappropriate

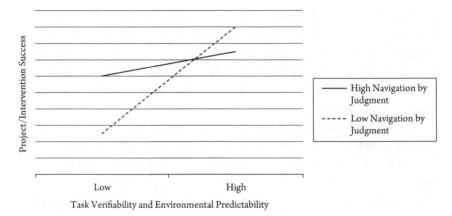

*Figure 1.1* Stylized Relationship between Navigation Strategy and Success. Low Navigation by Judgment and top-down control will serve international development organizations (IDOs) well in highly predictable environments and highly verifiable projects. As environmental predictability and/or project verifiability fall, so will development project success for all IDOs. However, Navigation by Judgment will mediate this relationship, with more Navigation by Judgment the better IDO strategy in low-predictability environments and for low-verifiability projects.

action (e.g., fraud, corruption) and the negative media headlines that come with it. Insecure agencies will choose to minimize negative headlines rather than maximize overall performance. Insecure IDOs will also want to generate numbers that they can report to political authorizers. Output measurement can create the appearance of effectiveness even when low project verifiability runs the risk of measures becoming unmoored from broader agency and project goals, thus orienting agents toward generating numbers rather than investing their time more productively. This book will argue that there is sometimes a tension between appearing successful and actually achieving success. Where this is true, insecure IDOs may use tight control to achieve the former at the expense of the latter.

## The Data

The range of foreign aid efforts is almost mind-boggling—IDOs are involved in education, health, infrastructure, public financial management, anticorruption efforts, judicial reform, and much, much more. Indeed, it is difficult to come up with a public-sector activity in which IDOs are entirely absent. The broad spread of IDOs and their projects across much of the developing world and virtually the entire range of the public sector provides an ideal research environment for a study of comparative organizational performance. By comparing the functioning of IDOs across countries and tasks, we can learn much about the circumstances under which Navigation by Judgment is most, and least, helpful. This book draws on two main sources of empirics to help address these questions.

First, I use an original cross-IDO dataset composed of over 14,000 unique development projects from 9 IDOs in 178 countries and over 200 sectors that were evaluated between 1973 and 2013, which I call the *Project Performance Database (PPD)*.[23] One of the key features of the PPD is that it includes for each project a holistic score of overall project performance—a measure of the overall success of a given project.

While the World Bank has long made their project outcome data available in a publicly accessible database, no other organization currently does so; as such the PPD is the world's largest database of development project outcomes.[24] To the World Bank data the PPD adds project results data from the Asian Development Bank (AsDB); the United Kingdom's Department for International Development (DFID); the European Commission (EC); the Global Fund to Fight AIDS, Tuberculosis, and Malaria (GFATM); the German Technical Cooperation Agency (GiZ); the German Development Bank (KfW); the International Fund for Agricultural Development (IFAD); and the Japan International Cooperation Agency (JICA). Chapter 5 and Appendix I provide additional information on the data collection process and criteria for inclusion; and Appendix II provides additional econometrics, including explorations of the PPD's quality and reliability. The PPD is available for public use and can be accessed via my website danhonig.info.[25]

Second, I employ eight case studies of IDOs implementing development projects. These eight case studies allow comparison of two IDOs, the US Agency for International Development (USAID) and UK Department for International Development (DFID). As Chapter 4 will establish, USAID and DFID have markedly different political constraints; thus my theory would predict these IDOs will engage in markedly different navigation strategies. The case studies examine whether USAID and DFID engage in different navigation strategies, how authorizing environments influence navigation strategy differences, and how navigation strategy differences influence comparative project performance. The case studies examine USAID and DFID projects in two countries with markedly different levels of stability and predictability (Liberia and South Africa) and two sectors of markedly different project verifiability (capacity building and health). This two-by-two-by-two design yields eight case studies, with four cases per unit of observation in any two-way comparison. That is to say, there are four USAID case studies and four DFID case studies, four Liberia case studies and four South Africa case studies, four capacity-building case studies and four health case studies. Figure 1.2 depicts this graphically. In each pair of cases I compare the navigation strategy of projects and the extent to which projects achieved their goals. More detail on qualitative data collection and methods can be found in Appendix I.

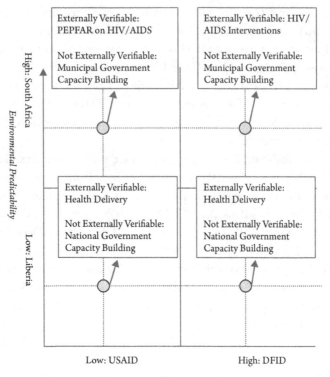

*Figure 1.2*  Case Study Schematic. This book examines four case study pairs, or eight case studies, examining two international development organizations of varying propensity to Navigate by Judgment in two environments of varying predictability in two sectors of varying project verifiability.

## Structure of the Book

Part I of this book theorizes what Navigation by Judgment is and why we might expect it to sometimes be useful. The next chapter, chapter 2, addresses the costs and benefits of Navigation by Judgment relative to the costs and benefits of Navigation from the Top. This chapter differentiates Navigation by Judgment from its first cousins, autonomy and discretion.

Chapter 3 animates the individuals who must actually do the judging in IDO Navigation by Judgment, the IDO's field agents. It argues that job design and agent quality and motivation are linked. An IDO's navigation strategy thus has an important part to play in the attraction and retention of highly qualified and intrinsically motivated agents. Chapter 4 shifts the focus from IDO agents to IDO principals, exploring how political authorizing environments can constrain IDOs' choice of navigation strategy. When authorizing environments are insecure, IDO management will engage in more top-down control than otherwise appropriate.

Part II turns to empirical tests regarding the relative performance of navigation strategies. Chapter 5 introduces the PPD and qualitative case studies in substantially more detail. Chapter 5 also operationalizes the key concepts of Navigation by Judgment, environmental predictability, and project verifiability for use in quantitative analysis. Chapter 6 brings quantitative analysis of the PPD data and the Liberia case studies to bear in exploring the role environmental predictability plays in explaining how different IDO navigation strategies impact project performance. Chapter 7 shifts to the role of project verifiability, examining how differences in performance are linked to the extent to which output quantification and management are viable management strategies for a given task and project. Chapter 7 draws on both the PPD and the South Africa case study data in exploring the role of project verifiability.

Part III explores implications of Part II's findings. Chapter 8 examines the principal-agent relationships between IDOs, their authorizers, and their field agents as well as examining the role of implementing contractors in light of Part II's findings. Chapter 9 concludes, exploring how IDOs might change to improve the match between navigation strategy and development project context in light of this book's findings. Chapter 9 also explores the implications of this book for scholars and those beyond the aid industry.

This book is at its core about the trade-off between central and agent control in the management of foreign aid projects; the next chapter, Chapter 2, explores this trade-off. Chapter 2 introduces Navigation by Judgment in more depth and when and why we might expect Navigation by Judgment to prove useful to IDOs in the implementation of foreign aid projects.

# 2

# When to Let Go

## *The Costs and Benefits of Navigation by Judgment*

A teacher sits in her classroom and sips her morning coffee. In these precious minutes before students arrive, she looks over the lesson plan on her tablet computer. If this teacher works for Bridge International Academies in Mombasa, Kenya, she is reviewing a lesson script composed by master teachers who have likely never seen her school or her students.[1] This script includes the precise words the teacher should say, prompts her to pause where master teachers believe appropriate, and instructs her as to how long each subtopic is to be discussed. The script also instructs the teacher when to make eye contact with students and when to snap her fingers to draw students' attention. As the teacher goes through her day, the tablet will record detailed usage information with every tap of the screen and transmit this information back to Bridge's management.

Nearby, a teacher at a government school sits in his classroom and similarly contemplates the day ahead. He is guided by his experience in the classroom and his knowledge of his students. The lesson plan he is reviewing is his own. While this teacher has consulted unenforced government guidelines in devising his plan, no one controls what happens in his classroom but him. He has the power to adjust the pace of the class and the emphasis of the lesson. But this is far from the effective limits of this teacher's control; the teacher also has the power to teach an entirely different subject if he thinks it is appropriate or even to exert no effort and teach nothing at all.[2]

This chapter outlines Navigation by Judgment. *Navigation by Judgment* is an organizational strategy in which front-line employees are able to meaningfully guide their organization's work based upon their judgments. Key to Navigation by Judgment is that this judgment guides not merely the application of policy but also substantive strategic direction. The government school at which the second teacher works is Navigating by Judgment. At the other end of the navigation spectrum, Bridge International Academies is Navigating from the Top. Navigation by Judgment and Navigation from the Top are ideal types. Very few organizations will sit at either extreme on this continuum; the example schools are rare in occupying extreme positions in the Navigation by Judgment–Navigation from the Top continuum.

This chapter first distinguishes Navigation by Judgment from autonomy and discretion, which I view as related but distinct concepts. The chapter then discusses the basic framework for weighing the costs and benefits of organizational navigation led by top-down managerial controls versus front-line employee judgment: the trade-off between principal control and agent initiative. After outlining the contrasting advantages of principal control on the one hand and agent control on the other, this chapter turns to a discussion of the circumstances in which one set of advantages is likely to dominate for international development organizations (IDOs). Whether IDOs will fare better with tight principal control or by letting front-line employees lead depends on the type of project undertaken and the environment in which the project takes place.

## Navigation by Judgment: What It Is and How It Differs from Autonomy and Discretion

Putting front-line employees, whom this book will largely refer to as *field agents*, in control brings to mind the notions of bureaucratic discretion and organizational autonomy. This section disentangles Navigation by Judgment from discretion and autonomy with the aim of clarifying the distinctions between these ideas as well as showing why organizational autonomy is a necessary but not sufficient condition for Navigation by Judgment.

Agent discretion normally refers to agents' use of judgment over a circumscribed range of decisions, normally as regards implementation of already agreed strategy. Discretion tends to be the property of an individual rather than an organization; we talk of "agent discretion" but tend not to discuss "organizational discretion." The U.S. Department of Labor has a notably elegant description of "discretion and independent judgment" that connects quite straightforwardly to Navigation by Judgment.[3] According to the U.S. government:

> Discretion and independent judgment involves the comparison and the evaluation of possible courses of conduct, and acting or making a decision after the various possibilities have been considered. The exercise of discretion and independent judgment must be more than the use of skill in applying well-established techniques, procedures or specific standards described in manuals or other sources. The exercise of discretion and independent judgment implies that one has authority to make an independent choice, free from immediate direction or supervision.[4]

Key to both discretion and to Navigation by Judgment is independent choice, the use of judgment, and freedom from supervision. That said, to Navigate by Judgment an organization must allow a degree of agent discretion that goes beyond the typical uses of the term. To fully Navigate by Judgment, the zone of agent discretion must include strategic direction and policy, not just individual cases and tactics. An organization that uses Navigation by Judgment empowers its front-line agents not just to implement, or to exercise judgment in a limited sphere of choice, but to substantively lead what the organization does.

Navigation by Judgment is an organizational property; the term is intended to focus attention on organizational management choices. In a sense, Navigation by Judgment is the organizational choice to employ a relatively extreme degree of discretion. "Organizational Navigation by Judgment" could be alternately defined as "an organizational management strategy in which the organization gives agents an extremely large degree of discretion, extending to policy decisions and strategic revision of organizational interventions." Navigation by Judgment is the organizational choice to embrace an extreme form of agent discretion such that discretion is no longer discrete or tightly bounded to particular narrow choices or domains.

The term "autonomy," unlike "discretion," is often applied to organizations, agencies, and firms; scholars frequently discuss "organizational autonomy."[5] But while autonomy may be at the same unit of analysis as Navigation by Judgment—the organization, rather than the agent—autonomy is unsatisfying as a way of describing agents' use of judgment as the primary guide to an organization's actions. Autonomy is conventionally understood as freedom *from*—that is, the absence of constraints—rather than the presence of the use of field agent judgment (or any other particular quality) in organizational decision-making.

Organizational autonomy's relationship with organizational Navigation by Judgment is perhaps most clearly illustrated via a stylized example. Sheila owns the Novel Toy Company. The Novel Toy Company manufactures a novel children's toy of Sheila's invention in her fully owned factory. The Novel Toy Company controls distribution and marketing and is bound by no contract to meet any particular standards. This organization is, in the conventional sense of the term, fully autonomous. Sheila does not report to a board of directors, shareholders, politicians, or any other actors; she can choose her organization's navigation strategy without constraint. The novelty of the toy suggests that there is not even a market mechanism that might force conventional standards for the good onto the manufacturing process. Sheila still decides that the best way to monitor her employees is via tight, top-down process controls. Sheila chooses, then, to give her agents no ability to use their judgment in determining what the company produces or how it is produced. The Novel Toy Company is an organization that is both fully autonomous and has little Navigation by Judgment.

Organizational autonomy and Navigation by Judgment are by no means independent of one another, however. It is hard to imagine a firm in the inverse position of the Novel Toy Company, one that has very little organizational autonomy but a great deal of Navigation by Judgment. An organization that does not have autonomy is unlikely to Navigate by Judgment, as it will be very difficult to justify having done so to those above—whether "those above" are executive boards, politicians, or shareholders. Chapter 4 will explore IDOs' relationship with political authorizers in more detail.

If an organization lacks autonomy, it will be unlikely to free its agents from top-down control. Table 2.1 provides a stylized description of the relationship between organizational autonomy and organizational Navigation by Judgment. Organizations with low levels of autonomy are unable to Navigate by Judgment. This does not mean high-autonomy organizations will always choose to Navigate by Judgment; autonomy merely allows high-autonomy organizations to consider Navigation by Judgment as a strategy. Navigation by Judgment is "on the menu" of potential strategies for high-autonomy organizations but not for their low-autonomy peers.

## The Tension between Agent Initiative and Principal Control

In a variety of contexts, good decisions sometimes rely on elements of a situation that are partially unobservable to others who are not immediately present. In these contexts the assessments of agents cannot be directly verified, or proven, to their principals. A therapist needs to decide whether to pursue a particular avenue of interrogation with a patient. A loan officer needs to decide whether to

*Table 2.1*  **Organizational Autonomy and Navigation Strategy. IDOs with greater autonomy will alter their navigation strategy appropriately to recipient country environment and project type. Low-autonomy IDOs will be unable to adjust appropriately and will Navigate from the Top even where this is not the best strategy**

|  | *Navigation by Judgment* | *Navigation from the Top* |
| --- | --- | --- |
| **High Organizational Autonomy** | Likely Where Appropriate | Likely Where Appropriate |
| **Low Organizational Autonomy** | Highly Unlikely | Highly Likely |

award a "character loan" to an applicant; the loan officer needs to judge whether the client is trustworthy. Subtle judgments about context, and "gut instincts" regarding how best to proceed, will be incorporated by an organization that Navigates by Judgment but may be excluded by inappropriate top-down controls, including inappropriate measurement and reporting schemes.

Economics Nobel Prize winner Jean Tirole, in collaboration with Philippe Aghion, frames the tension between management control and agent action as a trade-off between principal control and agent initiative.[6] Navigation by Judgment has the distinct advantage of incorporating agent knowledge and inducing agents to take initiative; however, this comes at the cost of principal control. This tension between agent initiative and judgment on the one hand and principal control and monitoring on the other is central to what makes the choice of navigation strategy so difficult. There are advantages to both agent initiative and principal control, but they cannot be simultaneously realized.

Aghion and Tirole's tension between agent initiative and principal control has echoes in a variety of literatures. In public administration, both theory and empirics point to the notion that inducing agent investment in expertise requires a loosening of principal control, as only agents with the ability to make use of expertise will work to cultivate it.[7] From management theory comes the need for organizational control decisions in light of firms' need to incorporate tacit knowledge.[8] From political science comes James Scott's claim that top-down planning precludes "metis" or "knowledge embedded in local experience."[9] The common thread in these views is that top-down control precludes agent use of what cannot be codified. I will use the Aghion and Tirole formulation in this book because I find it the most intuitive; virtually all of what follows could alternatively have been theorized from these various traditions.[10]

The next two sections outline the advantages to an organization of Navigation by Judgment and Navigation from the Top, respectively.

## The Benefits of Navigation by Judgment and Putting Agents in Charge

This section describes the benefits of Navigation by Judgment that may be precluded by top-down control, then turns to the unproductive distortions top-down control may induce that Navigation by Judgment avoids. When good organizational performance depends on things agents can know and their supervisors cannot (such as regarding local context), Aghion and Tirole suggest it is critical that agents have not just formal but "real" authority.[11] This means agents need to be given not just the formal ability to make judgments but also that the organizational incentives agents face encourage agents' use of their judgment.

Aghion and Tirole argue that agents without an incentive to gather information to which they have access but their principals do not – i.e. asymmetric information – will not put in the time and effort to learn what the organization needs to know to make good decisions.

Asymmetric information can include soft information. Soft information is defined as information that a skilled observer might use to inform his or her decisions, but that "cannot be directly verified by anyone other than the agent who produces it."[12] Soft information is perhaps most easily understood as the informational cousin of tacit knowledge or subtle expertise, inasmuch as a key feature of soft information is the difficulty of codifying this information for transmission to others.[13] Soft information is local, contextually bound information that is difficult to put into a formal report or an email back to headquarters. Tight principal control means agents will not gather asymmetric information, including soft information. Organizations with tight principal control will thus not be able to use this information in making decisions or planning new projects. Principal control will preclude principals from benefiting from soft information that is by definition impossible to verify by distant supervisors.

An example may help illustrate this central tension. Imagine Steve, an IDO representative sitting in his organization's well-appointed office in a developing country capital. Steve's choice this afternoon is between playing tennis and scheduling a meeting with government representatives with whom an education project is ongoing. Imagine Steve's IDO is like Bridge International Academies, with Steve following a tightly dictated set of steps.[14] If Steve will be unable to influence or change the project in any way as a result of the meeting, he has very little incentive to get in his Land Rover and go to the meeting. The compound is lovely; why not spend the afternoon improving his backhand? The same basic logic that applies to initiative taking and Steve's meeting applies to soft information. That is, Steve won't gather soft information if he can't make use of it. But for soft information to be used, Steve's organization must allow him to take substantive action on the basis of information that the organization by definition cannot verify. In other words, for Steve to gather soft information requires the organization to trust Steve's judgment.

Retired U.S. General Stanley McChrystal and his coauthors' description of Iraq counterinsurgency (COIN) operations provides a case study of what I would call the relationship between agent initiative, soft information, and Navigation by Judgment in practice.[15] McChrystal describes Iraq as a complex, unfamiliar, and difficult-to-understand environment in which existing management practice based on top-down command and control was inappropriate. His answer was to devise "new rules of engagement for a complex world."[16] These rules of engagement focused on "letting go" of central control, relying instead on "empowered execution" by field agents.[17] As McChrystal puts it, "In the old model, subordinates provided information and leaders disseminated commands. We reversed it: we had our leaders provide information so that subordinates, armed with context, understanding, and connectivity, could take the initiative and make decisions."[18] McChrystal is quite explicit that to make this work required a conscious decision to not control agents.[19] In shifting COIN operations toward Navigation by Judgment, McChrystal chose agent initiative and soft information over principal control and standardization, which resulted in marked success.

McChrystal's account also highlights the other key advantage of Navigation by Judgment: flexibility. Principal control may impede organizational response to changing contexts. Putting more control in the hands of agents empowers actors who are better placed to rapidly respond when flexibility and adaptation is needed, while simultaneously reducing the control mechanisms (review procedures, approval processes, etc.) that might impede rapid response. Less principal control will thus be associated with a greater ability to adapt to changing circumstances in implementation. Flexibility is complementary, but distinct, from the asymmetric (soft) information channel; flexibility is in greater demand when contexts change more rapidly, whereas the direct returns to soft information may persist irrespective of the rate of environmental change.

## The Distortions of Top-Down Control That Navigation by Judgment Avoids

This description of Navigation by Judgment's potential benefits has thus far focused on what principal control precludes—what agents can do in the absence of control. Not Navigating by Judgment, and instead Navigating from the Top, may also induce unproductive distortions that an organization that chooses Navigation by Judgment will avoid.[20] Given the difficulty of directly observing agent action, IDOs' primary tool of agent control is the setting of performance targets and requiring reporting against them.[21] A recent Organization for Economic Cooperation and Development (OECD) review of the U.S. Agency for International Development (USAID) finds that USAID uses "approximately 200 standard indicators (recently reduced from 500), and many more custom indicators" in their monitoring and evaluation of projects.[22]

An oft-repeated management axiom asserts that "what gets measured gets managed." Requiring reporting against externally verifiable measures allows principals a means of specifying behavior when monitoring could not otherwise occur. By design, "pay for performance" schemes deploy measurement as a form of agent control to shape what agents do. Target setting and reporting requirements can be forms of control that, no less than rules or direct oversight, augur for principal control over agent initiative and use of judgment. These indicators orient agent action, thus acting as a de facto management tool irrespective of whether their intent was in fact to put control in the principal's hands. In an echo of Heisenberg's uncertainty principle, top-down controls, including setting targets and measuring performance relative to them, changes the behavior of the assessed.[23]

Target setting is not a simple thing to get right; the difficulty increases in the complex contexts in which IDOs operate.[24] International development organizations operate in an environment where it is very difficult in many cases to observe outcomes, and in any case it is difficult to attribute outcomes to IDO efforts. If infant mortality declines in a country, it is difficult to estimate the extent to which an IDO's health or economic development projects have contributed to that outcome. It is unsurprising, then, that IDOs focus their target setting on discrete outputs directly attributable to projects such as the construction of a clinic or the training of nurses.[25] Where outputs and outcomes are well correlated, this will not be a problem; but an output-based reporting framework raises the risk of constructing many clinics but not actually improving health outcomes. This risk varies by IDO project, as the section of this chapter on project verifiability will discuss. As Kerr put it over forty years ago, there is potential for IDOs to engage in "the folly of rewarding A while hoping for B."[26]

Agents may invest time and effort in achieving the target that is being evaluated, but consequently agents underinvest in what is not being measured; this is known in contract theory as a "multitask" problem.[27] It is also possible for a given measure to be a good proxy before it is used for management purposes, with the value of the measure collapsing when it is used for control purposes.[28] One example of the breakdown in the world of foreign aid is, arguably, the focus on educational enrollment—getting kids into classrooms around the world. So central was this thrust that increasing primary enrollment was one of the eight Millennium Development Goals, the globally agreed objectives for international development between 2000 and 2015 against which both IDOs and national governments reported. As a result, many, many more students are in class. However, as eloquently captured in the title of Pritchett's <u>Schooling Ain't Learning</u>, the relationship between enrollment and educational achievement has broken down as enrollment levels have climbed.[29] Many more children may be sitting in their chairs, but little additional learning is taking place. This, too, has an echo in the literature on military COIN operations; as one RAND report puts it, in COIN operations "metrics can lead to a tendency to develop short-term solutions for long-term problems."[30]

There are, then, many distinct advantages to Navigation by Judgment. Navigation by Judgment can induce better organizational performance by incorporating asymmetric (soft) information, stimulating agents' use of initiative, and increasing organizational flexibility. Navigation by Judgment can also avoid the distortions that may result from inappropriate performance measurement. That said, there are also many benefits to tight principal control, which the next section explores.

## The Benefits of Principal Control and Navigation from the Top

The benefits of Navigation by Judgment must be balanced against its costs. Putting more control in the hands of field agents also means those agents will find it easier to engage in a range of actions, including those that may be illegal or undesired. This includes both outright corruption as well as capture.[31] Capture—when an agent ceases to become an effective representative of their organization as the agent becomes unduly influenced by the individuals and environment with which they interact—is very much a live issue for IDOs.[32] International development organizations are concerned that as they send individual agents to distant locales, where they spend much of their time interacting with domestic agents in the recipient countries, their agents' interests will become aligned with something other than the best interests of the organization.[33] Agents will be more susceptible to capture with less principal control.

Less constrained agents may also simply act in a manner other than that desired by their principals.[34] In principal-agent terms, agents may have objective functions that do not match those of principals, and thus they may wish to do different things. When the misalignment between principals' and agents' interests is sufficiently large, tightly controlling agents may be the best course of action for principals even if in so doing there are substantial losses of soft information, agent initiative, and flexibility. In addition, agent judgment can simply be wrong even when well intentioned, as chapter 3 will explore more fully. An IDO that gives agents more control will have more to fear from fallible agent judgments.

Principal control also produces more standardized behavior. If an organization Navigates by Judgment, it is likely that different agents will make different choices in response to similar prompts. By shifting control to agent judgments, an organization may allow more scope for bias and prejudice.[35] Where standardization is critical to good outcomes—the organizational equivalent of baking a cake, where following a precise recipe is likely to yield the best results—less principal control will likely induce variation that will be detrimental to organizational performance.[36]

Chapter 1 introduced the image of Lewis and Clark's 1804 navigation from St. Louis to Oregon, contrasting it with 2015's strategy of using Google Maps.

Modern tools can sometimes make 1804 challenges more like those of 2015. In the Kenyan school example above, Bridge International Academies engaged in very little Navigation by Judgment. While rigorous impact evaluation of Bridge has yet to emerge, Bridge suggests its students pass Kenyan national exams at higher rates than do public school students.[37] Many smart people seem to believe Bridge's model likely to prove a useful innovation—Bridge's investors include the Chan Zuckerberg Initiative, the Bill & Melinda Gates Foundation, the Omidyar Network, the World Bank's International Finance Corporation, and leading venture capital firms including Pershing Square and Khosla Ventures.[38] Perhaps something as seemingly unpredictable and judgment-laden as teaching a class of students can be improved upon by employing tight monitoring, measurement, and top-down control.

Navigation by Judgment's lack of standardization is also likely to result in organizational interventions that do not proceed in a linear, ex ante predictable manner. This means organizations that choose to Navigate by Judgment will need to manage something other than day-to-day outputs in order to provide agents with the slack to act in the manner they see as best. Navigation by Judgment cannot coexist with Bridge International Academy's management techniques, which may be beneficial. Navigation by Judgment also precludes providing high-powered performance incentives, directly rewarding agents by paying for performance. The management and contract theory literatures make clear that paying for performance is a powerful and sometimes effective tool for driving agents to perform, particularly when performance is observable and clearly attributable to individual agents.[39]

Navigation by Judgment has substantial drawbacks. There are potential costs to relying on the initiative and judgment of field agents to steer organizational direction, just as there are costs to tight principal control. The next section explores whether quantitative targets and performance measurement are truly in tension with Navigation by Judgment, as the discussion thus far has suggested. This chapter then turns to when Navigation by Judgment is likely to be a superior organizational strategy to Navigation from the Top and vice versa.

## Are Quantitative Target Setting and Navigation by Judgment Really in Tension with One Another?

When is performance measurement and orientation toward quantitative targets in fact a tool of Navigation from the Top, and when can it be compatible with reliance on agent judgment to guide interventions? To say that metrics *can* induce distortions is not to suggest that measurement is *necessarily* unproductive and distortionary. In the world of foreign aid, advocates of both cash on delivery aid and results-based financing argue for conditioning aid on the accomplishment of long-term quantifiable outcomes.[40] By remaining agnostic as to how outcomes are achieved and rewarding their achievement with financing, advocates note that focusing measurement and control on outcomes will give implementers autonomy. Implementers could use that autonomy to allow the implementation of interventions to be guided by the judgments of field agents so long as that strategy produced the desired outcomes—to Navigate by Judgment to some degree.[41]

A managerial focus on outcomes as summary performance measures is likely to be a good idea when there are externally verifiable outcomes that can be independently measured and that do not incentivize overinvestment of agent effort in the elements of the job that are measured at the expense of those elements of the job that are not.[42] Success in contracting on outcomes also requires an environment where intervening events are unlikely to require a radical rethinking of what needs to be done or how performance is to be measured.[43] As these conditions suggest, contracting on outcomes is often not practicable in delivering foreign aid.[44] Reliable outcome measures are hard to identify; data are difficult to collect; success and failure depend on too many things beyond an IDO (or developing country government's) control, making attribution difficult; outside shocks are too frequent.[45] As a result, the focus of measurement for IDOs remains project outputs. To illustrate: a recent report examined the reporting practices of nongovernmental organizations (NGOs) that implement humanitarian relief projects.[46] The report classifies 1,680 performance indicators used by eleven NGOs in measuring and reporting on their performance. More than 50 percent of the metrics were process or input indicators; a further 24 percent were output indicators. Only 1 percent of indicators focused on the ultimate impact of projects.[47] Chapter 9 will return to these issues, revisiting where project management can be improved by altering the timing or nature of measurement to allow a degree of Navigation by Judgment.[48]

In practice, then, it is rare that development assistance measurement and reporting occurs at a level where it is compatible with any degree of Navigation by Judgment. A skeptic might object that the illustrative data discussed in this section, and indeed this chapter as a whole, conflate the management of projects and the means via which projects are evaluated. I would argue that there is a reason the development industry twins monitoring and evaluation—"M&E" in industry parlance. An organization that wants a good evaluation will drive agents to produce what the evaluation will capture, thus turning evaluation criteria into a managerial tool of monitoring and control. The case studies employed in Part II will provide multiple examples in which reporting requirements act as a form of top-down control, precluding Navigation by Judgment. [49]

# When Will IDOs be Better Served by Letting Go of Top-Down Control?

Recognizing that Navigation by Judgment has benefits and costs is fine, as far as it goes. So is noting that Navigation from the Top and principal control are not without their drawbacks. But IDOs, and organizations more broadly, need to actually choose a navigation strategy. When will more or less Navigation by Judgment be a good idea? When and where should principals in fact let go of the reins, giving up tight control?

Table 2.2 summarizes key elements of the discussion thus far, highlighting in some sense the best case for both strategies.

Chapter 1 introduced the contrast beween "1804" problems and "2015" problems. When Lewis and Clark set off from St. Louis in 1804, they had no map to guide them and virtually no knowledge of what lay ahead. International development organizations are in substantially more fortunate data environments, even at the extreme; there is arguably nowhere IDOs work where prior knowledge is as scarce as it was for Lewis and Clark. What's more, in the contexts in which the least is known, there is ample ability to communicate back to headquarters. That said, I suspect most readers will agree that there is no equivalent of Google Maps to guide IDOs' navigation.

The less 2015 a context, the greater the returns to Navigation by Judgment. The less 2015 a problem, the greater the returns to agent initiative, soft information, and flexibility as compared to tight principal control, oversight and reporting, and standardized behavior. But what makes a problem "2015"—what are

Table 2.2   **Summary of Key Benefits of Navigation by Judgment and Navigation from the Top. The stylized "ideal type" navigation strategies have advantages that are in distinct tension with one another; to reap the benefits of one often means forgoing the benefits of the other. "*" indicates that chapter 3 will further develop these features of Navigation by Judgment and Navigation from the Top**

| *Navigation by Judgment* | *Navigation from the Top* |
| --- | --- |
| Agent initiative | Principal control |
| Soft Information | Oversight |
| Flexibility | Standardized behavior |
| May induce intrinsic motivation* | May induce extrinsic motivation |
| Avoids distortions of performance measurement | Avoids fallible agent judgment* |

the relevant features of Google Maps? How can we get empirical leverage on what precisely is likely to make Navigation by Judgment more successful? I propose two features that affect the "2015-ness" of a particular project.

First is the *environmental predictability* of the context, the extent to which things are likely to change in ways that cannot be foreseen and planned for. Google Maps is less useful when it cannot keep up with changing circumstances. Google Maps cannot tell us when a tree closes a rural road or animals block one's way. My home is under a mile from the White House; I frequently see cars stuck in traffic due to protests, rallies, and marches of which I presume Google Maps is unaware. The more frequently things change in ways principals, and top-down controls, cannot foresee, the greater the returns to soft information and flexibility.

Second is *project external verifiability*, a project's projected tractability to management based around counting and quantifying without inducing the unproductive distortions discussed above. If the relevant features of a road cannot be turned into the 0s and 1s that underlie all computer code, they cannot be put in Google Maps' database. And if Google Maps cannot display the relevant features of the road, it will not be helpful to rely on Google Maps to navigate.

## Environmental Predictability

As IDO project implementation occurs, many things may impact how interventions ought to proceed. Some changes are foreseeable, and thus a smart project plan could account for these contingencies. However, there are frequently what former U.S. Secretary of Defense Donald Rumsfeld once referred to as "unknown unknowns."[50] We know that things we have not anticipated may, in fact, occur; somewhat frustratingly, just knowing that the unanticipated may occur does not itself allow us to strengthen our anticipatory skills and plan accordingly.

A number of mutually supporting channels link greater unpredictability to a greater need for Navigation by Judgment. First, top-down controls may impede rapid response when contexts do indeed change. A need to seek approval from above is likely to diminish an organization's flexibility and thus the efficiency with which an organization responds to changes. An organization that Navigates by Judgment puts more authority in the hands of the actors who can respond most rapidly to shifting circumstances.

Second, some "unknown unknowns" may be unforeseeable when a project commences but nonetheless predictable at some time before they occur. When a hypothetical project to provide youth vocational skills in collaboration with the Ministry of Youth and Sports begins, the Minister may appear to be a valuable ally to the IDO field agent running the project. However, a year into implementation, the Minister falls out of favor with the Prime Minister and is likely to lose his job; the current Minister's likely successor would be inclined to marginalize a project closely associated with her predecessor. A wise and well-informed IDO field agent, foreseeing this possibility, may begin to include more career civil servants in the steering committee of the project and consult the Minister himself less. Such a decision requires Navigation by Judgment and soft information. An IDO that does not Navigate by Judgment will have more poorly informed agents who would in any case be less able to act on their own unverifiable judgments.[51]

Third, environments vary with regards to legibility—the extent to which they can be understood from a distance.[52] In the context of international development, this might be understood as the correlation of de jure structures with de facto reality. In those developing countries characterized by higher levels of legibility, the name on the door of a government unit is well correlated with the activities that take place within. In others, this is not the case; formal organizational charts bear little resemblance to reality. Formal structures and hierarchy vary with regards to whether they are good indicators, for example, of whose approval is needed in practice to ensure a project will proceed. The greater the gap between structures and reality, the greater the returns to soft information and thus to Navigation by Judgment.

Legibility and predictability are conceptually distinct—one could imagine a government that worked through very formal structures but was still vulnerable to many unforeseeable shocks. Predictability and legibility are highly correlated, however; countries with weaker, less formalized systems are also those where a range of unpredictable events related to government turnover and conflict are more likely to occur. In less legible environments, it will be hard for anyone other than field agents to make judgments about how to proceed in designing and implementing projects.

More unpredictability increases the chance that top-down controls will impose costly inflexibility. More unpredictability also raises the value of what top-down controls can preclude. More unpredictable environments require more flexibility and more demand for organizations to make use of asymmetric (soft) information. This, then, gives rise to my first hypothesis—*Returns to Navigation by Judgment will rise as unpredictability rises.*

## Project Verifiability

As noted earlier in this chapter, a focus on reporting outputs may lead to a breakdown of the correlation between the measures on which reporting occurs and the broader goals these measures were intended to achieve. Measurement leads to greater production of whatever is measured; the question is in some ways one of when that is likely to be a good thing and when it is a bad thing. Some IDO projects are more likely to suffer breakdowns in the correlation between outputs and outcomes than others.[53] The greater the chance of breakdown, the lower the degree of *project external verifiability*.

My use of project external verifiability is not intended to indicate whether there are in fact project outputs that can be observed, quantified, and reported. Project verifiability, as I define it, is a measure of the extent to which using project outputs for control purposes is likely to work well. A more precise, though unwieldy, name for project verifiability might be "manage-ability based on short-term externally verifiable outputs." A project's degree of verifiability is not a retrospective measure of whether top-down control has worked but rather an estimation of how well management by output measurement is likely to work in expectation. Project verifiability captures the extent to which outputs are likely to remain tightly correlated with a project's goals or the susceptibility of the best possible output measure is subject to distortions. As previously noted, these distortions may take the form of concentrating agent focus on the monitorable part of a complex project—a multitask problem. They may also take the form of causing the output measure to degrade in value as a proxy for the project's ultimate goal.

Project verifiability not only depends on the goal a project aims to achieve but also reflects on the precise manner in which an IDO wishes to make progress toward that goal. Imagine a project aimed at improving the health of HIV+ patients; in this case, the goal focuses on delivering antiretroviral drugs. The administration of drugs can be easily quantified, and there is little concern that somehow the taking of drugs (a measurable output) will become unmoored from helping HIV/AIDS patients. This would be, in my sense, a highly verifiable project.[54]

Imagine a different project with the same goal—improving the health of HIV+ patients—instead focuses on building health clinics in areas with high HIV prevalence rates and training community groups to operate the newly built clinics (the outputs). It is quite easy to monitor the actual construction of a clinic using top-down controls and to verify the quality of the clinic's construction once completed. This is less true of the group trainings which form an integral part of the project's impact on the community. Constructing clinics does not in and of itself improve health care; there is the possibility that clinics may be built without improving patient health if they are not used properly or used at all. If agents focus on the measurable clinic construction to the detriment of the training, there will be little improvement in HIV patient health. This latter project is less verifiable than the drug delivery project.

The more externally verifiable a project, the less useful Navigation by Judgment is likely to be.[55] In highly verifiable projects, output measures are likely to serve as good guides for agents and thus for projects. Indeed, in the most externally verifiable projects—building a dam or delivering antiretroviral drugs—I expect Navigation by Judgment to be unhelpful on net. Why rely on fallible agent judgment when one can instead rely on, and incentivize agents to deliver, clear, stable, accurate, and nondistortionary measures of performance? This, then, gives rise to my second hypothesis—*Returns to Navigation by Judgment will rise as project verifiability falls.*

Figure 1.1 in chapter 1 depicted the combined expectations of the two hypotheses articulated here graphically. Navigation from the Top will be to an IDO's advantage when the challenges the IDO faces are relatively straightforward and the correct course of action is well understood in advance. As my two key measures—enviromental predictability and project verifiability—fall, IDOs will face challenges that are more 1804 and less 2015. All IDOs will see their performance suffer as the going gets tougher. However an IDO that can Navigate by Judgment will be relatively better able to cope with tougher, and more unknown, terrain.

## Stocktaking: This Chapter and the Rest of Part I

This chapter illustrates what Navigation by Judgment is and some of its basic costs and benefits relative to Navigation from the Top. It also argues for when we might expect Navigation by Judgment to perform better than Navigation from the Top and vice versa. Navigation by Judgment allows an organization's direction and mission to be substantially directed by the judgments of field-level operators. Navigation by Judgment requires not just a formal delegation of authority but also the design of organizational processes and procedures that reward the use of authority. Navigation by Judgment requires agent initiative at the expense of principal control. Employing Navigation by Judgment has distinct costs for an organization in diminishing principal control; it also has distinct benefits.

This chapter argues that IDOs will sometimes, but by no means always, do better by letting go of central control. If this chapter is the "what" and "when" of Navigation by Judgment, the rest of Part I will expand on the "why" and "who." Chapter 4 will focus on the "why," exploring how authorizing environments may prompt IDOs to Navigate from the Top even where it is not the navigation strategy most likely to lead to Project Success. The next chapter, Chapter 3, will focus on the "who"—the individuals doing the judging and the agents themselves. If an IDO relies on their judgment, can IDO agents be trusted to make the right decisions? In the following chapter, I will explore the implications for agent quality, agent recruitment, and the motivation of organizational Navigation by Judgment.

# Agents

## *Who Does the Judging?*

This chapter examines the actors doing the judging in Navigation by Judgment—front-line agents. For international development organizations (IDOs), front-line agents are employees who live and work in developing countries—the IDO's field staff. What makes these field staff tick? When are they more or less likely to make good policy if given the freedom to do so? This chapter first introduces the central issue—the motivation of agents and the impact of agents' motivation on job design and principal supervision. It then discusses the relationship between agent quality and job design through both selection and treatment effects. It next turns to the fallibility of judgment even when agents have the best of intentions. This chapter argues that there is a mutually reinforcing equilibrium between organizational Navigation by Judgment and agents who are more likely to make productive (though still imperfect) use of the greater scope for independent action provided by Navigation by Judgment.

## Agent Motivation: When Does It Need to be Induced?

Navigation by Judgment is a strategy that places more power in the hands of field agents at the expense of the control and oversight held by their supervisors. Whether this strategy is likely to lead to better or worse net performance thus depends critically on who the agents are. A recent study of World Bank project performance found that the identity of a project's manager explains twice as much of the variance in outcomes as does the identity of the country in which the project occurs.[1]

If agents are primarily interested in maximizing budgets and not in accomplishing the organization's goals, then top-down controls are likely necessary, even if they preclude some actions that might improve organizational performance.[2] On the other hand, voices from Economics Nobel laureate Elinor Ostrom to former U.S. Agency for International Development (USAID) administrator Andrew Natsios have suggested that development requires local knowledge, agent discretion, and adaptability.[3] These views suggest that agents can and will utilize granted autonomy for good, not ill. Less monitoring may result in better performance at a lower cost for the principal.

Over a half-century ago, Massachusetts Institute of Technology professor Douglas McGregor argued for a distinction between two starkly contrasting theories of employee motivation, which he termed "Theory X" and "Theory Y."[4] Theory X is a management style consistent with the view that agents will not act in the absence of close supervision and tight controls and that extrinsic motivation is required to stimulate good performance. Theory X is appropriate, then, when agents will do things that do not serve the principal's interests in the absence of top-down control.

McGregor's Theory Y, on the other hand, envisions very different employees. In Theory Y, a firm's employees accomplish goals because they are intrinsically motivated. In this type of firm, close supervision and tight controls over employees are not just unnecessary—they are counterproductive.

Noted political scientist Jane Mansbridge has made a somewhat parallel distinction regarding public agencies and accountability.[5] She argues that principal-agent theory has led scholars to view public accountability as being based on sanctions alone, with better performance stemming from oversight and punishment for bad behavior. Sanctions may be the best solution when, as Mansbridge puts it, we are "in contexts of justified distrust."[6] When agents can be trusted, however, Mansbridge argues that trust-based accountability will be the superior strategy for motivating good performance.

Management structure not only follows agent motivation but also influences the mix of agents an organization has to work with. As Mansbridge puts it, "Sanction-based accountability not only stems from distrust; it creates distrust."[7] Treating agents as if they need tight controls, then, can be a self-fulfilling prophecy. The following section examines three distinct mechanisms via which this might take place. First, agents' motivation may be changed by exposure to the organization's culture and management practices; there is an organizational treatment effect. Second, Theory Y agents are more likely to enter firms that have job designs that give them the ability to flourish; organizational Navigation by Judgment will attract more Theory Y agents. Third, conditional on entering, Theory Y types are less likely to exit a firm that Navigates by Judgment. Intrinsically motivated agents are also less likely to grow frustrated and exit the firm in favor of other opportunities that grant them greater independence and autonomy.

## Treatment Effects: Making Agents
## Trustworthy by Trusting Them

Theory X and Theory Y are not innate types determined at birth; examples of the very same agents transitioning between types abound.[8] One illustration is the case of General Motors' (GM) Fremont Assembly plant. The plant closed in 1982 in part because its employees were, in the words of *their own union representative*, "the worst workforce in the automobile industry in the United States."[9] In 1984 the plant reopened as NUMMI, the first joint venture between Toyota and GM. Eighty-five percent of the workers hired by NUMMI came from the GM-Fremont workforce, a concession to the United Automobile Workers that represented the plant.[10] Those rehired included "the old union hierarchy"; demonstrating the relative powerlessness of NUMMI management to choose employees, the rehired workers included a number of former GM-Fremont workers who failed an initial drug screening.[11]

By far the biggest new ingredient at NUMMI was Toyota's management system. This management system sought "to build an atmosphere of trust and common purpose."[12] A key feature was the ability of workers to take initiative—to report problems, suggest improvements, and even stop the production line if need be.[13] As one pair of management scholars put it, the Toyota system requires that an agent "exercise considerable judgment in identifying potential problems, and must believe that he or she will not be penalized for potentially stopping the line. No formal contract can specify the conditions under which stopping the line is an appropriate thing to do."[14]

What were the results of these changes—what Philippe Aghion and Jean Tirole might term a relative shift toward agent initiative and away from principal control? "By the end of 1986, NUMMI's productivity was higher than that of any other GM facility and more than twice that of its predecessor, GM-Fremont."[15] As John Shook, an industrial anthropologist hired by Toyota to work at NUMMI, put it:

> The absenteeism that had regularly reached 20% or more? It immediately fell to a steady 2%. The quality that had been GM's worst? In just one year, it became GM's best. All with the exact same workers, including the old troublemakers. The only thing that changed was the production and management system—and, somehow, the culture.[16]

The identity of the workers had not changed, but their behavior certainly did. Key to this process was a change in job structure, which in turn altered workers' motivation. Theory X GM employees became Theory Y NUMMI employees.

Psychology's self-determination theory argues that autonomy is a critical element of cultivating intrinsic motivation, with intrinsic motivation crowded out by a management system that controls agent action by orienting agents toward external carrots and sticks.[17] Intrinsic motivation can be extinguished by extrinsic rewards or punishments and by monitoring and evaluation schemes.[18] Pay for performance and a focus on extrinsic targets can reduce agents' intrinsic motivation, shifting focus to instrumental (reward-linked) goals.[19] Creating pay-for-performance schemes or imposing penalties can shift a Theory Y employee toward embodying more traits consistent with Theory X. As NUMMI illustrates, the opposite is also true; Theory X employees can become more intrinsically motivated. Adam Grant's experimental work has demonstrated that prosocial motivation increases when agents are able to see the significant purpose of their work and feel connected to those who benefit from their labors.[20]

Intrinsic motivation is necessary for Navigation by Judgment to succeed, but it is not sufficient; agents must also be knowledgeable. Chapter 2 argued, following Aghion and Tirole, that there is a causal link between Navigation by Judgment and agent knowledge, increasing the soft information agents have about a given context.[21] Navigation by Judgment is also, Sean Gailmard and John Patty argue, likely to increase agents' investment in cultivating expertise.[22] By cultivating expertise, organizations will allow agents to see themselves as trusted professionals and thus make agents more likely to hold each other and themselves accountable via the internalization of professional norms.[23] Navigation by Judgment is associated with improvements in agent motivation, knowledge, and expertise. These improvements also make it more likely that Navigation by Judgment will succeed.

The next section considers entry into and exit from organizations. Agents like being trusted. Agents like being able to act autonomously. Agents like Navigation by Judgment. Agents thus will be differentially attracted to firms that exhibit greater Navigation by Judgment, and they will differentially exit firms that exhibit less Navigation by Judgment. Where an organization can recruit a skilled and intrinsically motivated group of employees, there will be no need to change agents from Theory X types to Theory Y types. The challenge instead for an organization will be to avoid changing agents for the worse, reducing intrinsic motivation or prompting motivated and skilled agents to exit the organization.

## Entering and Exiting Firms and Careers: Selection Effects and Navigation by Judgment

If agents desire autonomy and purpose in their work, then firms that provide opportunities for the exercise of judgment will see a greater number of applicants, all else being equal. Firms that Navigate by Judgment will be able to choose higher-quality, more motivated agents. Being able to exercise greater decision-making power is often more desirable for employees than moving up an organizational hierarchy.[24] While agent quality is difficult to observe directly, job autonomy is positively associated with employee motivation and job satisfaction.[25] Schoolteachers in America are more satisfied, and more likely to remain in education, if they report greater "teacher control over classroom activities"; that is, greater organizational Navigation by Judgment.[26]

While differential positive selection may lead to more Theory Y and fewer Theory X applicants for positions at a firm that Navigates by Judgment, there is still the underlying question of the pool of agents. If the labor force in a given field is full of agents for whom Mansbridge's justified distrust is appropriate, it may not matter that a firm that Navigates by Judgment has a slightly more trustworthy mix of applicants. In evaluating the likely effects of Navigation by Judgment, we care about the actual level of intrinsic motivation and skill in the workforce, not just the marginal difference between one organization and its peers.

Happily for our case, there are good reasons to believe the agents who populate IDOs are likely already positively selected for motivation and skill relative to the general population. They are certainly a well-educated group of employees; for example, of the approximately 2,500 professional employees at the International Monetary Fund (IMF) in 2015, over 2,000 held master's degrees and 775 held PhDs.[27] Many employees of IDOs are not maximizing financial rewards in their current positions given their qualifications; for example, while PhD holders in the IMF are on the whole quite well compensated, it is also likely that many would receive even higher wages at private-sector financial institutions. Seeking and retaining employment that does not maximize personal income is arguably suggestive evidence that something other than extrinsic rewards is an agent's primary motivator. International development organizations' socially beneficial mission increases the likelihood that employees have a desire to advance their organization's goals.[28] If agents share their principal's goals, there is less need to ensure that agents do not act in ways counter to the principal's desires.[29]

There is also suggestive evidence of differential selection into international humanitarian and development organizations. In systematic surveys, employees of international organizations exhibit different motivational mixes than the general public of their home countries.[30] Work on the United Nations (UN) perhaps provides an even better analogue to IDOs. United Nations employees rank "serving a good cause" as the second-most important of seventeen factors for joining the UN system (salary was tenth).[31] Employees in the UN system exhibit very high levels of concern for others, suggesting that these employees have policy motivation—that they care about the outcomes of the organizations for which they work.[32]

Agent burnout and exit, both from specific IDOs and the industry as a whole, are substantial concerns in the aid industry.[33] Just as organizational navigation strategy can attract more intrinsically motivated and higher-quality agents, navigation strategy can also repel these Theory Y agents. If better-quality employees prefer control over their work, they will be more likely to stay in organizations that grant them more autonomy.[34] If employees are prosocially motivated, those facing tight principal control "may find themselves increasingly frustrated as time passes, as their hopes to contribute are dashed."[35]

In U.S. federal agencies where managers have lower levels of influence over policy relative to their supervisors or political authorizers, employees are more likely to express an intention to exit the agency.[36] When U.S. presidents centralize control in the executive, it induces greater exit by the bureaucrats who formerly had the ability to impact policy and now see their potential for impact reduced.[37] For UN employees, a greater frustration with "red tape"—bureaucratic processes that constrain independent action—is associated with greater desire to exit the UN system.[38]

Stephen Snook's account of the U.S. Agency for International Development (USAID) in Tanzania during the 1980s and 1990s explicitly links an increasing focus on quantification and measurement to more control by principals relative to field agents, and in turn to the exit of qualified staff. As early as mid-1985, USAID's office in Tanzania began receiving instructions focusing on the need for externally verifiable data; USAID headquarters in Washington, DC indicated that "benchmarks need to be specific and quantified as much as possible."[39] Relatedly, the "center of power" began to shift upward from USAID missions in the field to administrators based in USAID's Washington headquarters.[40] This changed the nature of agents' jobs. One of Snook's interviewees argued that USAID stopped being "a hands-on, implementation-focused organization doing in-the-dirt development" and had become "a bank."[41] This had an impact on staff exit and staff entry; as the interviewee put it, "[USAID] attracts different personalities now. The hands-on people wanted to do development work; the 'bankers' are bean counters."[42] As USAID's navigation strategy moved away from Navigation by Judgment, USAID lost motivated field staff.

To investigate whether there is a systematic relationship between organizational navigation strategy and turnover for IDOs, I attempted to collect turnover statistics from every IDO for whom propensity to Navigate by Judgment scores can be calculated; chapter 5 will explain these scores in detail. While a number of IDOs have published documents noting their concerns over high turnover rates, I was able to find credible turnover data for only eight IDOs; these data are displayed in Figure 3.1.[43] In this limited sample, Navigation by Judgment–prone

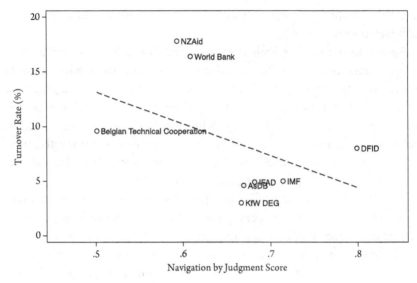

*Figure 3.1* Navigation by Judgment and Staff Turnover. Consistent with broader theory, international development organizations with lower propensity to Navigate by Judgment see higher rates of staff turnover.

IDOs see higher turnover rates than their more Navigation by Judgment–prone peers. While far from econometrically rigorous, these data are suggestive of a relationship between organizational navigation strategy and staff propensity to exit for IDOs.[44]

## Agent Motivation and Control Systems: A Case of Multiple Equilibria?

Twenty years ago Judith Tendler examined the surprising government agency successes of one rural Brazilian state with a history of underpaid, unmotivated, unhappy, and unproductive civil servants.[45] Changes in administrative structure that included greater use of Navigation by Judgment—giving field agents more autonomy and discretion—had almost magical effects. A sense of mission and purpose helped agencies accomplish remarkable things even in the absence of substantial agent compensation. Employee turnover fell. Client satisfaction improved. What is true in Brazil seems to be true in Ghana and Nigeria; there is a positive association between autonomy and the performance of the civil service.[46] If lightly compensated civil servants can make productive use of greater Navigation by Judgment, it seems even more likely that highly trained and well-compensated IDO personnel will be able to productively guide projects when given the opportunity to do so.

There are multiple stable equilibria that an organization and its agents can reach with regards to job design, motivation, and agent knowledge.[47] At one extreme there is a Theory X equilibrium with dissatisfied agents who have little autonomy or incentive to learn anything, or act productively, without explicit rewards for doing so. This seems to describe the GM-Fremont plant; unmotivated agents at odds with management will act in unproductive ways in the absence of tight controls. There is also a Theory Y equilibrium with higher-quality, motivated, and satisfied agents with a greater level of autonomy and ability to exercise judgment. This Theory Y equilibrium is also associated with greater investment in the development of expertise by agents and greater retention of this expertise by organizations.[48] In this Theory Y equilibrium, tight principal control is not just unnecessary; it is also counterproductive.

## How Theory Y Can Go Wrong

The theory Y equilibrium described in the preceding section is not a salve for all organizational ailments. Motivated, knowledgeable agents can reduce, but by no means eliminate, the risk of agent action undesired by principals, such as fraud, corruption, and malfeasance. Indeed, given enough agents and enough time, the existence of some undesired agent actions, and "bad" agents, is arguably not just probable but nearly certain. In addition, bad intent is not the only possible risk from relying on agents' judgments. Even the best-intentioned agents can make mistakes of omission and commission. Judgments are often wrong, even massively so.

Take the case of doctors, who must often rely on their experience-laden judgments. In my research for this book I read thousands of pages regarding medical decision-making.[49] For a time I thought an organizing image for chapter 1 would be doctors performing standard operations (e.g., appendix removal) versus highly specialized surgery (e.g., open heart, brain). In the former case, I think intuition suggests that standard operating procedures and an adequately trained surgeon are sufficient; in the latter, a true expert relying on their judgment seems the superior choice. This image has the advantage of easily connecting to how the growth of metrics as a control mechanism constrains Navigation by Judgment by highlighting the procedure codes and time-per-patient analyses against which doctors chafe. As one doctor put it, "Those who see medicine as a business rather than a calling push for care to be apportioned in fixed units and tout efficiency. A doctor's office is not an assembly line. Turning it into one is a sure way to blunt communication, foster mistakes, and rupture the partnership between patient and physician."[50]

Seems great, right? Perfectly suited to my purposes. One problem: while trusting the best doctors to Navigate by Judgment might well be an excellent idea, there is compelling evidence that in some important ways doctors' judgments are not at all reliable. Diagnostic errors occur during approximately 5 percent of medical outpatient visits; this comes to about *twelve million* annual mistakes in the United States alone.[51] Doctors also seem to be barely more statistically literate than the general population, a substantial problem for a profession that is often called upon to, for example, explain test results to patients.[52] Doctors making consequential errors of judgment need not be inexperienced, poorly trained, intentionally neglectful, corrupt, or drunk on the job. They are simply wrong, despite presumably the best intentions.

It would be foolhardy to try to recount in just a few paragraphs the various ways even the best-intentioned human judgment can systematically fail, given the number of volumes dedicated to this topic. One could see the entire field of behavioral economics as an exploration of just some of the myriad systematic sources of error in human judgment. Suffice it to say, people's judgments are wrong. A lot.

Nonetheless, if I was faced with a rare, mysterious condition or a highly specialized problem requiring the expert judgment of surgeons, I would need to rely on a doctor's judgments. I might not be fully comfortable doing so; but I would nonetheless in these unlikely circumstances prefer a doctor's judgments to the best computer algorithm or standardized course of care. Lewis and Clark made a lot of mistakes, too. Were it on offer, I would not choose Meriwether Lewis and William Clark's guidance over that of Google Maps in attempting to cross the Rocky Mountains today. In 1804, however, Google Maps was not yet available.

Navigation by Judgment is not likely to be the best organizational management strategy where Google Maps works well. Navigation by Judgment is a second-best solution—an alternative for when there is no perfect data, no stable and predictable environment. It is an organizational management strategy for organizations that face problems and contexts that are more 1804 and less 2015. The less well top-down controls rely on verifiable information to the exclusion of soft information, the more likely Navigation by Judgment and reliance on highly fallible human judgment is likely to be a prudent organizational strategy.

## Conclusion

A common objection put forward to granting agents more autonomy where it might otherwise be desirable to do so is that the agents are not of adequate quality to be able to make use of the granted autonomy. I believe this objection may sometimes confuse cause and effect. Agents may be of lower quality in part *because* of the lack of autonomy. Giving agents autonomy may help to retain better agents among the existing pool as well as attract additional high-quality agents. International development organizations differentially attract and retain prosocially motivated Theory Y–type agents who are likely to productively utilize the greater scope for independent action provided by organizational Navigation by Judgment. The ability to engage in meaningful autonomous action—making and using judgments—also has the effect of inducing more agent motivation, thus allowing a relaxation of principal control.

There is every reason to think critically about the operators of the system in whose care performance ultimately rests—the "who" of Navigation by Judgment. This chapter argues that the relevant elements of "who"—including agent motivation, expertise, and overall quality—is not a static feature of an organization's agents. Navigation by Judgment requires high-quality, intrinsically motivated agents. There are good reasons to believe that IDO agents may well be sufficiently high-quality and intrinsically motivated to make good use of Navigation by Judgment, and that Navigation by Judgment may induce improvements in agent quality via treatment and selection effects.

A shift toward greater Navigation by Judgment for organizations facing 1804 problems may be beneficial to an organization's performance in the long term, even when the starting point is not an agency full of satisfied, intrinsically motivated agents. Navigation by Judgment might begin a transformation process in an organization via treatment effects in the short to medium term and selection effects in the medium to long term. Mansbridge notes that sanctions-based accountability can induce distrust by agents; I argue that trusting agents to Navigate by Judgment can also induce trust and increase motivation.

Even the best-intentioned and most knowledgeable agents will make errors in their use of judgment. The high levels of agent quality and motivation this chapter predicts for an IDO that Navigates by Judgment reduces the expected rate of misuse and mistaken judgment and thus increases the probability that Navigation by Judgment will prove superior when facing 1804 problems. This is consistent with the view that Navigation by Judgment may prove the superior strategy only where environments are not predictable and projects not easily verifiable.

The next chapter, chapter 4, will explore how organizations choose navigation strategies—or more precisely what precludes organizations from choosing to Navigate by Judgment where appropriate. Chapter 4 explores the relationship of IDOs to their authorizing environments, suggesting these environments are one reason why organizations might choose not to Navigate by Judgment even when it can be helpful. As noted earlier in this chapter, organizational

Navigation by Judgment will inevitably lead to more incidents of malfeasance and mistaken agent judgment even when Navigation by Judgment works best. The next chapter will explore how a need to minimize headline-grabbing mistakes and demonstrate success to authorizers precludes IDOs' use of Navigation by Judgment.

# 4

# Authorizing Environments and the Perils of Legitimacy Seeking

This chapter explores how authorizing environments can prompt international development organizations (IDOs) to get navigation strategy "wrong." It would seem natural that IDOs—indeed, all organizations—would evolve appropriate management practices for their organizational goals. Why would we ever observe less than fully efficient management practices? Why would IDOs not employ Navigation by Judgment where it might advance an IDO's goals?

Firms, both public and private, often manage agents in ways that can be improved. The profession of management consulting and substantial strands of the academic fields of management and organizational behavior all speak to the frequent mismatch of management practice to organizational objectives. This chapter focuses on one source of variation in mismatch for IDOs: the structural differences facing IDOs that stem from differences in authorizing environments. Organizational behavior scholarship has long accepted that organizational strategies are determined in part by the need to access critical resources.[1] For public organizations, political authorizing environments are critical gatekeepers to resources, controlling the funding, the mandate, and the very survival of public agencies.

Authorizing environments are the collection of actors to whom organizations are accountable. Both public- and private-sector organizations must respond to their authorizing environments. Organizations also respond to the shadow of their authorizing environments. By "shadow," I mean the threat of future authorizer sanction, which in turn affects management's actions and navigation strategies.[2] Firms frequently adjust their behavior in anticipation of their authorizing environment's reaction. When Amazon's management considers how Amazon's board of directors will receive news of a new product launch and alters their plans accordingly, Amazon is responding to its authorizing environment. When Hillary Clinton worried about quarterly capitalism, arguing that "everything is focused on the next earnings report or the short-term share price . . . the result is too little attention on the sources of long-term growth,"[3] she voiced concerns about the effect of the shadow of private-sector firms' authorizing environments on firms' time horizons and behavior. Clinton's concern is linked to the distortions of quantitative reporting (e.g. earnings reports and share prices), as are this book's.

Public-sector organizations are also concerned with the shadow of their authorizing environments. One clear, if fictional, example of the shadow of authorizing environments trickling down a hierarchy in public agencies comes from HBO's *The Wire*, set in Baltimore. To give the appearance that crime is declining—an effort tied to Baltimore's mayor, who would like to claim that the city is becoming safer as a way to bolster his approval while running for reelection—crimes are reclassified downward. Felonies are recorded as misdemeanors and thus crime statistics improve, although crime itself is unchanged. This manipulation of statistics is a central focus of conversation all the way down the chain of command. The desire for "the numbers" flows from the chief of police, to the deputy for operations, to the majors who command districts, and, ultimately, to the front-line police officers who patrol the streets. The looming shadow of the police department's authorizing environment influences management practice, in turn focusing field agent (police officer) attention away from actual performance and toward reporting on that performance.

Figure 4.1 presents a stylized principal-agent framework showing the relationship between political authorizing environments, IDO headquarters, and

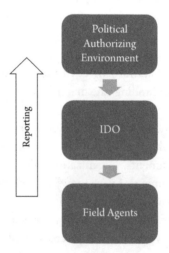

*Figure 4.1* Stylized Principal-Agent Framework for IDOs. International development organizations (IDOs) are agents of their political principals, and IDO management are in turn principals who delegate to field agents. From the perspective of the IDO, then, agents must perform actions that will be perceived as satisfactory by political authorizing principals.

field agents.[4] When IDOs "manage up" to their political authorizers, this will affect how IDO management interacts with IDO field agents.

This chapter connects authorizing environments to IDO pursuit of legitimacy-seeking measurement and reporting practices, suggesting that reporting regimes and a top-down navigation strategy can persist even when not contributing to organizational success. If authorizing environments limit organizational autonomy they will, following the logic of chapter 2, limit Navigation by Judgment.

## Not All Authorizing Environments Are Equal: Contrasting USAID and DFID

The relationship between political principals and IDOs plays a critical role in how IDOs function and what they deliver.[5] Different IDOs have very different relationships with their authorizing environments.[6] The expected probability of sanctions for failure or reputation-damaging cases of corruption and fraud varies by IDO. As such, the "length" of the authorizing environment's shadow varies; some IDOs worry about how their performance will be viewed by authorizers to a much greater degree than do others.

There are many possible reasons for this variation in IDOs' authorizing environment.[7] To name but a few: Countries vary in political culture, colonial history, and the degree to which their pasts are linked to the exploitation of the developing world. Donor nations are differentially involved in the affairs of the developing world more broadly, and they may also value aid as a tool of national strategy differently. Different donor-country publics vary widely in their support for foreign aid.[8] What differences in authorizing environments look like in practice can perhaps best be seen through a comparative example.

The U.S. Agency for International Development (USAID) and U.K. Department for International Development (DFID) are two IDOs that show clear differences in authorizing environment insecurity. The formal status of an agency and its level of formal independence have long been thought of as important features of agency independence and insulation from political oversight.[9] There are differences in formal status in USAID and DFID: DFID is a separate ministry run by a cabinet-level minister; while USAID is subordinate to a cabinet secretary, reporting to the U.S. secretary of state. DFID's leadership has power and access that USAID's does not, a sign of the relative importance and authorizing environment security of DFID vis-à-vis USAID. If the volume of legislation controlling an agency is any guide to how insulated agencies are from politics, this is another measure on which DFID and USAID vary markedly. The U.S. Foreign Assistance Act runs over three hundred printed pages; comparable United Kingdom (U.K.) legislation runs fewer than forty pages.[10]

The United Kingdom has much higher levels of foreign aid funding than the United States, suggestive of greater support for foreign aid in the U.K. legislature than the U.S. Congress.[11] DFID's budget is also much more stable, with a continued high level of funding enshrined in legislation.[12] By contrast, USAID's budget is quite unstable, with no long-term budgetary commitments. USAID's budget, unlike DFID's, involves heavy use of "earmarks" that prespecify what funds must be used for; by one Congressional Research Service estimate, earmarks comprise almost 75 percent of USAID's budget.[13] USAID has greater insecurity in a very real and tangible sense than does DFID. It is much more likely that USAID's funding will be directed in particular directions by legislators or cut. Shorter budget cycles put pressure to show results more frequently, and the general sense is that USAID is on a tighter "leash" than is DFID.

These authorizing environment differences are associated with observable differences in how the two political authorizing environments respond to common shocks. The 2008 fiscal crisis constrained government budgets in both the United Kingdom and the United States. DFID and USAID received quite different treatment consistent with the view that they are held in very different regard relative to other agencies by their respective political authorizers; DFID's budget was protected (indeed, it increased markedly in both real and relative terms) in the years that followed, while USAID's budget was not. Indeed, literally the very first public statement given by the Obama-Biden campaign in 2008 following the collapse of Lehman Brothers and the beginning of the financial crisis was a pledge to reevaluate their campaign's previous commitment to increasing foreign aid.[14]

More recently, the spring of 2017 saw both U.K. and U.S. politics moving in a broadly populist direction following the 2016 U.S. presidential election and 2016 U.K. vote to exit the European Union (EU), respectively. Criticism of foreign aid has risen in both countries as critics note the pressing domestic problems on which aid funds might be spent. In the United Kingdom, this has meant discussion of whether to revise the current law requiring the U.K. government to spend .7 percent of Gross National Income (GNI, the UN development spending goal) on foreign aid; the United Kingdom is the only G7 nation with such a legislated commitment.[15] In the end Theresa May, head of the governing Tory Party, decided in April 2017 not to attempt to change the .7 percent commitment currently enshrined in law.[16] By contrast, President Donald Trump's March 2017 initial budget proposal included cutting USAID funding by over one-third and recommended consolidating USAID into the U.S. Department of State.[17]

In both the United States and the United Kingdom, aid advocates currently feel themselves to be on the defensive; as to what happens in either country in the years to come, only time will tell. That said, "being on the defensive" has quite different meanings in the two countries. United Kingdom aid advocates find themselves defending, for the time being successfully, government spending on aid at .7 percent of GNI. In the United States, aid advocates find themselves arguing against proposed cuts that would lower U.S. spending on aid from approximately .18 percent of GNI to approximately .11 percent.[18] This would lower U.S. spending from its current relative level of about 25 percent of U.K. spending to about 16 percent of the U.K. spending level, adjusting for the size of the two nations' economies. In the United States, advocates also need to defend the very existence of USAID; in the United Kingdom, DFID's continued existence is not a question of mainstream debate. The USAID and DFID simply live in two different political realities as regards the level and stability of the broader political authorizing environment's commitment to foreign aid.

My personal experience in researching this book provides one last example of an observable difference plausibly linked to differential IDO authorizing environment insecurity. One might expect a more insecure organization to be more reticent to share information regarding its projects; this is precisely the impression I have been left with. In researching USAID and DFID projects, I filed parallel requests under the U.S. and U.K. Freedom of Information Acts on USAID and DFID, respectively.

The DFID request was initially made in May 2013; following an initial back and forth, the request was fulfilled and all requested information was provided in July 2013. The USAID request was initially made in June 2013; after many, many rounds of emails and frequent follow-up I received what USAID considered a final reply to my request in September 2015, more than two years later. This reply, in addition to being vastly more delayed, was much less comprehensive and responsive to my request compared to DFID's parallel disclosure. Most notably, USAID's response entirely ignored two of the projects regarding which information was requested. As a result I filed an appeal; after more than a year and half of delay, my appeal was granted in August 2017. However, as this book went to press at the end of 2017 no additional information had been disclosed by USAID despite multiple queries.[19] While not initially intended as an audit study, the stark difference between the two IDOs' responses to parallel requests is consistent with the view that USAID is much more insecure and thus much more resistant to disclosure. This echoes the work of Abby Wood and David Lewis, who find an association between U.S. agency politicization and relative lack of response to Freedom of Information Act requests.[20] These scholars theorize that there is a broader tension between (in this book's terms) authorizing environment insecurity and organizational success—that "efforts to make agencies responsive to elected officials may hurt management performance."[21]

The next section explores how authorizing environment constraint impacts the functioning of IDOs. It argues that more insecure IDOs are more risk-averse, less flexible, and more likely to engage in legitimacy-seeking measurement. Thus more insecure IDOs are unable to Navigate by Judgment where appropriate.

## The Impact of Authorizing Environment Insecurity on IDOs

Insecure agencies may take fewer risks, even when risk taking would benefit the agency.[22] There are two distinct senses in which agency risk aversion can lead to lower average outcomes. First, an agency that needs to show success quickly may choose a modest "quick win" over a chance at a bigger impact over the longer term.[23] An insecure IDO is akin to an insecure baseball general manager (the actor responsible for signing free agents, arranging trades, etc.) interested in showing short-term success to retain his job. A general manager on the "hot seat" may focus on winning in the short term even if doing so means lessening the team's long-term chances of success.[24]

Second, a politically insecure agency may more greatly fear what IDOs sometimes call "reputational risks." When foreign aid attracts the attention of the press and public in developed countries, it is often because something has gone wrong, such as an incidence of corruption or fraud. DFID's risk management guidance notes that reputational risks include situations where "failure would attract UK headlines."[25] As an Organization for Economic Cooperation and Development (OECD) report puts it in discussing donor reputational risk, "Even small transgressions can become a major scandal if taken out of context . . . the financial and development consequences of exposed corruption or mismanagement are typically small in relation to the whole [donor] portfolio, but the reputational damage can be much greater."[26] A more insecure IDO will have more to fear from bad headlines, and thus may avoid any risk of bad headlines even if that risk is also associated with greater development impact on average. Attempting to avoid any headline-grabbing failures may also preclude an IDO from maximizing success.

As seen from the perspective of an agency in need of justifying itself, one attractive feature of measurement and reporting is measurement's role in making the activities of the organization seem legitimate.[27] Insecure IDOs are much more likely to be concerned with demonstrating that they have been successful to authorizers. In the public sector, measurement has increasingly become critical to justifying continued funding and building legitimacy as part of a broader discourse on accountability and control; the spread of performance measurement is often linked with legitimacy seeking.[28] The use of measurement as a management practice to build the confidence of external audiences is nicely illustrated by the formal text of the U.S. government's performance measurement act, the Government Performance and Results Act (GPRA). The GPRA lists as its first purpose to "improve the confidence of the American people in the capability of the federal government, by systematically holding Federal agencies accountable for achieving program results."[29] The U.S. federal performance measurement regime, then, is explicit that one of its goals is legitimacy seeking.

The reason for measurement is in part to *appear* successful; when appearing successful and actually accomplishing the organization's objectives are in tension, the latter is likely to be sacrificed in favor of the former. By measuring things and meeting targets, even when those targets are not well linked to ultimate organizational goals, organizations can appear to be performing to political authorizers.[30] The greater the pressure to report organizational results, the greater will be the use of performance measurement and target setting inside an organization to generate the data that can then be reported.[31] Target setting does more than simply add an additional reporting step to agents' workload; as chapter 2 argued, when pressure is put upon measures for control purposes, measures change what agents and organizations actually do.

Insecure agencies are likely to engage in greater principal control at the expense of agent initiative. This is both because principal control is likely to better generate standardized data that can be used for legitimacy-seeking purposes and because tight control limits opportunities for agent malfeasance or bad action that might serve as a reputational risk for agencies. If authorizing environments are such that organizations will be penalized for failure, they will attempt to avoid failing. Ironically, an agency oriented toward documenting and reporting success may thus not be able to codify and learn from failure.[32]

## Application to the USAID-DFID Comparison

USAID and DFID are by their own admission very different organizations as regards risk-taking. USAID describes itself as having a "conservative risk appetite"; by contrast, DFID describes itself as having "a relatively high risk appetite, and [DFID] is often willing to tolerate high levels of risk where there are substantial potential benefits."[33] USAID's reporting to the State Department also creates conflict between what the USAID Inspector General's Office has called "the State Department's budget and programming for shorter-term politically strategic goals" and "USAID's longer-term development planning."[34] This mismatch in the agencies' time horizons is another source of constraint that may impede appropriate risk-taking, and navigation strategy, by USAID.

In addition, USAID stands out with regards to its top-down control of aid and the extent to which it uses output measurement to control projects. The OECD Development Assistance Committee's recent peer review of USAID— essentially a report written by other IDOs regarding USAID's systems—finds that USAID's need for authorization from Washington constrains its operating flexibility.[35] The OECD review also noted that USAID country offices "are operating with—and have to report on—an excessive number of indicators."[36] As noted in chapter 1, former USAID administrator Andrew Natsios has described USAID as suffering from "Obsessive Measurement Disorder (OMD), an intellectual dysfunction rooted in the notion that counting everything in government programs . . . will produce better policy choices and improve management."[37] Natsios links this desire for measures directly to authorizing environments and argues that these legitimacy-seeking measures detract from field agent performance. As Natsios puts it, "Demands of the oversight committees of Congress for ever more information, more control systems, and more reports have diverted professional USAID (and now MCC) staff from program work to data collection and reporting requirements."[38]

USAID may also sometimes avoid codifying its failures lest the agency be called to task for having wasted taxpayer dollars.[39] Consistent with this view, DFID has historically put much more of an emphasis on evaluation and learning than has USAID.[40] USAID and DFID keep very different kinds of records on performance. When DFID projects are complete, DFID assigns projects an overall success rating. This means noting that some projects fail and why this failure has occurred.[41] USAID, by contrast, does *not* give its projects an overall assessment of project success. For all the data USAID collects on project outputs, it does not systematically collect data that would make some projects appear unsuccessful. As a result, citizens and legislators interested in overall USAID performance are left with a great deal of data but little understanding of what projects have worked and which have not. Interested parties can currently get a report on USAID's performance against 4,206 discrete outputs.[42] One can learn that, in 2015, USAID in Albania delivered 1,894 person hours of training in trade and investment capacity-building supported by U.S. government assistance.[43] However, there is no straightforward way to determine if USAID Albania's training on trade and investment was effective or what might make it more so. By not systematically codifying failure, USAID may diminish its ability to learn. Relatedly, USAID interviewees were much more likely to ask to be made anonymous than their DFID counterparts; this may well be because they believed USAID would be less tolerant of dissent or criticism.

Chapter 3 argued that we should expect more Navigation by Judgment to be associated with better motivated and happier agents. If indeed insecure authorizing environments constrain IDO Navigation by Judgment, then a more insecure authorizing environment ought to be associated with differences in employee motivation and satisfaction. This does indeed seem to be the case for DFID and USAID. USAID is in the bottom half on U.S. federal employee satisfaction surveys.[44] DFID, on the other hand, is among the top 10 percent of U.K. agencies on employee engagement.[45] DFID and USAID are IDOs engaged in similar tasks, drawing from presumably parallel universes of civil servants. The most straightforward explanation for these differences in relative satisfaction is that the experiences of working at DFID and USAID are quite different.

Theory suggests insecure authorizing environments will be associated with less risk-taking, greater principal control, and greater use of legitimacy-seeking output measurement. A preliminary comparison of USAID and DFID, the two IDOs whose projects and management practices will be examined in greater depth, provides support for the notion that these dynamics apply to IDOs.

## Intra-national and Intra-IDO Variation in Authorizing Environment

Not all agencies of a single government operate under the same level of insecurity. In the United States the Department of Defense and the Environmental Protection Agency report to the same authorizing environment but nonetheless face differential political authorizing insecurity. This is true of IDOs as well; two agencies reporting to the same authorizing environment can have markedly different relationships with authorizers.

Recent proposals to reform U.S. foreign assistance have included many suggestions that USAID would largely cease to exist but very few that threatened the existence of the Millennium Challenge Corporation, another IDO that delivers U.S. foreign aid. Indeed, both the Republican 2015 budget and a 2016 proposal by the conservative Heritage Foundation call for cutting USAID in favor of, as one commentator put it, "elevating the Millennium Challenge Corporation (MCC) as the lead foreign assistance agency."[46] Part of what differentiates the MCC and USAID is the relative reputation of the two agencies. As Dan Carpenter has powerfully argued, agencies can cultivate reputations for competence that give them greater effective autonomy.[47] The MCC has a reputation for competence relative to USAID that—irrespective of the merits—serves to insulate the agency from political pressures.[48]

Just as different agencies can have different effective authorizing environments, so too can different units within agencies. This may be a product of a given unit's relative reputation for competence or incompetence. It also may be due to differences in agency history (mergers, creation under different governments, etc.) or the nature of the tasks some units pursue relative to others. Within USAID the sections of the agency related to "disaster relief and rehabilitation" are given more flexibility than most USAID departments, presumably due to the need for expeditious response.[49] These sections of USAID also tend to have a better reputation than USAID as a whole.[50] One of the USAID projects that will be examined in Part II operated under this relatively more flexible regime, allowing a suggestive look at within-IDO variation in authorizing environment and whether it had any impact on project outcomes.

## Success for Whom? Multiple Principals and Competing Priorities

This chapter has assumed that political principals in fact desire successful projects and that where management practice undermines delivery it is an error, not an intentional act. But is this really the case? One key feature of public agencies in general and IDOs in particular is that they report to many principals.[51] The greater the extent to which authorizers believe IDO staff have goals that differ from their own, the less likely Navigation by Judgment will be used to forward authorizers' ends.[52] Perhaps ineffective aid is in the interests of legislators who oppose aid. Seen this way, an inefficient navigation strategy would be a strategic choice rather than an error.[53]

Analyzing the overlap of objectives is thus, as in any principal-agent problem, a critical step to determining the causes of IDO navigation strategy. That said, the tension in foreign aid *implementation* is distinct from the tension in foreign aid *allocation*. Aid allocation—whether aid ought to exist, at what level of funding, and what countries ought to receive funds—is certainly a contentious issue. Aid allocation is very much a tool of donor-country domestic politics, and it is certainly at least sometimes used to accomplish political ends.[54] This may reasonably lead to some aid being less effective than it might have been; if the motivation for an allocation is political in nature, it may suggest that allocation is motivated by something other than maximizing development impact across all possible uses/countries/sectors for a given IDO.

The focus in this work on the success of IDO projects in delivering on their goals means the political economy of aid allocation and goal prioritization is largely taken as a given. The question here is whether funding that has been allotted for a particular purpose – however that allocation might have occurred – in fact accomplishes the goal towards which it is allotted. Even when aid allocation and goal determination is motivated by politics, aid is then structured into discrete projects.[55] It is hard to imagine that many stakeholders often see a given project's failure as a better outcome than that project's success, all else equal. An incomplete, unusable dam does not obviously serve a donor nation, political entity, or economic interest group.

One possible exception might be a developed-country politician who wishes for foreign aid to stop and thus conceivably has an incentive for aid to fail so as to be able to advocate for aid's elimination. Consistent with this logic, in the

U.S. Congress aid skeptics have been a strong voice for measurement and rigorous assessment of development impact.[56] Some of this focus may be intended to expose aid's ineffectiveness; but it seems a bridge too far to suggest that aid skeptics' oversight efforts are meant to *induce* ineffectiveness. In my experience, the clear message—both on and off the record—from aid skeptics is that, while they may wish some aid to be eliminated, they also wish for development assistance to be as effective as possible so long as it does exist. At the risk of naiveté I, for one, believe them. I believe that many authorizers who have been pursuing tight oversight, accountability, and measurement have been doing so under the impression that these controls improve aid effectiveness. Part I of this book is an argument that this view may be mistaken—that tight control will not in fact improve aid effectiveness. But to be mistaken about whether control will improve aid effectiveness is a far cry from authorizers in fact pursuing tight control in an effort to make aid less effective.

## Conclusion: Authorizing Environments and Part I in Summary

Writing in 1975, political scientist Judith Tendler, following a period of observation inside USAID, argued:

> It has been generally recognized that criticism of the foreign aid program weakened [USAID] and kept it from doing what it wanted to do. Less understood is the fact that the process of living with criticism profoundly affected what the agency *wanted* to do and what it was capable of doing.[57]

Insecure political authorizing environments do not just constrain agency actions; they change agency strategy. This need not be because authorizers (e.g., congressional representatives) intervene in, or are even aware of, specific projects. The threat or fear of future behavior can change agency navigation strategy.

Navigation by Judgment is risky. It requires IDO management to give up control to field agents, something that will be hard to justify to political authorizers if projects do not succeed or some agents engage in bad behavior (as some inevitably will). By inducing greater risk aversion and more legitimacy-seeking use of measures, the shadow of authorizing environments changes the behavior of IDOs in ways that limit Navigation by Judgment. When IDOs focus not on actually succeeding but rather on demonstrating that the organization is succeeding, it is likely that target setting and reporting will preclude Navigation by Judgment to an IDO's detriment.

The great irony is that the push from authorizing environments is, in my view, often well intentioned. It makes all the sense in the world to demand results in exchange for funds, particularly when those funds come from citizens and taxpayers. Where Navigation by Judgment is critical to success, however, these efforts will sometimes be self-defeating, like trying to hold on to a handful of sand—the tighter one squeezes, the less sand remains in one's hand.

This is not to suggest that an agency with an extremely secure authorizing environment will in fact always choose to Navigate by Judgment. A secure agency simply has Navigation by Judgment available as an alternative, in contrast to a perfectly insecure agency. Political authorizing environments do not determine navigation strategy; they merely influence the range of navigation options available on a given agency's "menu" and change the perceived risk (and thus cost) of various options. As will be seen in Part II of this book, this is not always to the detriment of USAID's projects as compared to DFID's; more Navigation by Judgment is not always a good thing.

This chapter brings part I to a close. Part I of this book has focused on providing a fuller picture of what navigation is, why we might sometimes expect it to lead to better outcomes, and what might preclude IDOs from fully making use of agents' judgment where appropriate. Chapter 2 examined what Navigation by Judgment is and when Navigation by Judgment will be most useful to an organization. Chapter 3 focused on agents—those in fact using their perceptions and judgment in determining the organization's course when Navigating by Judgment. This chapter has examined why some IDOs may not employ Navigation by Judgment even when it is likely to improve performance.

The next three chapters comprise Part II of this book, examining empirically when Navigation by Judgment is associated with better IDO performance and why. The next chapter, chapter 5, formalizes Part I's theory. Chapter 5 also explores in more depth the data that will form the basis of Part II's empirical tests—the Project Performance Database and qualitative case study pairs. Chapters 6 and 7 then use these data to test this book's hypotheses.

# PART II

# HOW DOES NAVIGATION BY JUDGMENT FARE IN PRACTICE?

# 5

# How to Know What Works Better, When

*Data, Methods, and Empirical Operationalization*

Chapter 2 introduced the costs and benefits of Navigation by Judgment and Navigation from the Top, with a particular focus (given its centrality for international development organizations [IDOs]) on output target-setting and reporting as a tool of tight principal control. Chapter 3 then added to this picture, exploring issues around agent motivation and quality. Chapter 4 argued that political authorizing environments can keep IDOs from Navigating by Judgment when appropriate.

This chapter serves as a bridge between Part I's theorizing and Part II's empirical tests. This chapter will first revisit the hypotheses initially put forward in chapter 2 and then operationalize the key dependent and independent variables. The chapter then introduces the empirical strategy, exploring the quantitative and qualitative methods and data that chapters 6 and 7 will use to test the hypotheses. The reader uninterested in these somewhat technical details may wish to pass over this material, returning to the narrative at the beginning of the next chapter.

## Hypotheses Revisited

The empirical strategy that is the backbone of Part II relies on considering when the virtues of Navigation by Judgment are likely to outweigh those of Navigation from the Top and vice versa. Chapter 2 states two key hypotheses. First, *Returns to Navigation by Judgment will rise as environmental unpredictability rises.* The empirical implication of this hypothesis is that the interaction between environmental unpredictability and Navigation by Judgment will have a positive relationship with Project Success. The converse is also true; as unpredictability falls—as environments become more predictable—returns to Navigation by Judgment in terms of Project Success will also fall.

Second, *Returns to Navigation by Judgment will rise as project verifiability falls.* The empirical implication of this hypothesis is that the interaction between project verifiability and Navigation by Judgment will have an inverse relationship with Project Success. The converse is also true; as projects are more externally verifiable, returns to Navigation by Judgment vis-à-vis Project Success will fall.

Figure 5.1 (first presented as Figure 1.1 in chapter 1) depicts the stylized relationships I predict among Navigation by Judgment, the mediating variables of environmental unpredictability and project verifiability, and Project Success. To be clear, Figure 5.1 is a stylized depiction, based on no data whatsoever. I predict that Navigation by Judgment will prove a superior strategy when environments are predictable and projects externally verifiable. Figure 5.1 suggests that there will be some point on each spectrum above which Navigation by Judgment will be an inferior strategy and below which Navigation by Judgment will be a superior strategy.

An organization that Navigates by Judgment will increasingly outperform an organization that does not as the challenges IDO projects face increase in their "1804-ness" and decrease in their "2015-ness", as introduced in chapter 1. This is not to say that an organization that Navigates by Judgment will see its performance actually improve in more difficult to navigate contexts; I hypothesize that it will be harder for virtually all organizations to operate in contexts that are

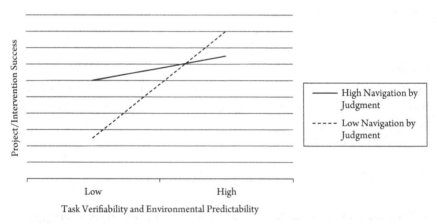

*Figure 5.1* Stylized Relationship between Navigation Strategy and Success. Low Navigation by Judgment and top-down control will serve international development organizations (IDOs) well in highly predictable environments and highly verifiable projects. As environmental predictability and/or project verifiability fall, so will development project success for all IDOs. However, Navigation by Judgment will mediate this relationship, with more Navigation by Judgment the better IDO strategy in low-predictability environments and for low-verifiability projects.

less predictable and to deliver projects that are less verifiable. Put another way, an organization that Navigates by Judgment will see much less of a decline as it shifts from more 2015 to more 1804 contexts than will an organization that does not Navigate by Judgment.

## Testing the Relationship: One Empirical Strategy, Two Complementary Methods

I will engage in two broad methods to test the relationship between Navigation by Judgment and success across context: (1) econometric analysis of project outcome data; and (2) carefully chosen pairs of case studies directly examining development projects. These methods are chosen to be mutually reinforcing parts of a single empirical strategy—the shortcomings of one method are, to the extent possible, addressed by the other. This section describes the methods, the data that will be used in testing the hypotheses, and the operationalization of key variables.

Chapter 4 provides an exogenous source of IDO variation in navigation strategy—the insecurity of political authorizing environments—that the empirical strategy, both qualitative and quantitative, will exploit. The greater the insecurity of a given IDO, the less likely that IDO is to Navigate by Judgment even when doing so will improve a project's chance of succeeding. The extent to which an IDO is likely to Navigate by Judgment for use in quantitative analysis, then, is measured in part via the degree of authorizing environment insecurity a given IDO faces. As to the qualitative empirics, the clear contrast between the authorizing environments faced by the U.S. Agency for International Development (USAID) and the United Kingdom's Department for International Development (DFID) forms a key part of the qualitative case selection strategy. By examining projects of IDOs with markedly contrasting levels of IDO authorizing environment insecurity, the qualitative empirics can speak to whether in fact IDO authorizing environments are associated with differences in IDO navigation strategy in practice. If indeed IDO navigation strategies do vary by authorizing environment, this case selection strategy facilitates direct comparison of Project Success in projects managed by IDOs employing markedly different navigation strategies.

## Quantitative Methods, Operationalization, and Data

This section first introduces the data on discrete project performance the quantitative empirics will employ, discussing its composition and collection. It then

operationalizes the key variables used in the quantitative analysis, prevents summary statistics of these variables, and introduces the econometric model. This
section closes by discussing shortcomings of the data, putting the quantitative
analysis in the context of the broader empirical strategy.

## The Project Performance Database

As discussed in chapter 1, projects are discrete time- and place-bound mechanisms meant to achieve discrete ends in service of broader development results
(goals). In addition to the (largely output) measures against which project
performance is evaluated in the short term, many IDOs also engage in broader
evaluation of projects, often substantially after the fact; these evaluations are
meant to capture project achievement of goals, not just delivery of outputs.
I have compiled a database of evaluations from nine IDOs between 1973 and
2013, which I call the "Project Performance Database" (PPD). The PPD contains data on over 14,000 unique projects in 178 recipient environments.[1] The
PPD is unique among large foreign aid datasets in including a measure of overall
Project Success. The public PPD is available for download and use at my website,
danhonig.info. Figure 5.2 shows the distribution of projects across countries,
demonstrating the wide range of countries in which projects occur.

The nine IDOs whose data comprise the PPD are the European Commission
(EC), DFID, the Asian Development Bank (AsDB), the Global Fund to Fight
AIDS, Tuberculosis and Malaria (GFATM), the German Development Bank
(KfW), the World Bank (WB), the Japan International Cooperation Agency
(JICA), the German Society for International Cooperation (GIZ), and the
International Fund for Agricultural Development (IFAD). The World Bank data
is public and easily downloadable. For two of these IDOs (DFID and the AsDB),
the data included in the PPD came from formal public information processes.
For three IDOs (the EC, GFATM, and KfW), Project Success data was released
on request or after negotiation with the organization.[2] For the remaining three
IDOs (GIZ, JICA, and IFAD), the data were assembled from individual project
completion reports by Odesk-contracted research assistants under my supervision, with the compiled data then sent back to the originating agency for comment and/or correction.[3] Table 5.1 summarizes the sourcing process for each
included IDO.

There are two basic reasons more IDOs are not included in the PPD. First,
many IDOs do not in fact assign an overall holistic success rating to projects. The
USAID is one such example: while USAID collects (as chapter 4 notes) copious
data on outputs, it does not assign projects holistic success ratings. As there is
no overall measure of Project Success for USAID, USAID projects are not in the

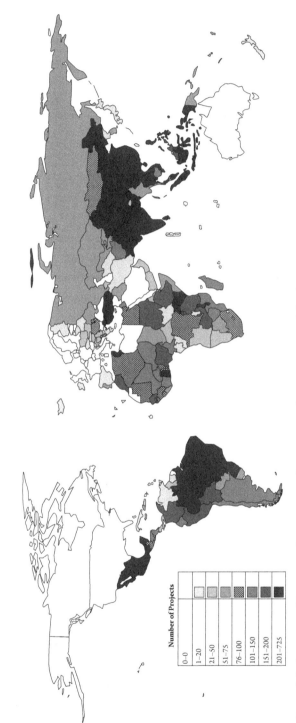

**Number of Projects**

| | |
|---|---|
| □ | 0–0 |
| | 1–20 |
| | 21–50 |
| | 51–75 |
| | 76–100 |
| | 101–150 |
| | 151–200 |
| | 201–725 |

*Figure 5.2* Overview of Projects in the Project Performance Database. International development organizations engage in projects across a wide range of settings.

*Table 5.1* **IDO-by-IDO Sourcing Process. Only the World Bank's data is public and accessible in a usable form; for all other IDOs additional coding, request, or negotiation was necessary to assemble the PPD**

| IDO Name | Sourcing Process |
|---|---|
| Asian Development Bank (ADB) | Public Information Process |
| UK Department for International Development (DFID) | Public Information Process |
| European Commission (EC) | Negotiated Release |
| Global Fund for AIDS, TB, Malaria (GFATM) | Released on Request |
| German Agency for Technical Cooperation (GIZ) | Coded from Public Documents |
| German Development Bank (KfW) | Negotiated Release |
| International Fund for Agricultural Development (IFAD) | Coded from Public Documents |
| Japanese International Cooperation Agency (JICA) | Coded from Public Documents |
| World Bank (WB) | Already Public |

PPD. Second, for some IDOs I could not get access to Project Success data that does exist (e.g., the African Development Bank). More detail on the data collection, cleaning, and coding process can be found in Appendix I.

In addition to IDO name and Project Success ratings,[4] other variables in the PPD include recipient country; project sector; project size; project start, end, and evaluation dates; project name; evaluation type (where IDOs conduct multiple kinds of evaluations); and the nature of the assistance (grant or loan).

## Operationalizing Project Success

A project's overall Project Success rating is the key dependent variable for regression analyses in chapters 6 and 7. Project Success ratings are assigned on a six-point Likert-type scale, with 6 as "highly satisfactory" and 1 as "highly unsatisfactory."[5] Holistic Project Success ratings can be assigned by IDO staff, external evaluation departments, or independent evaluators. The underlying construct employed by different IDOs for measuring the success of projects is relatively consistent, with Organization for Economic Cooperation and Development (OECD) standards in place. A given project's rating is intended to incorporate a project's relevance, effectiveness, efficiency, sustainability, and impact.[6]

This is, of course, a less than fully precise standard as to what constitutes success. Success may be defined differently for different IDOs or in different sectors. Fixed effects by IDO, sector, and recipient country partially help control for these potential sources of bias; however they do so incompletely, as variation might occur on the project level.[7] Data quality and evaluation bias are potential threats to validity, which will be discussed later in the chapter and treated in robustness checks in Appendix II.

It is also possible for the data to be accurate in the sense of correctly reflecting an organization's assessment but for that assessment to bear little connection to the actual performance of the project. To the extent possible, I have also attempted to validate these evaluations by turning to primary documentation. The World Bank uniquely allows access to archived primary project documents.[8] These documents include correspondence among project staff and between World Bank staff and national governments, back-to-office reports and (often handwritten) notes by those monitoring projects, detailed financial and performance indicators, and detailed evaluation reports. For approximately a dozen projects I reviewed archival documents at length, focusing on cases in which similar projects (such as the first and second phases of a particular project in a particular country) received quite different ratings. One might therefore be particularly doubtful about the reliability of project ratings in these cases, and I thus selected cases where I thought it was particularly likely that source material would contradict assigned project ratings. In reviewing the archival documents (which in every case occurred many months after identifying the projects to be reviewed), I intentionally proceeded without knowledge of which projects were more or less successful and attempted to generate my own rating from the primary documentation. I cannot say that my rating on a six-point scale always matched the World Bank's score precisely. Indeed, this would be troubling if true, since evaluators also engage in conversations with project personnel, recipient-government officials, and project beneficiaries, transcripts of which are not included in the archived files. However, there were no cases in which my self-generated rating differed by more than one point from the World Bank's official rating on a six-point scale. In short, in this small sample, success and failure do seem to be different and map onto real features of IDO projects.

## Operationalizing Navigation by Judgment

There is no established measure for Navigation by Judgment. As such, I combine the implications of chapters 2 and 4 in constructing a measure. Chapter 2 argues that a necessary part of Navigation by Judgment is the devolution of control from an organization's headquarters. Chapter 4 argues political authorizing environments can constrain organizational autonomy, precluding Navigation by Judgment.

In 2005 IDOs and recipient countries came together to agree on the Paris Declaration, a set of principles for achieving more effective aid tied to measurable targets.[9] Follow-up Paris Declaration monitoring surveys focused on a variety of elements of aid delivery, including the practices of IDOs. The monitoring surveys asked both donors and recipient countries for reports on their own and each other's practices (i.e., recipient countries also reported on donor behavior). From the quantitative indicators that formed part of the monitoring surveys I construct proxies for IDO "propensity to devolve control" and IDO "authorizing environment insecurity."[10]

The authorizing environment insecurity measure is constructed from two indicators. These indicators are, first, the degree to which aid is untied; that is, the extent to which it is not required that funds be spent on goods and services produced by the donor country. A high level of tied aid is a sign of an IDO's need to build political consensus for aid by serving domestic political constituencies and thus a more insecure IDO relationship with its political authorizing environment. The second indicator is the predictability of aid. The Paris Declaration asked donors to report formal projections of disbursements for future years; the monitoring surveys compare the last (that is, most recent) ex-ante projection of aid spending in a given year to the actual volume of aid disbursed.[11] Previous scholarship suggests that deviations from estimated sums are linked to IDO funding insecurity and political interference in IDO funding levels and direction.[12]

The propensity to devolve control measures are constructed from three indicators examining an IDO's project implementation behaviors. There is no available measure of IDO behavior with regards to their own agents; there are, however, systematic measures of IDO behavior as regards recipient-country governments and the frequency with which IDOs let go of control in favor of implementation led by these governments. Many of the same factors that I theorize drive IDOs' inappropriate retention of principal control vis-à-vis their agents—such as reputational risk and a desire to ensure short-term delivery are successful at the expense of long-term development goals—should also reduce an IDOs' propensity to hand over substantive control to developing-country governments. I use IDO control tendencies toward recipient governments as a proxy for IDO control tendencies toward their own agents. The specific measures employed are the use of recipient-country public financial management (PFM) systems; the use of recipient-country procurement systems; and the avoidance of parallel implementation units.[13]

In chapter 4 I argued that more insecure authorizing environments constrain IDO devolution of control to agents. An observable implication of this theory is that scores on the authorizing environment insecurity measure should be well correlated with the devolution propensity measure, inasmuch as the former influences the latter. This is indeed the case, with the devolution propensity and authorizing environment constraint measures reasonably well correlated (.41). I combine these five indicators into a simple scale of propensity to Navigate by Judgment ranging from 0 to 1, coded so that higher scores on the scale represent lower levels of political authorizing insecurity and higher IDO propensity to devolve control.[14]

A principal components analysis suggests this simple average is a more intuitive solution that will yield similar results to formal use of principal components; in any case results are robust to using a principal components approach. Appendix II presents the relevant technical information (e.g., eigenvector scree plots and component loading tables). The overall scale has a Cronbach's alpha of .825.[15] This provides reasonable confidence that these measures and the two subscales map the same essential facts regarding IDOs and thus provide suggestive evidence for my conjecture that political constraints do in fact trickle down to IDOs' engagements in the field.

I validated the Navigation by Judgment propensity scale with a more direct measure of Navigation by Judgment in practice. I conducted a small-scale direct field survey of aid experts—individuals who have substantial development experience or whose jobs bring them into contact with a wide variety of donors.[16] A typical role for one of these respondents would be a senior position in the aid management unit of a recipient government's ministry of finance. Respondents rated a number of development agencies (including but not limited to those in the sample) on a scale of 1 to 7 in response to the following question:

> To what degree do you believe the in-country field office/bureau of the agencies listed below (presented in random order) are enabled to make decisions with a significant impact on the direction, nature, or quality of development projects? Please only respond for those agencies you have had exposure to either via working with the agencies or discussions with colleagues.

The survey N is 28, with varying coverage for different donors.[17] This is a small but well-informed sample; methodological studies suggest small numbers of high-quality respondents will prove more accurate than significantly larger samples that lack expertise.[18] This survey measure is well correlated with the Paris Declaration monitoring survey–based propensity to Navigate by Judgment scale (.73).[19] The survey measure provides additional confidence in the accuracy of the Paris Declaration–based measure and serves as an alternate, direct measure of IDO propensity to Navigate by Judgment.

## Environmental Unpredictability

This work will operationalize environmental unpredictability by focusing on differential state fragility. Predictability and fragility are often linked explicitly in development practice, with practitioners speaking about the difficult and unpredictable nature of fragile state environments.[20] As the World Bank puts it, fragile states are "more unstable and unpredictable" than their less fragile peers.[21] Fragility is in some sense the likelihood that the current equilibrium will break down or change rapidly. The focus of this work is not on fragile states as a class—that is, on those at the very extreme of the state fragility measure. The hypotheses above are intended to apply to the entire range of state fragility, and thus comparisons will be made across the entire universe of developing countries.

Chapter 2 argued that unpredictability is also closely linked to legibility—to the ability of those distant from a context to be able to make sense of it based on what they can observe from afar (thus relying on data that is externally verifiable). Fragile states are also less legible; systems are less formalized (e.g., official roles are often only weakly correlated to actual power relationships). As Raymond Muhula, a Liberia-based World Bank Public Sector Reform specialist, put it when I interviewed him while researching this book, "Engaging in a fragile state with the ambitions of HQ staff is a driver of failure; when you sit in HQ and when you sit here you see things vastly differently." Fragile environments are more difficult to navigate without soft information. The more fragile a state, the less predictable the environment, all else equal.

Environmental unpredictability is measured via the Polity IV State Fragility Index (SFI).[22] This index incorporates security, governance, economic development, and social development measures and has two subscales: effectiveness and legitimacy. The two subscales are highly correlated (.66) and Cronbach's alpha (.78), which suggests that they map the same underlying construct.[23] While the analysis which follows looks at the aggregate SFI measure, results are robust to dropping either subscale. The SFI varies at the country-year level, with every country holding an annual SFI score from 1994 to the present.

## Project Verifiability

To differentiate between projects of varying external verifiability, I use OECD Development Assistance Committee (DAC) sector and purpose codes, standard classifications for projects that are assigned to projects by IDOs themselves.[24] Even the more specific of these (the five-digit purpose codes) leave much to be desired. One can't look, for example, at the delivery of antiretroviral drugs to HIV/AIDS patients specifically, as the relevant sector (sexually transmitted disease control including HIV/AIDS) includes public awareness and social marketing campaigns, strengthening of countries' HIV/AIDS response programs, and projects that focus on prevention in addition to treatment, as well as entirely unrelated sexually transmitted diseases (STDs) such as syphilis. One might wish to zero in on vaccine delivery, but this is under a code (basic health care) that also includes such things as nutrition services, support for nursing care, and strengthening of rural health systems.

As such, this work cannot systematically code sectors as having more or less verifiable projects. That said, while many sectors contain projects with a wide range of project verifiability, there are a handful of sector codes in which projects are more clearly clustered at the extremes of verifiability. Sector codes focused on the construction of physical infrastructure contain projects that are highly likely to be relatively verifiable, and sector codes focused on administrative reforms or management are highly likely to contain relatively unverifiable projects. As a second-best alternative, chapter 7 focuses on subgroup analysis, utilizing related sectors at relative extremes of likely project verifiability.

## Summary Statistics of Key Variables

Having now discussed the operationalization of Project Success, propensity to Navigate by Judgment, and environmental unpredictability, Table 5.2 presents summary statistics.

The coverage of the State Fragility Index (the measure of environmental predictability) only begins in 1994. This effectively limits the analysis to the nearly 10,000 project evaluations concluded since 1994.[25] Figure 5.3 displays the distribution of the State Fragility Index observations. The key measure of environmental unpredictability has a reasonably normal distribution and reasonable density in the tails of the distribution. This allows us to confidently estimate interaction effects, on which the following econometric model will focus.

Appendix Tables II.1 and II.2 provide additional summary statistics regarding the key dependent variable, Project Success. A key weakness of these data is the modest number of IDOs in the sample. Throughout the analysis which follows I will take care to ensure this small "2nd-level N" is not leading to spurious conclusions. In particular, I employ quite simple and straightforward econometric models to minimize the chance that these models are "overfit," with results driven by the relative lack of variation in outcome data as compared to the number of explanatory variables.

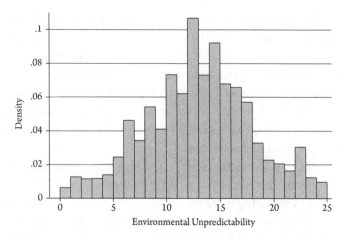

*Figure 5.3* Histogram of Environmental Unpredictability. The State Fragility Index, the key measure of environmental unpredictability, is relatively normally distributed.

*Table 5.2* **Summary Statistics for Key Variables**

| Variable | Obs | Mean | Std.Dev. | Min | Max |
|---|---|---|---|---|---|
| **Overall Project Success** (6 pt scale) | 14617 | 4.234 | 1.204 | 1 | 6 |
| **Environmental Unpredictability (State Fragility Index)** | 9312 | 12.522 | 4.993 | 0 | 25 |
| **Project Size (USD Millions)** | 9716 | 38.887 | 117.067 | .004 | 6308.998 |
| **Navigation by Judgment Propensity (from Paris Declaration monitoring)** | 14617 | .649 | .066 | .559 | .799 |

## Econometric Model and Data Limitations

The model for project $i$ in recipient country $j$ by IDO $k$ generalizes to

$$\text{Project Success}_{i,j,k} = \beta_1 * \text{Environmental Unpredictability}_j + \beta_2 * \text{Environmental Unpredictability}_j * \text{Propensity to Navigate by Judgment}_k + \beta_3 * \text{Controls}_i + \text{Fixed Effects}_j + \text{Fixed Effects}_k + \epsilon_i$$

The key empirical prediction is that the coefficient on $\beta_2$ will be positive and statistically significant; that Project Success$_{i,j,k}$ will increasingly benefit from Propensity to Navigate by Judgment$_k$ as Environmental Unpredictability$_j$ rises.

One key shortcoming of the dependent variable, Project Success, is that it is not amenable to direct interorganizational comparisons; there is no reason to believe that one IDO's rating of "4" is in fact more successful than another IDO's rating of "3." Any (constant) systematic differences among IDO evaluation criteria or measurement standards are addressed in two ways: by including IDO $k$ fixed effects in the models below (thus generating results that leverage intra-IDO comparisons across projects); and by normalizing project ratings using IDO-specific z-scores where fixed effects are not employed. The measure of propensity to Navigate by Judgment employed here varies at the IDO $k$ level and is time-invariant. This means that the measure is colinear to IDO $k$ fixed effects. As a result, quantitative analysis cannot directly compare IDOs' performance—it cannot say that, for example, KfW projects were more successful than IFAD projects in country X while IFAD projects were more successful than KfW projects in country Y.

The quantitative analysis instead focuses on the differential performance of IDOs with varying levels of propensity to Navigate by Judgment in interaction with other explanatory variables. This takes advantage of the fact that a rating of 4 given by KfW means a project was more successful than a project assigned a 3 by KfW, while a 2 given by IFAD means a project was less successful than one given a 3 by IFAD. It is possible, then, for the quantitative analysis to yield conclusions in the style of (as a hypothetical example) "KfW projects are more successful in country X than country Y, while IFAD projects are more successful in country Y than country X". Inter-IDO comparisons can be made implicitly by contrasting different patterns of intra-IDO variation in Project Success.

In a literal sense, using IDO fixed effects removes the mean of the dependent variable—Project Success—for each IDO. This also means we need not trust that projects are as successful than donors say they are to believe the results of this model. Table 5.2 indicates that the average project scores a 4.2 on a six-point scale; as one commenter on a draft of this work put it, this number is "unbelievably high. Literally."[26] It seems possible, even highly likely, that the average project is not in fact a clear success. This will not affect the econometric model so long as for a given IDO higher numbers are still associated with greater success; so long as a project scoring a 6 is more successful than a 4, a 4 more than a 2, etc. By de-meaning Project Success, we also avoid spurious conclusions about absolute levels of successfulness.

An IDO's propensity to Navigate by Judgment is not static over time and place in practice, of course. That the measure of propensity to Navigate by Judgment varies at the organizational level is not intended to suggest there is not IDO-recipient and IDO-recipient-year variation in Navigation by Judgment. It would be ideal to have time-varying data for every IDO, including variation at the country or, better yet, project level. In the absence of better measures, the question for this analysis is how likely it is that the lack of more granular measures biases these results. Controls and robustness tests presented in chapter 6 and in Appendix II attempt to probe these results to limit the risk of spurious interpretations.[27]

## Quantitative Methods in Sum

The section has aimed for a "goldilocks" level of detail—not too much or too little. Different readers will have different views on this, of course. The reader who would prefer more detail on the data collection will find more in Appendix I. The reader concerned about the quality of these data or the potential for evaluation bias, selection issues, measurement validity, sensitivity of the results to features of the modeling, the uniqueness of the Navigation by Judgment scale, decomposition of measures, and much more ought turn to Appendix II. Appendix II has a wide range of additional information, data quality checks, alternative specifications, and placebo tests; it may make sense to explore Appendix II after examining the primary quantitative results in chapters 6 and 7.

The quantitative data has substantial limitations. There is no temporal variation in the key independent variable, propensity to Navigate by Judgment. There is no inter-IDO comparability in the key outcome measure, Project Success. I feel toward these data as Winston Churchill did toward democracy as a system of government; these are the worst possible data on IDO performance . . . except for all other data.[28]

The econometric analysis attempts to analyze these data in such a way as to wring valuable insight from this messy and flawed source. The advantage of the quantitative analysis is breadth—the ability of the analysis to incorporate a wide range of projects. The quantitative analysis cannot, however, directly compare the relative performance of two IDOs operating in a single context; nor can it provide great insight regarding mechanisms.

This book has hypothesized a somewhat complicated causal chain—from political authorizing environments to constraints on IDO management strategy to actual constraints on agents in the field. The quantitative analysis can be no more than suggestive in these regards. Econometric analysis can provide support (or not) that the observable implications of the theory are as hypothesized, but it cannot say much about why this is the case or whether the theory is correct vis-à-vis an alternative theory with similar observable implications. As such, this quantitative analysis is just one-half of this book's empirical strategy; the other half of that strategy, leveraging qualitative case study research, is described next.

# Qualitative Methods and Data

This section describes in detail how the case studies were chosen and briefly describes data collection methods. It then describes the role that qualitative cases play in the overall empirical strategy.

## Case Selection

Chapter 4 introduced the marked difference in authorizing environments faced by USAID and DFID. The case selection strategy exploits this difference, examining USAID and DFID projects in contexts of varying environmental predictability and project verifiability. USAID and DFID were chosen for their relatively parallel status—as aid agencies of two allied Anglophone countries—but seemingly quite dissimilar levels of authorizing environment insecurity. The propensity to Navigate by Judgment score for each IDO supports the view that these differences in authorizing environments do indeed lead to different propensities to Navigate by Judgment; USAID has a score of .36, thirtieth among the thirty-three IDOs for whom Paris Declaration monitoring surveys allow the calculation of scores. DFID, on the other hand, has a score of .80, second among the thirty-three IDOs.[29] Thus the case studies implicitly serve as another check on the validity of the propensity to Navigate by Judgment measure, examining whether USAID and DFID do indeed navigate in starkly different ways as the measure would suggest.

The case studies examine USAID and DFID in two countries that vary markedly in terms of environmental predictability, South Africa and Liberia. On the State Fragility Index used to measure environmental unpredictability in the quantitative analysis, Liberia scored a 16 in 2012.[30] This put Liberia closer to Iraq (20) and Afghanistan (22) in 2012 than it was to South Africa (8). The choice of Liberia as one of the countries in which to examine IDO performance was a natural one given my previous work experience in the country.[31] South Africa seemed the natural country with which to pair Liberia. It is also in sub-Saharan Africa and is Anglophone (thus facilitating fieldwork). South Africa is relatively stable and predictable among developing countries; also, to be completely honest, it is a country I was interested in learning more about. Given my previous involvement with IDOs in Liberia, I took care to ensure that none of the Liberian cases involved IDO projects with which I had been substantially involved; in many cases I had not previously been aware of the projects before selecting them. Having known many of the actors involved in the Liberian cases (particularly on the government of Liberia side) for many years might be seen by some as compromising—as auguring toward something less than complete objectivity. I would argue experience has its benefits in access, honesty in inter-viewee response, and understanding of the perspectives and motivations of par-ticular actors.

In selecting case studies of varying project verifiability, I intentionally focused on sectors with differential likelihood of verifiable projects rather than directly choosing projects that were differentially verifiable. I selected on sectors rather than directly on projects in part because in many cases it was difficult to determine a project's verifiability before closely examining the project. Engaging in such close examination of projects before selecting cases raised the prospect of unintentional bias in case selection, which I wanted to avoid.

There are also more substantive advantages to selecting sectors for case studies rather than projects directly. Part I suggests authorizing environment insecurity and IDO navigation strategy affect not just the performance but also the design of projects. Chapter 2 makes clear that two projects may have the same goal but different levels of project verifiability. Choosing sectors rather than projects allowed me to examine not just how differences in navigation strategy affected project performance conditional on the project's verifiability—the qualitative equivalent of block randomization—but also how IDO choice of project within sectors varied. Choosing sectors thus allowed a richer examination of how two IDOs with markedly contrasting authorizing environments and propensity to Navigate by Judgment scores fared in attempting to achieve similar goals.

The sectors I chose were government capacity-building and health. Government capacity-building seemed to me to be a sector where projects would likely have low project verifiability; improving the government's ability to deliver seemed a hard thing to manage via output measures. As a contrasting sector I chose health, a sector that is often—but not always—focused on highly verifiable outputs, such as the delivery of antiretroviral drugs. These sectors had the additional advantage of being fairly well populated by IDO projects, thus increasing the chance in expectation that I would be able to find closely matched USAID and DFID projects in a particular country and sector.

In choosing the specific projects to examine in each country and sector, I primarily used the OECD development assistance database to which both USAID and DFID report all projects.[32] I looked for USAID and DFID proj-ects in each of the four country-sector pairs—South African health, Liberian capacity building, etc.—with the most similar goals. In some case pairs, this led to incredibly similar projects—for example, in South Africa USAID and DFID had essentially parallel projects focused on municipal government finan-cial management and execution capacity that occurred at the same time. In all case pairs, there was reasonable similarity of project goals, and thus a common standard against which to evaluate a project's relative instrumental success in reaching those goals.

Some of these case studies came to cover multiple discrete projects from a single IDO in a single sector, as multiple projects served the same goal for the IDO. As such the unit of analysis in the case studies shifts at times from discrete projects to an IDO's overall pursuit of a particular development goal in a country over a given period of time. I refer to this as the IDO's "interventions," or, when referring to projects that followed one another in pursuing a goal, an IDO's "arc of interventions."

Tables 5.3 and 5.4 show the specific USAID and DFID projects that will be examined. The vast majority of these projects are ultimately implemented not by the IDOs themselves but by contractors. For the most part, the additional level of complexity introduced by this contracting of delivery will not be a primary focus of the case studies, inasmuch as the use of contractors is common for both USAID and DFID; however, there will be some comparison of differences in how similar contracting structures operated in practice for the two IDOs. Chapter 8 will discuss the implications of this book's findings for the use of contractors by IDOs more generally.

*Table 5.3* **Schematic of USAID Interventions and Case Studies.\* Indicates the end date is the time period discussed in interviews regarding the intervention, rather than the end date of the intervention itself**

|  | *Low Environmental Unpredictability: South Africa* | *High Environmental Unpredictability: Liberia* |
| --- | --- | --- |
| **Low Project Verifiability: Capacity Building** | Local Governance Support Program (LGSP) phase 2, 2004–2010: implemented by RTI International | Building Reform and Recovery through Democratic Governance (BRDG), 2006–2008: Implemented by Development Alternatives Incorporated (DAI) for the Office of Transitional Initiatives (OTI) |
| **High Project Verifiability: Health** | President's Emergency Plan For AIDS Relief (PEPFAR), 2003–2013\*; various implementers | Rebuilding Basic Health Services (RBHS), 2008–2013\*: Implemented by JSI<br>Fixed Amount Reimbursement Agreement (FARA), 2011–2014\* |

*Table 5.4* **Schematic of USAID Interventions and Case Studies. * Indicates the end date is the time period discussed in interviews regarding the intervention, rather than the end date of the intervention itself. Liberia's health-sector pooled fund was begun by DFID but is not exclusively a DFID mechanism**

|  | *Low Environmental Unpredictability: South Africa* | *High Environmental Unpredictability: Liberia* |
|---|---|---|
| **Low Project Verifiability: Capacity Building** | Consolidation of Municipal Transformation Programme (CMTP), 2003–2009: implemented by Deloitte | Support to Civil Service Capacity Building (CISCAB), 2007–2010: Implemented by Adam Smith International |
| **High Project Verifiability: Health** | HIV/AIDS Multisectoral Programme (MSP), 2003–2008; implemented initially by Futures Group, succeeded by HLSP | Support to the Office of Financial Management (OFM), 2007–2010: Implemented by Price Waterhouse Coopers |
|  | Rapid Response Health Fund (RRHF), 2008–2009; implemented by HLSP | Health Sector Pooled Fund (PF), 2008–2014* |
|  | Strengthening South Africa's Response to HIV and Health (SARRAH), 2010–2013*; implemented by HLSP |  |

## Data Collection Methods

The case study pairs draw from primary documents (including those acquired by U.S. Freedom of Information Act and U.K. Freedom of Information requests) and semistructured interviews, the majority of which occurred in Liberia and South Africa in the spring and summer of 2013 (for Liberia, May–June 2013; for South Africa, July–August 2013). Notably for the Liberian health cases, this means the vast majority of the interviews occurred prior to the Ebola outbreak in West Africa, which began in late 2013. Ebola was at the time of interviews an "unknown unknown," a tragic future shock unforeseen and unforeseeable for Liberia.

In total I conducted approximately 300 hours of interviews with approximately 140 individuals across the eight case studies. Appendix Tables I.1, I.2, I.3, and I.4 provide the full list of interviewees by case study. For many of the

South African interviews I employed transcription services, creating written records I was then able to reference, review, and interrogate.[33] The majority of interviews were recorded, allowing me to listen to individual interviews multiple times and confirm and clarify my notes.[34] I focused on finding interviewees who had been at a senior level in making decisions for each project, complementing their perspective with that of their subordinates, their supervisors at headquarters, and other stakeholders—for example, where relevant I interviewed project beneficiaries and recipient government officials who were responsible for or interacted substantially with a given project. I also spoke to individuals involved in the design of each project to understand how the project came to be and what motivated critical design choices.

Interviewees were told that no comment would be attributed to them by name without their explicit permission. As such, the interviews are cited via randomly generated numbers and the date of the interview. In all cases where quotations are attributed to specific individuals, the interviewee indicated either this specific quote, or the interview as a whole, were attributable; attributed quotes are not associated with interview numbers, as doing so would serve to de-anonymize any other statements the interviewee made. Some individuals requested anonymity as well; these individuals are listed under the tables of interviewees as "Anonymous." Appendix I contains additional information on data collection and interview methods.

## Case Study Construction

The case studies provide an opportunity to understand the relationship between political authorizing environment, organizational navigation strategy, and Project Success with a greater degree of detail. These cases allow for a much more direct examination of the role of mechanisms for better understanding the pathway between navigation strategy and success. The case study pairs also allow for direct comparison of different organizations' success in a given context.

For each case study, I examine three distinct phases: the design, implementation, and (where necessary) revision of projects. I identify critical decisions in each phase and the process via which they were made, with a particular focus on the degree of initiative and judgment exercised by field agents and constraints on same. I also explore reporting requirements and agents' motivations and considerations when determining whether to act or what choice to make. I then examine the relative performance and levels of success of each project and intervention. Success is defined instrumentally; I use as my measure of a project's success the degree to which the project accomplished the goals the project set for itself.

The case studies provide two opportunities for examining variation beyond the USAID-DFID comparison. First, USAID's South African health projects were under the larger umbrella of the U.S. government's President's Emergency

Plan for AIDS Relief (PEPFAR). The U.S. Centers for Disease Control (CDC) also executed South African PEPFAR projects, allowing for a comparison of the navigation strategy of two U.S. agencies engaged in nearly identical work in the same recipient-country environment.

Second, USAID's Liberia capacity-building project was managed by USAID's Office of Transitional Initiatives, which enjoys more flexibility than other units at USAID. While this was not intentional—I did not know the managing unit of any USAID or DFID project at the time case selection occurred—it is in many ways fortunate, as it allows an examination of intra-IDO variation in navigation strategy. This intra-IDO variation is, as chapter 4 argued, perfectly consistent with the theory that political authorizing environments are an important, but far from the only, source of variation in navigation strategy.

## Case Study Role in the Broader Empirical Strategy

The qualitative case studies, then, allow for an examination of how authorizing environments and IDO rules, targets, measures, and reporting requirements affect the behavior of agents in the field and the course of IDO projects and interventions. The case studies allow for an examination of the design, implementation, and revision of projects and the role that principal control and agent judgment play in these critical junctures. The case pairs allow a direct comparison of success for two very different IDOs in four distinct contexts that vary by level of environmental predictability and sector, with sectors chosen so as to provide a contrast in the tractability of potential projects to management by externally verifiable measures. By comparing across case pairs, the case study design also allows an examination of whether environmental predictability and project verifiability are important mediators of the relationship between navigation strategy and Project Success.

The qualitative and quantitative strategies are designed to be mutually supportive. The quantitative data do not allow direct interorganizational comparisons of success; the qualitative strategy does just this. The qualitative cases, while chosen to maximize variation, could be outliers in unobservable ways; the broad coverage of the PPD means the quantitative analysis does not suffer from the same concerns. If the two strategies lead to mutually supportive results in line with this chapter's predictions, this will provide strong evidence for the underlying theory.

## Conclusion and the Rest of Part II

This chapter has formalized expectations regarding when Navigation by Judgment is likely to prove successful and outlined how these hypotheses will be tested. Fifteen years ago, the economist Avinash Dixit argued that what the study of public organizations lacked was empirics that do not "seek sweeping universal findings of success or failure of performance-based incentives or privatization, but should try to relate success or failure to specific characteristics like multiple dimensions and principals, observability of outputs and inputs, and so on."[35] Part II of this book answers Dixit's call, exploring the interaction of organizational strategy with specific characteristics of project observability and environment.

The next two chapters test this book's hypotheses, connecting navigation strategy and performance directly. Chapter 6 focuses primarily on the role of environmental unpredictability in mediating the effects of Navigation by Judgment, leveraging the PPD and the case studies in relatively unpredictable Liberia. Chapter 7 focuses primarily on project external verifiability, using the PPD and the case studies from South Africa; this allows a focus on the differences in project verifiability without the potential confounding influence of an unpredictable environment. Collectively, the rest of Part II explores the evidence as to when, where, and why Navigation by Judgment succeeds or fails.

# Journey without Maps

*Environmental Unpredictability and Navigation Strategy*

This chapter investigates whether the quantitative and qualitative data support the claim that Navigation by Judgment has greater returns in terms of Project Success in more unpredictable environments for international development organizations (IDOs).[1] This chapter also helps us better understand how precisely Navigation by Judgment affects Project Success. The chapter first examines the role that an IDO's propensity to Navigate by Judgment plays in the relationship between IDO Project Success and environmental unpredictability. It then turns to qualitative cases, examining two pairs of interventions in Liberia. These case studies compare U.S. Agency for International Development (USAID) and U.K. Department for International Development (DFID) performance in Liberia's unpredictable environment as both IDOs attempt to achieve similar goals in health-sector and government capacity-building interventions.

## Quantitative Analysis: Does Navigation by Judgment Help IDOs Cope with Greater Environmental Unpredictability?

Chapter 5 introduced the data employed in the quantitative analysis, including summary statistics, descriptions of scale construction, and much more. As such, this section turns immediately to empirical results. Table 6.1 reports core findings on the relationship between Navigation by Judgment and environmental unpredictability in the success of IDO projects. Inasmuch as Table 6.1 represents the core empirical results—and thus this small table is in some sense the primary product of well over a thousand hours of work in collecting and cleaning data even before turning to analysis—I hope the reader will permit me to linger a bit on this table and its implications.

Table 6.1 **Navigation by Judgment Mediates the Relationship Between Environmental Predictability and IDO Project Success. While all IDOs see performance decline as environments become less predictable, more Navigation by Judgment–prone IDOs have substantially smaller declines. Ordinary least squares (OLS) regression**

| DV: Project Success (6-pt scale) | (1) | (2) | (3) | (4) | (5) | (6) | (7) |
|---|---|---|---|---|---|---|---|
| Environmental Unpredictability | −0.170*** | −0.171*** | −0.149*** | −0.147*** | −0.112*** | −0.107*** | −0.0868*** |
| | (0.0194) | (0.0222) | (0.0237) | (0.0262) | (0.0317) | (0.0335) | (0.0361) |
| Env Unpredict*Nav by Judg | 0.205*** | 0.206*** | 0.187*** | 0.180*** | 0.113** | 0.104** | 0.107* |
| | (0.0292) | (0.0322) | (0.0344) | (0.0373) | (0.0500) | (0.0517) | (0.0550) |
| Project size (USD Millions) | | 0.000585*** | | 0.000413*** | | 0.000566*** | |
| | | (0.000126) | | (0000131) | | (0.000166) | |
| Constant | 4.724*** | 4.739*** | 4.186*** | 4.231*** | 6.037*** | 6.113*** | 4.817*** |
| | (0.0314) | (0.0400) | (0.179) | (0.197) | (1.087) | (1.052) | (1.091) |
| IDO Fixed Effects | Y | Y | Y | Y | Y | Y | Y |
| Recipient Fixed Effects | N | N | Y | Y | N | N | Y |
| Sector Fixed Effects | N | N | N | N | Y | Y | Y |
| R²-Within | 0.029 | 0.024 | 0.081 | 0.080 | 0.086 | 0.091 | 0.143 |
| R²-Between | 0.0T0 | 0.106 | 0.081 | 0.119 | 0.362 | 0.558 | .336 |
| Observations | 9312 | 7247 | 9312 | 7247 | 7370 | 5446 | 7370 |

Standard errors in parentheses

* p<0.05, ** p<0.01, *** p<0.001

The first row in Table 6.1 tells us there is a robust and statistically significant negative relationship between environmental unpredictability and overall Project Success. Environmental unpredictability is associated with less successful project evaluations for IDOs on average. All models include IDO fixed effects.[2] This means that the model's comparison is being made within each IDO's projects, comparing whether a given IDO—for example, the Asian Development Bank—sees more successful projects on average in more or less unpredictable environments (as measured, per chapter 5, by the State Fragility Index). Models 3 and 4 in Table 6.1 incorporate recipient-country fixed effects, thus focusing only on changes in environmental predictability within recipient countries over time. Models 5 and 6 incorporate sector fixed effects, controlling for sectors at the most fine-grained level available, the 222 unique five-digit Organization for Economic Cooperation and Development (OECD) Development Assistance Committee Creditor Reporting System (CRS) purpose sectors. Findings are robust to focusing on differences in performance within sectors as well.

If Project Success ratings in the Project Performance Database (PPD) introduced in chapter 5 were simply arbitrarily assigned, we would expect no relationship between Project Success and environmental unpredictability. If in harder to monitor unpredictable environments all projects were declared more successful, we would expect environmental unpredictability to be associated with higher success ratings. But instead we see the relationship that this book's theory, and arguably intuition, would predict: as environments become (in Chapter 1's language) more 1804 and less 2015—as the implementation journey becomes less tractable to pre-drawn maps—IDO Project Success falls. It seems that Project Success ratings contain useful information.

As noted in chapter 5, the key empirical prediction regards the interaction between Navigation by Judgment propensity and environmental unpredictability. This is the variable that allows us purchase on whether more Navigation by Judgment–prone IDOs are able to cope more successfully with greater environmental unpredictability than their less Navigation by Judgment–prone peers. The second row of Table 6.1 indicates that this interaction term is positive and statistically significant, suggesting that Navigation by Judgment does indeed play an important role in allowing an IDO to cope with greater environmental unpredictability. Once again, this result holds when focusing on within-sector or within-recipient-country data.

Figure 6.1 draws from Model 1 of Table 6.2 to graphically represent differential performance by level of Navigation by Judgment. Note that the y-intercepts, and thus the relative level of the two lines in Figure 6.1, do not contain useful information. The direct effect of propensity to Navigate by Judgment is absorbed by IDO fixed effects, making the vertical positions of the two lines arbitrary. What *is* informative is the differential slopes of the two lines—the differential

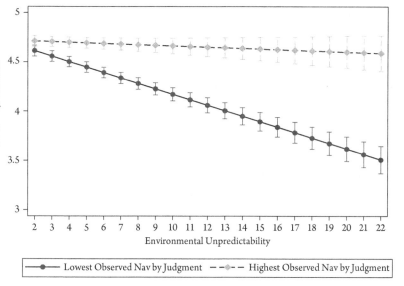

*Figure 6.1* Returns to Navigation by Judgment in Countries of Differential Predictability. More Navigation by Judgment–prone IDOs see much more consistent performance than do less Navigation by Judgment–prone IDOs as environmental predictability varies. Bars around each point estimate represent 95% confidence intervals. The "lowest-observed" Navigation by Judgment propensity score in the PPD is .56 on a zero to one scale and the "highest-observed" is .80; these represent the extremes of Navigation by Judgment propensity in the sample data. See Appendix Table II.14 for a full list of Navigation by Judgment propensity scores.

success in response to differential levels of success for IDOs of varying levels of propensity to Navigate by Judgment.

All IDOs perform better in more predictable, stable contexts than they do in less predictable environments. More Navigation by Judgment–prone IDOs perform better than their less Navigation by Judgment–prone peers in less pre- dictable environments relative to their own performance in more predictable environments. An IDO with relatively low levels of Navigation by Judgment sees over half a point (.5) of difference between its performance in a state like Armenia (SFI = 7 in 2014, or one standard deviation more stable than the mean) and its performance in a state like Nigeria (SFI = 17 in 2014, or one standard deviation below the mean). An IDO with relatively high levels of Navigation by Judgment experiences about .06 of a point, or one-tenth as much, performance differential in response to the same difference in environmental unpredictability.

Going from one extreme of environmental unpredictability to the other— a difference of 20 units—would move a project by the least Navigation by Judgment–prone IDO in the sample from the median, or 50th percentile, of Project Success (a 4.5) to below the 25th percentile (a 3.4; the 25th percentile of the distribution is 3.6). By contrast, a difference of 20 units of environmental unpredictability would move a project by the most Navigation by Judgment–prone IDO in the sample from a 4.5 to a 4.4, still well above the mean (4.2) of Project Success. Notably, this would cause the low Navigation by Judgment IDO's project to transition from "success" at the mean to "failure"; in using the World Bank's scale, for example, some scholars have chosen when compressing success to a binary measure to call any project scoring 4 and below "unsuccessful."[3]

These empirical findings are highly supportive of this book's theory. The following sections briefly discuss some of the main threats to validity of these results. Appendix II contains many dozens of additional pages of exploration of the underlying data and robustness tests.

## Selection

One natural concern might be that controlling for recipient and sector fixed effects does not account for the fact that different IDOs may make decisions about what projects to pursue in light of where projects would be more successful. Part I of this book suggests that more Navigation by Judgment–prone IDOs are also those IDOs more able to act autonomously. Perhaps more autonomous IDOs engage in greater strategic selection of recipient countries and sectors, placing themselves in a better position to succeed. While this selection effect would be a channel from Navigation by Judgment to differential IDO Project Success, it would be one that meant more Navigation by Judgment–prone IDOs were not in fact more successful than their less Navigation by Judgment–prone peers in actually delivering projects in more unpredictable environments relative to their own performance in more predictable environments.

To explore IDO project selection I construct a parallel dataset with the number of observations from each IDO in each country in each sector. If indeed differential propensity to Navigate by Judgment is working via selection of sectors and projects, we should see differential presence or absence of projects by level of environmental unpredictability. Table 6.2 replicates Table 6.1's regression model but substitutes the number of projects in each IDO-country-sector as the dependent variable. There are over 950,000 unique IDO-country-sectors, allowing quite a bit of precision in this selection estimate. Table 6.2 finds no selection along the main dimension of inquiry, the interaction between environmental unpredictability, and the propensity for Navigation by Judgment. This suggests that IDO selection of sectors and countries is not a systematic problem for the analysis presented above.

*Table 6.2*  **IDO Project Selection. IDOs of different levels of Navigation by Judgment propensity do not differentially select into more or less unpredictable recipient-country environments**

| DV: # of observations by IDO-country-sector | (1) | (2) | (3) | (4) |
|---|---|---|---|---|
| Environmental | −0.000102 | −0.000847 | −0.000102 | −0.000847 |
| Unpredictability | (0.000491) | (0.000475) | (0.000491) | (0.000475) |
| Env Unpred*Nav by Judg | 0.000594 | 0.000594 | 0.000594 | 0.000594 |
| | (0.000666) | (0.000666) | (0.000666) | (0.000666) |
| Constant | 0.00192 | 0.0174*** | −0.00474*** | 0.0107* |
| | (0.00129) | (0.00411) | (0.00118) | (0.00416) |
| IDO Fixed Effects | Y | Y | Y | Y |
| Recipient Fixed Effects | N | Y | N | Y |
| Sector Fixed Effects | N | N | Y | Y |
| $R^2$ | 0.007 | 0.014 | 0.015 | 0.021 |
| Observations | 957096 | 957096 | 957096 | 957096 |

Standard errors in parentheses
* $p<0.05$,** $p< 0.01$,*** $p <0.001$

In Appendix II, Table II.6 also adds time fixed effects to the controls in Table 6.1, demonstrating that the results in Table 6.1 are robust to controlling for time, time interacted with IDO, and time interacted with recipient-country fixed effects. The main results do not seem to be driven by the presence, absence, or success of IDOs over particular time periods.

## Additional Robustness Checks

There are myriad ways these results can be further interrogated. I pursue a range of tests in Appendix II to probe and extend these results.

To partially summarize, differential evaluation bias for different IDOs does not seem to be driving the relationship between propensity to Navigate by Judgment, environmental unpredictability, and success. If more Navigation by Judgment–prone IDOs were more likely to employ more generous internal evaluations (relative to less generous external evaluations) in more unpredictable environments than their less Navigation by Judgment–prone peers, the results in Table 6.1 might be a result of evaluation methods rather than actual performance differences. In Appendix II, Table II.5 controls for evaluation type; the primary results are unchanged. There may well be "grade inflation" in how IDOs evaluate their projects. However, there is no sign that differential evaluation bias is leading this econometric analysis to spurious conclusions.

It also does not seem to be quirks of measurement or subtle features of the construction of any of the key measures that are driving results. Using the survey measure of Navigation by Judgment or a principal-components approach does not alter findings. Treating success and failure as a binary outcome and employing logit models, or using ordered logits on the full original Likert-type scales, yields substantively identical results. So does dropping either subscale and any measure in the Navigation by Judgment scale drawn from the Paris Declaration monitoring surveys, such as using only the first wave of the Paris Declaration monitoring surveys; dropping any subscale of the measure of environmental unpredictability, the State Fragility Index; alternative clustering of standard errors; and many more such checks. Appendix II also presents the IDO-by-IDO relationship between environmental unpredictability and Project Success, explores variance in Project Success and how this varies with level of environmental unpredictability and propensity to Navigate by Judgment, and presents IDO-by-IDO summary statistics.

There is one last robustness check I wish to highlight. One might think that the measures I use as indicative of Navigation by Judgment are in fact just being a "good donor." This view would argue that, yes, donor practices matter; but it is a general suite of good practices, not specifically Navigation by Judgment, that is associated with being differentially able to make projects succeed in more unpredictable environments. In Appendix II, Table II.11 runs a placebo test, seeing if other scales of good donor practice—specifically, higher scores on the Quality of Official Development Assistance (QuODA) measure or the Commitment to Development Index (CDI)—are associated with more successful projects. These other measures of good donor practice do not show the same relationship with Project Success in interaction with environmental unpredictability as does the propensity to Navigate by Judgment. Scoring better on these measures of good donor practice may well be a good thing; higher scores are not, however, associated with a relatively greater ability of donors to cope with environmental unpredictability, as seen via Project Success ratings.

The empirical results above use a flawed dependent variable (Project Success) and a key independent variable (Navigation by Judgment propensity) that has no variation within IDO or over time. These features give rise to some of the many reasonable concerns one might have regarding the robustness of the key findings above. I have tried every way I can think of to disprove the primary results of Table 6.1. Nevertheless, they persist.

## Suggestive Quantitative Findings: Mechanisms

Chapter 2 suggested that there were multiple channels via which more Navigation by Judgment is helpful as environmental unprecitability rises. More Navigation by Judgment is helpful both in response to shocks (by encouraging flexibility) and in the face of lower environmental legibility (by enabling field agents to make sense of hard to understand environments). Appendix Table II.16 examines how IDOs of differential propensity to Navigate by Judgment are impacted by shocks (natural disasters) and finds suggestive but not statistically significant results that more Navigation by Judgment-prone IDOs cope better with disasters when they occur. Appendix Table II.15 examines legibility, exploring if a greater propensity to Navigate by Judgment is more helpful when countries rise in complexity (as proxied by ethnolinguistic fractionalization) and the World Bank's measure of "rule-based governance." For legibility the findings are substantially stronger than they are for shocks, with Navigation by Judgment associated with a differentially greater ability to deal with these more 1804 environments both across recipient countries and within recipient countries as they rise or fall on these measures over time. This suggests legibility plays an important role in making unpredictable environments more difficult contexts for projects to succeed.

One necessary condition for taking advantage of soft information is that agents actually be present to access locally observable but nonverifiable information. An observable implication of this is that IDOs that have a local office—with their own staff based in the country where the project is taking place—ought be more successful, and that this will be increasingly the case in more unpredictable environments. As reported in full in Appendix Table II.17, IDOs that are more likely to Navigate by Judgment may benefit more from the presence of an office in unpredictable environments after controlling for recipient-country fixed effects—that is, when comparing the presence of an office to other projects within the country where an office is not present. Having an office is not a universal boon to Project Success, however; IDOs with a lower propensity to Navigate by Judgment see no returns to the presence of a country office. This suggests that formal decentralization and establishment of local units are not sufficient to take advantage of soft information. Consistent with Philippe Aghion and Jean Tirole's model, agents need to have the incentive (the "real authority") to make use of information; mere presence of agents is insufficient.

## Linking Quantitative Empirics to the Qualitative Empirics

The econometric analysis supports the view that Navigation by Judgment has a substantial effect on project outcomes. Navigation by Judgment is most helpful to an IDO where environmental predictability is lowest. More Navigation by Judgment–prone IDOs perform better than their less autonomous peers in more unpredictable contexts relative to *their own* performance in other contexts.

The analysis thus far does not allow for the direct comparison of IDOs in situations of differential environmental unpredictability. The results thus far show more Navigation by Judgment–prone IDOs have more stable project performance than less Navigation by Judgment-prone IDOs as environmental unpredictability rises. "More stable" is not the same as "better"; that is, the econometric results are perfectly consistent with a view that all Navigation by Judgment–prone IDO projects are much less successful—but consistently much less successful—than those of less Navigation by Judgment–prone IDOs. The qualitative empirics allow us to directly examine the relative success of pairs of interventions that aimed to accomplish similar (or in some cases virtually identical) development goals from two IDOs of varying propensity to Navigate by Judgment—USAID and DFID. These empirics thus allow a direct test of the relative success of different IDOs' projects.

In addition, the quantitative findings on mechanisms reported in the preceding section are suggestive at best. The qualitative empirics can speak more directly to how precisely navigation strategy affects Project Success. The qualitative data can also say more about what in fact it means to "succeed" or "fail"; is it that Navigation by Judgment leads to clear and unambiguous success, or that a lack of Navigation by Judgment leads to clear and unambiguous failure? The qualitative case pairs discussed in the following section explore whether and how navigation strategy impacts relative Project Success.

# The Effect of USAID and DFID's Differential Navigation Strategies in Liberia's Unpredictable Environment

This section uses the four Liberia case studies to explore the relationship of Navigation by Judgment to Project Success, as well as the pathway that connects the two. It compares the performance of the U.K.'s Department for International Development (DFID) and the U.S. Agency for International Development (USAID) in a particularly unpredictable, and difficult to understand from afar (that is, low-legibility), environment: that of postconflict Liberia from 2006 to 2014. I first provide a brief background on Liberia during the period of the case study projects. I then turn to the case pairs themselves, examining first the Liberia health-sector case pair, then the Liberia capacity-building case pair.

Within each case pair I follow a similar structure. First, I introduce and provide some background on USAID and DFID's interventions and compare the navigation strategies of the interventions. I then compare the relative success of the interventions and link that level of success to navigation strategy. Appendix I describes my interview methods and practices in detail; the bulk of interviews were conducted in the summer of 2013, and thus the narrative largely uses 2013 as an endpoint. I used a semistructured interview process, meaning that to some extent I was open to interviews taking conversations, and thus these case studies, in unanticipated directions.

I try to balance a consistent structure for each case study with providing additional relevant detail about other elements of cases that speak to the themes of this book. This chapter additionally explores the differences between one of USAID's most flexible units (the Office of Transitional Initiatives), who managed USAID's Liberia capacity-building project, to USAID more broadly. In the Liberian health case I also conducted follow-up interviews, examining how the results of USAID and DFID's similar interventions fared in response to the shock of Ebola to the Liberian health system.

## Background and Context: Liberia, 2006–2013

The period 2006–2013 was a time of rapid change in Liberia. In January 2006, Ellen Johnson Sirleaf became sub-Saharan Africa's first democratically elected female head of state following a twenty-five-year period of Liberian history dominated by military coups, civil wars, and rule by warlords. Johnson Sirleaf's predecessor as president, Charles Taylor, was convicted of, as the judges put it, "some of the most heinous and brutal crimes recorded in human history" (including physical and sexual violence, use of child soldiers, terrorizing the civilian population, and enslavement) by the Special Court for Sierra Leone in 2012.[4] By contrast, Ellen Johnson Sirleaf was awarded the 2011 Nobel Peace Prize.

Liberia in 2006 was a country just emerging from a very dark period of its history. Infrastructure was scarce; there was no power grid anywhere in the country, and all electricity was provided by generators. Perhaps the only thing in shorter supply than physical infrastructure was skills. Liberia had some fifty physicians for a population of 3.5 million, with skilled professionals who could seek opportunities outside Liberia's borders having overwhelmingly done so over the previous quarter-century.[5] There was very little high-quality data via which to navigate; the last published census was that of 1974, and that census was of dubious quality.[6] Liberia was a country in distress, and one that had fallen from previous heights. The best estimates suggest gross domestic product (GDP) in 2005 was USD$160 per capita, or less than one-fifth Liberia's 1979 GDP per capita.[7]

*Table 6.3* **Diagram of Liberia Case Studies. * indicates the end date is the time period discussed in interviews regarding the intervention, rather than the end date of the intervention itself**

|  | *USAID* | *DFID* |
| --- | --- | --- |
| **Capacity Building** | Building Reform and Recovery through Democratic Governance (BRDG), 2006–2008: Implemented by Development Alternatives Incorporated for the Office of Transitional Initiatives (OTI) | Support to Civil Service Capacity Building (CISCAB), 2007– 2010: Implemented by Adam Smith International |
| **Health** | Rebuilding Basic Health Services (RBHS), 2008-2013*: Implemented by JSI | Support to the Office of Financial Management (OFM), 2007– 2010: Implemented by Price Waterhouse Coopers |
|  | Fixed Amount Reimbursement Agreement (FARA), 2011–2014* | Health Sector Pooled Fund, 2008–2014* |

By 2013 Liberia had seen stability for the better part of a decade and was one of the fastest-growing countries in the world, with economic growth of 8.3 percent in 2012.[8] The country had clearly transitioned from emergency recovery mode to the broad development space occupied by most other sub-Saharan African countries. Even in 2013 Liberia was far from a highly predictable environment, however. While stability had sprouted, there was much that remained to be done to ensure its roots were of adequate depth to stand firm in the storms the future might bring.

By examining the implementation of DFID and USAID's interventions over this period, we can see how different IDO navigation strategies were able to perform in Liberia's unpredictable environment. Table 6.3 provides an overview of the specific interventions that will be discussed below. The rest of this section will first examine USAID and DFID health-sector interventions in Liberia, then turn to DFID and USAID's approaches to government-wide capacity building.

## USAID and DFID Interventions in the Liberian Health Sector

The primary U.S. and U.K. aid agencies—USAID and DFID—employed markedly different navigation strategies in Liberia's health sector, as we will see. But this is not because the two international development organizations (IDOs) had fundamentally different analyses of the sector or different theories of how to improve the sector. Both USAID and DFID had the same basic strategy circa 2006—to support Liberia's minister of health, Dr. Walter Gwenigale, in his efforts to build a more capable Ministry of Health and Social Welfare and to guide greater resources through the ministry. [9] Gwenigale was widely seen as an honest, dedicated reformer, though one who faced a monumental challenge—turning a basically absent system in a country with some fifty doctors into a functioning public health infrastructure. [10]

In two separate "rounds" of interventions, USAID and DFID aimed to support the Liberian government's delivery of health services, allowing multiple points of comparison regarding navigation strategy and the shadow of the different U.S. and U.K. authorizing environments described in chapter 4. The health case studies thus examine multiple discrete projects for each IDO. The following section first introduces these interventions and their navigation strategy. It then compares the relative success of the interventions before linking this success to navigation strategy, allowing for an exploration of how navigation strategy impacted relative IDO intervention success.

### Comparing Interventions and Navigation Strategies

In some sense, DFID's first intervention in the Liberian health sector was a project it and USAID both might have implemented. One of the first things Gwenigale wished to do was improve the Ministry of Health's financial management. Appalled that his ministry could not even produce a simple financial statement, Gwenigale reached out to donors to support his efforts, requesting funding for equipment and advisors to help staff and train an Office of Financial Management (OFM). [11] The first IDO Gwenigale approached to support this goal was USAID, but the management of USAID Liberia was initially "not enthused" by the idea. [12] Gwenigale then approached the U.S. ambassador to Liberia directly. [13]

The U.S. ambassador was receptive and pushed USAID to engage; USAID estimated, however, that to stand up such an unusual project would require over a year of preparation. [14] On some interviewees' views, one element of what made this project nonstandard for USAID, and thus slow to commence, was how difficult it would be to set targets against which success could be measured. [15] Some within the Liberian Ministry of Health doubted USAID would ever actually implement, perceiving USAID's timeline as a "dragging of feet" in an effort to avoid implementing the project. [16] As a result of concerns regarding USAID's ability and desire to implement the project, the Ministry of Health approached DFID; DFID quickly committed to supporting the project.[17] This DFID decision was largely a judgment call made by DFID field personnel.[18] Support of the ministry's Office of Financial Management (OFM) thus became a DFID project rather than a USAID project largely due to the Liberian ministry of health's perception of DFID's relatively greater interest in providing this support.

While DFID's small office in Monrovia was technically reporting to its London headquarters via the much larger office in Sierra Leone, neither the Sierra Leone nor the U.K. offices played an active role in implementing DFID's OFM project. DFID personnel on the ground had a relatively free hand to manage as they saw fit.[19] In one example, the individual initially assigned by the implementing contractor to lead the support to OFM was seen by DFID field agents as not up to the job.[20] DFID field staff pushed for the individual's replacement. This change came quickly enough in the project's implementation that it would have been impossible for distant supervisors to see measures of poor performance. This decision, then, relied on soft information rather than data that supervisors could observe.

While USAID did not ultimately support the OFM project, USAID was actively involved in Liberia's health sector. The first major USAID project was a USD$52 million sector-wide project called Rebuilding Basic Health Services (RBHS), a single project that would focus on the whole of health systems.[21] RBHS focused both on direct service delivery, via nongovernmental organizations (NGOs) in seven of Liberia's fifteen counties (with a particular focus on five counties), and on strengthening the Liberian government's central Ministry of Health and county health teams.[22]

The USAID project was driven to a large extent by producing the output metrics on which the project reported to USAID.[23] Among the numbers reported in RBHS annual reports are the number and proportion of mothers delivering their babies in health facilities (3,043 deliveries, 14 percent coverage in 2009) and a count of the number of condoms distributed through the project (over 173,000 in 2009).[24] The 2009 report also contains information on "Key USAID Indicators." These include, among many others, the "Number of people trained with USG funds in malaria treatment or prevention," indicator 3.1.3.3 (73 people in 2009); and the "number of policies or guidelines developed or changed with USG assistance to improve access to and use of FP/RH service," indicator 3.1.7.5 (3 policies or guidelines in 2009).[25]

This USAID project also encouraged facilities that it funded to focus on counting and reporting performance, in part via performance-based contracts where providers were rewarded for meeting output targets.[26] Indeed, USAID's evaluation of RBHS saw reliance on, and promotion of, quantifiable targets as a key success; RBHS's 2011 performance evaluation articulates as the very first programmatic and technical strength of RBHS the introduction of "a data-driven culture in the national health care delivery system."[27]

DFID's Office of Financial Management project also had quantitative targets—but they were of a very different sort. The targets on which DFID's contractor had to report were longer term and included a large number of indicators only very tangentially related to sound financial management. For example, the very first indicator in the DFID project's logical framework—the document that links the project to outcomes—is to "reduce maternal and child mortality rates in Liberia."[28] A 10 percent reduction in mortality would make the project a success, according to its logical framework.[29]

Let's examine that 10 percent reduction target in a bit more detail. Reducing maternal and child mortality are laudable goals to be sure, and there is no doubt that better financial management can play an important role in improving the allocation of funds in the health sector as well as attracting new funds. As such clearly the OFM's success could be expected to have a positive impact on real health outcomes. That said, Liberia had myriad programs, from a variety of sources, devoted to reducing maternal and child mortality. Indeed, even without external intervention reaching DFID's 10 percent reduction target was quite likely, simply due to the end of Liberia's long conflict (and thus better access to existing formal and informal health facilities, meager though they might have been). It seems difficult to attribute gains on maternal and child mortality to the existence of the Office of Financial Management (OFM); and surely this state of affairs was perfectly predictable when the target was conceived. DFID's project "piggybacked" on other projects and secular trends in a way that allowed it to demonstrate "success" in a way that did not constrain what the project did in practice. Setting quantitative targets that did not depend on the project's activities resulted in measurement that in no way constrained DFID's Navigation by Judgment.

One small component of DFID's support for the Office of Financial Management project was to begin developing a Health Sector pooled fund that would fund activities in support of the newly created Government of Liberia National Health Plan. A pooled fund is a mechanism for channeling the support of multiple IDOs (who "pool" their resources). Pooled fund contributors are able to make more of a combined contribution toward their objectives while also lessening administrative costs for both IDOs and recipient governments. In the case of Liberia's health-sector fund, which is still operational, proposals are made to a steering committee composed of donors and the government (including both the Ministry of Health and the Ministry of Finance). Once there was agreement on the proposals, funds flowed from the pooled fund accounts through normal government channels (including the Office of Financial Management).[30] The pooled fund began operations in March 2008 when the fund received its

first funding from DFID.[31] The pooled fund then gained additional donor participation from Irish Aid in December 2008, followed by UNICEF and UNHCR.[32]

Some USAID officials wished to contribute to the pooled fund, a move
for which the Ministry of Health had also lobbied. However, congressional
restrictions regarding the commingling of funds in the health sector made this
impossible.[33] Congress directly precluded what for some in USAID would have
otherwise been the preferred solution; in this way, political authorizing environments very clearly constrained USAID's choice set.

USAID's alternative was to use a Fixed Amount Reimbursement Agreement
(FARA), via which USAID reimbursed the ministry based on explicitly measured performance in accomplishing discrete tasks. The FARA was explicitly
framed by one interviewee as an intentional effort to approximate the benefits
of the pooled fund within USAID's rules.[34] A number of interviewees noted
how innovative FARA was in comparison to other USAID programs, with one
interviewee calling it "about as innovative on the side of taking risk as I've seen
[at USAID]."[35] The FARA reimburses the Ministry of Health for spending in
accordance with a plan agreed between USAID and the Ministry of Health.
Reimbursements occur once the Ministry of Health accomplishes specifically
agreed benchmarks.[36] These benchmarks are all observable, generating clear
quantitative reports that can be transmitted up USAID's hierarchy and serve as a
firm objective basis for the release of funds.[37] One example of a FARA payment
indicator was "the percentage of [health] facilities receiving three supervision
visits during the quarter".[38] Indeed, USAID's policy guidance on FARAs globally
requires this measurement and reporting, saying "reimbursement is made upon
the physical completion of an activity, a sub-activity, or a quantifiable element
within an activity."[39]

Comparing the DFID-catalyzed pooled fund to USAID's FARA provides
a telling contrast in flexibility. Pooled fund resources can be deployed (and
revised) as the steering committee sees fit—that is, based on the judgments
of knowledgeable field-based actors. By contrast, FARA execution was fixed in
advance, with payments tied to meeting externally observable targets. Revisions
to FARA required a formal negotiation involving USAID headquarters.[40]

USAID and DFID had broadly the same goal: to strengthen the Liberian
health system. They also had a similar broad strategy to achieve that goal: to
build the capacity of the Liberian Ministry of Health and Social Welfare, including increasingly channeling funding and control via the ministry. They took
different navigation strategies toward that goal, a difference at least partially
attributable to rules and restrictions from USAID's political authorizing environment. The next section examines the relative success of USAID and DFID's
interventions.

## Establishing Levels of Success

How, then, do the interventions of the U.S. Agency for International Development (USAID) and the U.K.'s Department for International Development (DFID) compare in the Liberian health sector? As both agencies aimed to strengthen government health systems, their legacy in doing so seems a fair way to compare these interventions.

As of 2013 the Liberian Ministry of Health's Office of Financial Management (OFM), set up with the support of DFID's project, was a competent, widely praised unit functioning without external donor support.[41] Many actors noted that the DFID project led to a replacement of old, entrenched personnel with new systems and employees focused on good performance and prudent fiscal management.[42] In her January 2009 annual message (the rough equivalent of the U.S. State of the Union address), Liberian President Johnson Sirleaf singled out the Ministry of Health as the ministry to have advanced furthest in improving financial management systems. President Johnson Sirleaf also explicitly linked this improved financial management to the success of the OFM and the DFID-catalyzed pooled fund, saying, "The Ministry of Health has made the most progress in the establishment of financial management systems. In recognition of this achievement, the Pool Fund established last year for the sector attracted the support and the praise of several of our development partners."[43]

One actor described DFID's OFM project as "one of the more effective projects that I'm happy to have been part of,"[44] a view broadly representative of actors from DFID, the implementing contractor, and Liberian government officials. Improved financial systems also made routing funds through government systems more attractive. By one estimate, assets under management by the ministry rose from under USD$10 million in 2007 to nearly USD$70 million by 2012, with only a small fraction of that coming from government coffers.[45]

USAID's Rebuilding Basic Health Services (RBHS) project also had substantial impacts. It accomplished much in terms of service delivery as well as pioneering innovations such as performance-based financing that have since become national policy.[46] That said, this effective structure was outside the Liberian government, with (in the views of many inside and outside USAID) detrimental implications for the project's long-term ability to sustainably improve health systems—the project's primary goal.[47]

In response to open-ended questions regarding RBHS, it was striking how often individuals framed the project as, in the words of one individual, "basically running a parallel health system."[48] One concern raised was that this parallel system actually undermined government provision by offering higher salaries, which induced skilled providers to leave the public system for better pay. By one account, drivers and janitors for RBHS were making three times as much as skilled Ministry of Health workers.[49]

USAID's RBHS was a well-designed, well-executed project run by earnest, caring individuals.[50] The project made significant efforts to include the ministry in critical decisions to the extent the project structure allowed.[51] USAID's RBHS was nonetheless separate from the government, using a different operational approach—efficient but not necessarily transferrable to government, and thus possibly requiring perpetual external support. Little financial information flowed back to the ministry, making it difficult for the government to know precisely what was being accomplished or to get a holistic picture of spending in Liberia.[52]

As noted above, USAID and DFID then shifted their focuses in the Liberian health sector to funding direct Liberian government execution of health activities via FARA and the pooled fund, respectively. Liberian actors were universal in their support for the pooled fund as an important step in gaining control over the sector and in improving coordination. As Liberia's then chief medical officer and current minister of health Dr. Eunice Dahn put it, "From the word 'go,' from the time we established the pooled funding, the Ministry of Health has been in the driver's seat."[53] One study argued that, prior to the pooled fund, "Multiple donors funded multiple NGOs within a few geographic areas, which resulted in no clear sense of which organization was responsible for providing what services to what population."[54] The shift to the pooled fund—with NGOs contracted but funded from central ministry revenues—initially improved this coordination problem but with a decline in health delivery quality, as the Ministry of Health was unable to fill the supervision role previously played by donors.[55] The pooled fund steering committee responded by funding monitoring and evaluation from the pooled fund's resources, and performance improved.[56] As of 2013 NGOs were increasingly been held to account; performance by 2013 was well above levels in the period prior to pooled fund financing.[57] By the time of interviews in 2013, the pooled fund was a critical—and widely positively regarded—institutional feature of the Liberian health sector.[58]

USAID's FARA was also seen as a move in the right direction by a wide variety of actors as compared to other USAID health interventions.[59] The performance of health facilities transitioning from RBHS to FARA funding (and thus from USAID contractor to Liberian government management) also declined initially.[60] One observer characterized this as similar to the decline one might expect if there were a change in contractors between phases of a large USAID project.[61] Performance then improved, and FARA was largely seen as successful in delivering services.[62]

While FARA was largely seen as a success, it was not without its difficulties. The Liberian government was reimbursed for their spending by USAID only after verification of targets; this meant the Liberian government had to consistently find the money to "prefinance," as local actors put it, expenditures for FARA.[63] In Liberia's constrained fiscal environment, finding the money to finance operations was not always easy. One observer noted it was "quite optimistic to think a poor country is going to be able to prefinance a large USAID health portfolio."[64]

The FARA also placed a quite significant administrative burden on the Ministry of Health through a weekly FARA meeting involving senior Ministry of Health staff and USAID officials.[65] One senior ministry official described USAID as "guiding the process so that we can't make mistakes."[66] By all accounts, these meetings were critical to FARA's success. However, it is hard to imagine that the ministry would have been able to have a similar meeting with every donor were that to be required for fund distribution.

Both FARA and the pooled fund were designed to assist the Ministry of Health in delivering health services; these interventions both aimed to put the ministry in control. It is notable, then, that Ministry of Health actors saw FARA as less helpful, and less flexible, than the pooled fund.[67] Gwenigale, the minister of health when both FARA and the pooled fund were established, made clear that he preferred the pooled fund to FARA and saw FARA as very low risk for the U.S. government. As Gwenigale put it,

> The Americans are not taking any risk; because what they are doing is "use your money, if we want to we will pay you back or we will not pay you back if we don't accept what you have done." . . . They are not taking any risk by saying use your own money and we'll replace it.[68]

Viewing these arcs of support in aggregate, USAID delivered less than DFID even without adjusting for DFID's more modest level of spending. It is striking that DFID focused on interventions that more greatly empowered a recipient government that both USAID and DFID were interested in strengthening. DFID's interventions also were delivered in a way that naturally led to their continuation (including working more closely through the Ministry of Health). In the Liberian health sector, DFID's relative Navigation by Judgment was associated with greater levels of success in achieving the long-term development goal both USAID and DFID's interventions sought: strengthened government health delivery.

The Ebola crisis that began in March 2014 provides an opportunity to examine differences between the USAID's FARA and the pooled fund in response an unexpected exogenous shock to Liberia's health system.[69] The next section briefly examines how each intervention fared as Liberia coped with an "unknown unknown."

### Differential Responses to Ebola: The Pooled Fund and USAID's FARA

While not part of the initial hypotheses and interviews of my fieldwork, Ebola's tragic appearance allows an evaluation of which mechanism proved more beneficial in response to the kind of unpredictable exogenous shocks all too frequent for the world's least developed nations. Put another way, both FARA and the pooled fund sought to improve health systems. As such, examining which proved more helpful in response to a shock in the Liberian health system allows for further comparison of the relative flexibility and success of the two funding mechanisms.

Some FARA payment targets were altered to accommodate changed public health policies. In one example, a target relying on national meetings of health care professionals (imprudent given the risk such a meeting among health workers would facilitate Ebola transmission) was altered to allow county-level meetings.[70] But when Ebola ultimately interfered with the accomplishment of specific FARA targets, USAID responded by not making payments.[71] As one individual involved in FARA put it, "The deliverables are fixed; if they're not met, they're not met . . . .. You want to maintain the integrity of the mechanism."[72] USAID's FARA did "maintain the integrity of the mechanism"; as a result FARA failed to disburse funds to the Liberian government as it attempted to address the Ebola crisis.

The pooled fund focused largely on core health tasks during the Ebola crisis; however, the coordinator of the pooled fund, Miatta Gbanya, was detailed at the government's request to act as deputy national coordinator of the government of Liberia's overall Ebola response.[73] In this role, Gbanya played a substantial role in coordinating overall funding of the Ebola response, working to ensure financing flowed efficiently (rather than having multiple parties fund identical/duplicative things).[74]

While both FARA and the pooled fund focused primarily on their "core" pre-Ebola business throughout the crisis, the nature of the pooled fund meant that personnel and capacity were available to respond more dynamically to the country's overall health needs. The FARA proved itself less flexible and helpful in response to Ebola than did the pooled fund.

### Linking Success with Navigation Strategy

There is evidence that USAID pushed the bounds of the possible, abutting the limits of what its rules would allow, in the Liberian health sector. As such this case pair provides insight into where precisely the limits of the possible lie for USAID as well as differences between limits for USAID and DFID. In multiple specific ways—support for the Office of Financial Management and use of the pooled fund—DFID was able to act more autonomously, making decisions that were not possible for USAID. That DFID's health interventions were more successful in Liberia, and DFID employed greater Navigation by Judgment, does not necessarily mean that Navigation by Judgment played a causal role in DFID's great success. There are, however, a number of specific, discrete critical junctures in these projects that seem linked to DFID's greater Navigation by Judgment.

The DFID decision to fund the Office of Financial Management project seems a clear example of DFID's greater degree of Navigation by Judgment. The decision to quickly replace the initial OFM project lead also showed DFID's Navigation by Judgment. Field-level actors, confident in their judgments and in control of the project (from the point of view of their organization), pushed for a change not in de jure project rules but in de facto performance via the replacement of the key project personnel assigned by the contractor. This decision was in the view of a number of interviewees critical to the project's success.[75]

Political authorizing environments and top-down controls played a clear role in USAID's FARA. Congress prevented USAID from channeling funding via the pooled fund; DFID had no parallel authorizing environment constraint in channeling funding via the pooled fund. USAID instead implemented a project with the same objectives as the DFID-catalyzed pooled fund, one that pushed the envelope of what was possible for USAID. The FARA, USAID's alternative, is a mechanism that explicitly contracts on outputs and allows less Liberian government or IDO Navigation by Judgment than does the pooled fund. Even when pushing the boundaries of authorizing environment constraint, USAID still exhibits less organizational autonomy, more reporting and measurement, and less Navigation by Judgment than does DFID. USAID's greater constraints proved an awkward match for Liberia's environment.

DFID's Navigation by Judgment proved more successful in the Liberian health case pair due both to what Navigation by Judgment induced (e.g., the ability to use soft information in the OFM project) and what Navigation by Judgment avoided (e.g., the relative inflexibility of USAID's FARA). The next section turns to the other pair of Liberia cases, examining performance in USAID and DFID's attempts to strengthen the government of Liberia's ability to execute more generally.

## USAID and DFID Capacity-Building Projects in Liberia

The USAID and DFID both recognized the large capacity gaps in Liberia and the need to strengthen the government's ability to execute. As Liberian President Johnson Sirleaf put it:

> There you stand, trying to rebuild a nation in an environment of raised
> expectations and short patience, because everyone wants to see change

take place right away. After all, they voted for you because they had confidence in your ability to deliver—immediately. Only you cannot. Not
because of the lack of financial resources, but simply because the capacity to implement whatever change you have in mind does not exist.[76]

This case pair focuses on efforts by both the U.S. Agency for International
Development (USAID) and the U.K. Department for International
Development (DFID) to strengthen the government's ability to deliver across
its many functions. For DFID, their Civil Service Capacity Building (CISCAB)
project was pointed toward this goal. So was USAID's Building Reform and
Recovery through Democratic Governance (BRDG, pronounced "Bridge").[77]
The U.K.'s CISCAB and U.S.' BRDG may have had similar broad aims but differed substantially both in how they were managed and the tactics via which the
projects sought to achieve their aims.

The main focus of USAID's BRDG was to assist government ministries and
agencies in improving planning, communication, budgeting, and coordination—
that is, improving the ability of government to execute.[78] The USAID Office of
Transitional Initiatives (OTI) managed USAID's BRDG. The OTI is a relatively
flexible USAID unit, and the relationship between OTI and its contractors has
traditionally been more a partnership and less a supervisory relationship.[79]
We might expect, then, that OTI would be a unit more likely to Navigate by
Judgment when appropriate. By examining a pair of cases where USAID's efforts
were led by OTI, we can examine USAID's Navigation by Judgment as compared to DFID's when USAID's Navigation by Judgment is relatively likely to
Navigate by Judgment.

### Comparing Interventions and Navigation Strategies

There are indeed signs of greater Navigation by Judgment in the case of USAID
OTI's capacity-building efforts than in USAID's Liberia health projects. The
specific activities funded under BRDG were determined during implementation by the judgments of field personnel. The OTI project, BRDG, in the
end had 102 discrete components, from "Coaching Ministry Leaders" at the
Ministry of Education to "Administrative Support for the Liberian Judiciary"
at the Ministry of Justice.[80] The three discrete BRDG activities most often mentioned by interviewees were the establishment of the president's radio studio,
supporting youths' day activities held by the Ministry of Youth and Sports, and
short-term consulting to the Civil Service Agency on pay and grading reform.[81]
Some activities grew out of requests from Liberian government officials;[82] some
stemmed from the OTI and the contractor's reading of public messages from

Liberian government officials or issues raised in the popular press;[83] and some were identified by project staff themselves.[84]

Motivated staff, great working relationships, and a flexible and adaptive approach clearly served BRDG well. It is striking how many interviewees mentioned how different it was to work for, or interact with, BRDG compared to other USAID projects.[85] Specific features mentioned by interviewees included the greater power given to staff than in other USAID projects[86] and the speed of BRDG's decision making and execution as compared to other USAID projects.[87] Staff felt free to propose projects that were generated from their understanding of Liberia's needs—an understanding that incorporated soft information. Multiple interviewees noted that BRDG was relatively unique in that their work felt consequential, with their judgment able to impact program direction.[88] As one interviewee put it, there was "room for thinking on your own, for taking decisions."[89] Three Liberian respondents mentioned the greater flexibility of BRDG as a significant comparative strength.[90] This flexibility was also a strength of OTI mentioned by international staff.[91] USAID's BRDG project, then, seemed to exhibit greater Navigation by Judgment than the typical USAID project, perhaps due to the role USAID's Office of Transitional Initiative (OTI) played in managing the project. One of the results of this greater Navigation by Judgment was greater flexibility in responding to changing circumstances.

This is not to suggest that BRDG implementation was absolutely seamless—one interviewee reported an incident of procurement corruption, where someone buying goods on behalf of the project solicited bribes.[92] This incident is unique among the case studies in this book—there were no other projects in which an interviewee or source document revealed such clear malfeasance, and it is consistent with the notion that letting go of principal control increases the opportunity for corruption. While I cannot prove this empirically, my suspicion is that it may be that bribes were solicited, or other clear malfeasance and fraud were occasionally present, in other projects as well; what is remarkable here is the revelation of malfeasance, not its occurrence.

In any case, this occurrence of malfeasance needs to be set against the reported response of project staff. As reported by the same interviewee, who was also Liberian BRDG staff, the bribe solicitor's colleagues were very upset with the individual who had solicited bribes. As the interviewee put it, staff were upset that the accused was "ruining it for us . . . how dare you embarrass us this way."[93] The "it" that staff were presumably upset the incident of malfeasance might be "ruining" was the relatively unique culture, and ability to Navigate by Judgment, that project staff were enjoying. That project staff identified with the project, rather than their fellow Liberian (in a culture where soliciting bribes is far from unusual), strikes me as remarkable.

USAID's BRDG was unlike any other USAID project examined in Part II, with the choice of where to direct project support very much driven by field agent judgment. Each individual activity nonetheless required a substantial dose of verifiable output reporting. For each of the 102 discrete activities, BRDG had a report detailing delivery of procured supplies (BRDG did all purchasing, providing only in-kind financial support) or completion of trainings, drafting of manuals, and so on.[94] To take the two examples used above, for "Coaching Ministry Leaders" at the Department of Education this output reporting would have taken the form of a report with the number and perhaps names of ministry participants, days spent on the training, and topics covered.[95] For "Administrative Support for the Liberian Judiciary," this output reporting would have included proof of purchase and proof of delivery of the physical goods (computers, photocopiers, etc.) to recipients. Two BRDG staff members noted that proposals for projects that could not deliver discrete, quantifiable outputs were likely not to be approved by OTI for implementation.[96]

The U.K. Department for International Development (DFID) intervention that forms the other half of the Liberian capacity-building case pair is DFID's Civil Service Capacity Building (CISCAB) project.[97] The CISCAB project aimed to improve the civil service's ability to execute, and in so doing it sought to improve governance and service delivery.[98] This was a comprehensive civil service reform project, aimed at transforming the civil service. The project initially focused on developing a Civil Service Reform Strategy.[99] It then worked to implement the reform strategy, focusing on discrete components such as pay reform, civil service training, and developing standard procedures for the hiring and classification of civil servants.

DFID's CISCAB project also had reporting requirements. Quarterly "brief updates on project activities" and biannual reports to DFID on overall progress were both produced by DFID's implementing contractor.[100] These reports consisted entirely of narrative accounts rather than quantifiable output statistics.[101] The need to report, and specific targets, played very little role in CISCAB's implementation.[102]

DFID's project was substantially designed—indeed, generated—by DFID field staff.[103] The design of the project was based primarily on the judgment of DFID's field-level staff, then adjusted before implementation began in earnest as a result of the judgment of the implementing core team during an inception period in which the project was substantially revised.[104] The implementation team was given substantial scope to act in the manner they saw best, including modifying plans and activities when necessary, with DFID approval. Implementation decisions were left very much to the implementing team's discretion.[105] The DFID project also involved fairly substantial revisions driven by the judgment of personnel on the ground.[106] Plans and activities were altered when necessary with DFID approval.[107]

USAID's capacity-building project, BRDG, offered field agents some control, giving field agents the ability to use their judgment. However, the scope of this judgment was over the particular small, discrete activities to be funded rather than over the entirety of the project's direction and objectives. In contrast, DFID's capacity-building project, CISCAB, relied on the judgment of its field staff over a much greater scope of activity. This case pair, perhaps, nicely illustrates the difference between conventional uses of terms like "discretion" and my use of "Navigation by Judgment." Both DFID and USAID capability-building project staff could exercise a good deal of discretion. However, inasmuch as USAID's staff could apply this discretion only in narrower ways than could DFID's staff, USAID nonetheless exhibited a lesser degree of Navigation by Judgment than did DFID.

In some sense USAID and DFID had very different capacity-building interventions. USAID's intervention focused on a wide number of "quick wins"; DFID's was designed to be the beginning of an inevitably lengthy and complicated process of reforming the civil service. USAID's intervention was intentionally and explicitly opportunistic, investing where environmental conditions made success likely; DFID's aimed to tackle a difficult problem and alter environmental conditions. There is no direct process evidence relating this differential ambitiousness to political authorizing environments directly. That said, when attempting to accomplish similar capacity building goals in Liberia, the IDO that chapter 4 suggested faces greater authorizing environment contraint, USAID, designed a project that produced quantifiable small accomplishments. The less constrained IDO, DFID, chose a riskier, more ambitious project. This is consistent with the notion that more constrained IDOs are more risk-averse.

While there are certainly substantial differences in the ambitiousness of these projects, there are also striking similarities in this case pair. The capacity-building projects implemented by DFID and USAID were similar in financial size.[108] Most importantly for comparison of relative success, both projects had the same basic aims. These projects aimed at improving the ability of the Liberian government as a whole to deliver on whatever the particular mission of each agency might be. As such, it seems fair to compare their relative success in actually improving government functioning both in the short term and beyond the project's end.

### Establishing Levels of Success

The clearest impact of DFID's Civil Service Capacity Building (CISCAB) project was in the form of Liberia's Civil Service Reform Strategy. The strategy painted an ambitious agenda, including restructuring the civil service (including changes to political appointment powers), implementing biometric identification for civil servants, rationalizing and standardizing pay and grading, and skills train-ing.[109] This strategy still served as the government's principal guide for civil ser-vice reform at the time case-study interviews were conducted, and it was often referred to.[110] The quality of the strategy received substantial praise, and it was universally seen as a significant accomplishment owing much to CISCAB.[111]

In the latter phase of the DFID project, some elements of the project lan-guished. Despite repeated endorsement of the strategy and a push for reform from President Ellen Johnson Sirleaf, many ministers resisted changes that would have constrained their appointment powers.[112] Reforming appointment power was one small part of the larger civil service reform strategy; it is, how-ever, far and away the element of CISCAB that seems to have been most salient to actors at the time, and it is the most frequently recalled element of DFID's project.[113] Adding to CISCAB's troubles were internal tensions—both between the different Liberian institutions and within the project implementation team and between local consultants and international staff.[114]

That said, the government of Liberia seems to have acted in a way that sug-gests they found CISCAB, and DFID's support to civil service reform, quite valuable even toward the end of the project. When DFID indicated there would be no follow up "stage 2" funding to the project, Liberian President Johnson Sirleaf wrote then U.K. Prime Minister Gordon Brown asking for DFID funding of civil service reform efforts to continue.[115] Communication from one head of state to another about aid agency allocation decisions is quite unusual, particu-larly given the modest size of CISCAB.

President Johnson Sirleaf's letter did not alter DFID's stance, however. No further funding was allocated by DFID; DFID had decided to refocus their attention on Sierra Leone. On one account, Prime Minister Brown was briefed that any monies heading to Liberia would detract from Brown's efforts to sup-port health care in Sierra Leone.[116]

The end of DFID's CISCAB project in 2010 slowed the pace and trajectory of the government's civil service reform efforts.[117] As one interviewee put it, "what CISCAB was doing for [the Civil Service Agency]—to have to replace that—was really kind of difficult, to be frank . . . it put the entire reform of the [agency] back for some time."[118] Another interviewee remarked in 2013, three years after CISCAB's departure, "Ever since they [DFID] left, we have had a huge gap to trying to get back to the track that we were on. We were on a fast track to attain-ing our goals."[119]

By contrast, USAID's project, BRDG, didn't have a specific agency or sec-toral focus, and the benefits to each individual beneficiary were modest. As such, it's not surprising that beneficiaries sometimes had to be reminded of specific activities and support before commenting on BRDG.[120] In general, beneficiary organizations remembered appreciating the support, though not remembering it as particularly substantial or consequential.[121] USAID's BRDG is remembered for being quick, flexible, and broad, "just a phone call away,"[122] a project that was quick and practical—"a 'get started' project."[123] USAID's BRDG project, much like DFID's CISCAB, had no straightforward successor project, but BRDG's departure was met with no resistance from Liberian government actors.[124] The diffuse, multisectoral nature of BRDG meant that no stakeholders were as ill-affected by BRDG's end as they were by the close of DFID's CISCAB.

The diffuse nature of BRDG makes it harder to evaluate the impact of BRDG's efforts after the project's close. Some share of the physical infrastructure support for the Liberian government—including the president's radio studio and computers and office supplies in various agencies—was still in use at the time of interviews; less clear is any longer-term impact from the analytic work BRDG supported.[125]

So, which of these interventions was more successful? While both projects were well regarded by their beneficiaries and had short-term impacts, the DFID projects' impact on civil service reform left more long-lasting changes in the projects' shared goal—improving government capacity to execute—than the potpourri of activities supported by USAID. The departure of both projects was done without any real continuity to ensure that the activities initiated were to continue; however, the vocal opposition to the DFID project's departure and the extent to which actors clearly felt its absence speak to the greater value it had for beneficiaries.

## Linking Success with Navigation Strategy

DFID and USAID's capacity-building projects had the same broad goals and relatively equivalent budgets. But, as noted above, they were massively different in ambition. As one DFID official put it, CISCAB focused on "the unsung stuff—civil service reform is nasty, gritty, doesn't get much honors, doesn't get the plaudits, but it gets things done because it changes minds and it changes ways of doing things."[126] The DFID capacity-building project required a level of risk that USAID may have been unable to take on given its authorizing environment. As the DFID-prepared document laying out the plan for CISCAB prior to implementation puts it, "The fact has to be faced that post-conflict conditions in Liberia do provide a high level of risks to CISCAB . . . however if no attempt is made, conditions will never improve."[127] DFID CISCAB's success depended on its navigation strategy, inasmuch as CISCAB was designed in such a way that would have made top-down control difficult. This does not mean that there were no realized costs to Navigation by Judgment for DFID; tensions within the team implementing CISCAB, for example, stemmed in part from conflicts in work style that may have been mitigated had DFID exercised more top-down control.[128]

The USAID capacity building project, BRDG, focused on useful but relatively straightforward small accomplishments while demonstrating some, but a comparatively more limited, degree of Navigation by Judgment. USAID's BRDG only provided support when conditions were aligned for that support to be well received rather than trying to implement difficult structural changes. This strategy made USAID's project both less ambitious and less likely to experience the kind of political resistance that constrained the later phases of DFID's CISCAB. While BRDG suggests that USAID's focus on reportable outputs did not crowd out some use of soft information or flexibility, it also suggests the limits of a "mixed" strategy that pairs a degree of Navigation by Judgment with a need for discrete activities to have quantifiable outputs. Pursuing meaningful structural reforms in unpredictable environments may simply be unable to coexist with short-term output measurement.

### Comparative Liberia Case Study Performance in Sum: Navigation Strategy Success in Liberia's Unpredictable Environment

In Liberia's less predictable environment, a greater degree of Navigation by Judgment proved the superior strategy in both case pairs examined. In part, this is because of the longer-term effects, and continuation, of DFID's interventions. One senior Liberian government official, speaking about the lack of continuation of activities begun during a USAID intervention, said:

> In most of these projects sustainability is talked about, it's flagged as a priority, but it's really not. It's one of those things that makes sense to talk it, but the reality's quite different. People know that it's [the project's] not sustainable; the institutional arrangements are not worked out, especially the funding dries up, and everyone goes back to square zero.[129]

This insight applies to many of the USAID projects in Liberia, but less so to DFID's interventions. The end of DFID's focus on civil service reform may have led to a loss of momentum, but by no means a return to "square zero." The Ministry of Health's Office of Financial Management (OFM) and pooled fund continued to progress without active DFID involvement as well.

The in-country authority to make substantively significant implementation decisions was a critical part of success in these DFID projects; that this was the case seems related to the difficulty of understanding Liberia remotely. A DFID interviewee summarized this nicely in saying:

> There is a big difference [to being in-country] . . . any modifications
> or changes to implementing projects, it's easier to do so, and to under-
> stand why you're doing so, and to respond to the client requests in a
> more responsive manner if you're sitting in a country office and you're
> involved in the day-to-day context of what's going on. If you're remote,
> or if you're sitting in HQ, or you don't really have that personal rela-
> tionship or feel for the day-to-day implementation; or the difference
> between being a governance specialist, for example, or an administra-
> tor, you see it from a technical point of view as opposed to "oh well,
> I can't do it from an administrative point of view."[130]

This statement speaks to the importance of soft information and agent control. It also highlights the opacity (that is, the lack of legibility) of more unpredictable environments.

In Liberia DFID's Navigation by Judgment did not lead DFID's projects to unmitigated success. DFID's greater Navigation by Judgment nonetheless led to relatively greater success as compared to USAID in achieving USAID and DFID's shared goals in each agency's Liberian health and capacity-building interventions.

## Conclusion: Contrasting Performance as Maps Become Scarce

This chapter has examined how Navigation by Judgment and environmental unpredictability jointly affect International Development Organization (IDO) performance. The quantitative empirics examined a large sample of projects; indeed, the PPD is the largest dataset of IDO overall Project Success outcomes ever assembled. These empirics find a systematic relationship between pro-pensity to Navigate by Judgment and Project Success as environments become more unpredictable. The IDOs that are relatively less inclined to Navigate by Judgment fare worse, relative to their own performance otherwise, in less pre-dictable environments. This result remains robust even under a series of alterna-tive specifications and models, as outlined in Appendix II.

The case evidence focusing on USAID and DFID's relative performance in Liberia suggests that there is also an absolute difference in performance. A greater degree of Navigation by Judgment is associated with a greater degree of success in Liberia's relatively unpredictable environment. This is not primarily because some unexpected shock occurs in the Liberian cases to which greater

Navigation by Judgment allows DFID to better respond more flexibly or rapidly. Soft information and reliance on agent judgment seem to drive differential USAID and DFID performance in these case pairs even in the absence of such a shock. This speaks to the importance of legibility—the ability to be understood from afar—as a critical feature of environments for IDO choice of navigation strategy. There is more to say about these case study pairs and the light they shine on the theory developed in Part I. Chapter 8 will spend some time examining the link between political authorizing environments and IDO field agent actions in more detail.

The Liberian health case pair provides a clear example of authorizing environment limiting the menu of navigation options available to USAID. The Liberian capacity-building case pair illustrates that even near the extreme of USAID's within-agency variation of authorizing environment stability and flexibility, USAID was still less able to Navigate by Judgment than was DFID. In each case pair the DFID intervention exhibits substantially more Navigation by Judgment than its USAID counterpart. The IDO with the more insecure authorizing environment—USAID—is also the IDO substantially more invested in collecting quantitative data that might be used to justify itself, and much less likely to Navigate by Judgment. This chapter suggests, consistent with chapter 2's theory, that in a more unpredictable environment, greater Navigation by Judgment augurs for more success, and that consistent with chapter 4, political authorizing environments and reporting constrain the use of Navigation by Judgment.

The next chapter shifts focus more explicitly to examining the verifiability of projects—the extent to which different projects can be managed effectively using the externally observable measures that this chapter suggests USAID favors. Chapter 7 draws once more on the PPD, examining the roles played by sectors of differing project external verifiability in mediating the relationship between Navigation by Judgment and Project Success. It also examines the relative performance of USAID and DFID in a more predictable environment, that of South Africa. This book's theory anticipates that Navigation by Judgment will be less useful in South Africa than Liberia, given South Africa's greater predictability; this should be even more true when the nature of the development goal makes more verifiable projects are likely. The next chapter provides evidence as to whether this is in fact the case.

# Tailoring Management to Suit the Task

## Project Verifiability and Navigation Strategy

## Introduction

International development organizations (IDOs) are involved in a vast range of activities. Achieving the best possible results may require different navigation strategies depending on the nature of the project. Chapter 2 argued that one critical feature of projects is their verifiability. By "project verifiability," this book intends to connote not just the existence of observable project outputs—for example, the number of attendees at a training session. Rather, project verifiability captures the extent to which outputs are likely to remain tightly correlated with a project's goals, or the susceptibility of the best possible output measure to distortions.

For some projects, output data will be a good guide, allowing a Google Maps–style approach that uses externally verifiable information to drive agent behavior and project performance toward an IDO's goals. For these projects, this book predicts more IDO Navigation by Judgment will be associated with poorer IDO project performance. For less verifiable projects, chapter 2 predicts that a management strategy focused on driving agents to meet verifiable outputs will lead agents to reach measures at the expense of overall Project Success. In these projects, more Navigation by Judgment will be associated with better project performance. This chapter tests these predictions, exploring whether and how differences in the external verifiability of an intervention impacts the relative success of different IDO navigation strategies in achieving project goals.

This chapter begins by returning briefly to the Project Performance Database (PPD) to examine the role project verifiability plays in mediating the relationship between Navigation by Judgment and IDO project performance. It then turns to the case study pair where Navigation by Judgment is predicted to perform least well—when implementing a relatively verifiable project in a relatively predictable environment. This case pair examines the performance of the U.S. Agency for International Development (USAID) and U.K. Department for International Development (DFID) in attempting to support the HIV/AIDS response in South Africa. As USAID's interventions parallel those of the U.S. Centers for Disease Control (CDC) in the sector, this case pair also provides some additional leverage on understanding whether U.S. agencies differ in their navigation strategies and, if so, why they differ.

This chapter then turns to the fourth and final case pair, examining USAID and DFID performance in the South African municipal governance sector. This case pair is the one where DFID and USAID pursue the most similar interventions of all four case pairs. As a result, this case pair is particularly well suited for examining differences in these IDOs' choice of project navigation strategy and the impact of that choice. The chapter closes by reviewing Part II's empirics as a whole, bringing this part of the book to a close.

## Project Verifiability in the PPD

The standard method via which projects are classified—the Organization for Economic Cooperation and Development (OECD) Development Assistance Committee (DAC) coding scheme—leaves, as chapter 5 describes, much to be desired. The scheme does not allow anything like a systematic examination of the verifiability of particular projects, as even the most detailed coding level combines widely varying kinds of projects.[1]

There are, however, some sectors that are quite likely to contain highly verifiable projects. Sectors where projects focus on constructing physical infrastructure—such as building a road—lend themselves to output management. The quality of a road can be audited, and its design and construction follows a predictable path; a "Google Maps" navigation strategy is thus likely to yield good results. The claim is not that implementation in verifiable sectors will be seamless or trivially easy; indeed, there is a fair body of research that suggests there may well be a fair number of implementation challenges in, say, road construction.[2] The claim is that on net, top-down controls will fare better than relying on agent judgment in these contexts.

I compare IDO performance in highly verifiable sectors (that is, sectors highly likely to contain relatively verifiable projects) to performance in more difficult to verify related administrative sectors. The tables below replicate the primary econometric model examined in Table 6.1, but on subgroups of sectors. In highly verifiable sectors (e.g., road construction), I expect Navigation by Judgment to fare less well than Navigation from the Top. In less verifiable related sectors (e.g., transportation management), I expect to see the same relationship observed in chapter 6, with more Navigation by Judgment associated with better performance as environmental predictability rises.

Tables 7.1 and 7.2 suggest that the relationship between environmental predictability, Navigation by Judgment, and Project Success differs by sector external verifiability. Sector differences do seem to play a substantial role in explaining relative success within a given IDO's project portfolio.

Table 7.2 shows a strong relationship between the interaction of Navigation by Judgment propensity and environmental unpredictability when projects are likely to be relatively unverifiable. This contrasts with Table 7.1's mixed, and statistically insignificant, results. Figure 7.1 provides side-by-side graphs to make interpretation of these results a bit easier, graphing the relationships found in all sectors included in Tables 7.1 and 7.2.[3]

Consistent with chapter 5, in less externally verifiable sectors Navigation by Judgment has an even stronger relationship with Project Success than it did in chapter 6's empirics. However, it is not the case that a lower propensity to Navigate by Judgment is associated with better performance for more externally verifiable sectors as environmental unpredictability rises. That lower propensity to Navigate by Judgment is not associated with better performance in sectors like road and power line construction runs counter to this book's hypothesis that in more verifiable projects (and thus sectors) Navigation by Judgment will in fact impede success. Restricting the analysis only to more predictable environments (thus examining more externally verifiable sectors in environments where external shocks are relatively unlikely) does not alter these results.

This finding is, however, consistent with more Navigation by Judgment–prone IDOs focusing on externally verifiable data when appropriate. Chapter 2, and Table 2.1, suggested more autonomous IDOs—those that have a greater propensity to Navigate by Judgment—will rely on Navigation from the Top when it is appropriate. Less constrained IDOs are theorized to adjust their navigation strategy as appropriate. If more Navigation by Judgment–prone IDOs did not in fact Navigate by Judgment when projects could indeed be well managed using externally verifiable data, we might expect to see a relationship like that discussed above.

These results should not be interpreted as suggesting there is more actual variance in project outcomes as a whole in more externally verifiable sectors than their less externally verifiable comparators. The two samples are of quite similar mean and variance. The more externally verifiable sectors have 1,081 observations and a mean Project Success score of 4.31; the standard deviation of Project Success is 1.17. The less externally verifiable sectors have 1,575 observations and a mean Project Success score of 4.23; the standard deviation of Project Success is 1.11. While there are fewer observations in the more externally verifiable

Table 7.1 **Navigation by Judgment Does Not Systematically Mediate the Relationship between Environmental Predictability and IDO Project Success in Verifiable Sectors. Where projects are likely to be manageable based on outputs without distortions, Navigation by Judgment propensity does not differentiate IDOs in how environmental unpredictability impacts IDO Project Puccess**

| DV: Project Success (6-pt scale) | (1) Road Infrastructure and Transport | (2) Building Power Transmission Lines | (3) Agricultural Irrigation and Water | (4) Basic Drinking Water Supply and Sanitation |
|---|---|---|---|---|
| Environmental Unpredictability | −0.258*** | −0.829* | −0.384* | −0.175 |
| | (0.254) | (0.165) | (0.248) | (0.0979) |
| Env Unpredict*Nav by Judg | −0.350 | 0.206*** | 0.187*** | 0.180*** |
| | (0.410) | (0.272) | (0.398) | (0.152) |
| Constant | 5.007*** | 4.942*** | 4.548*** | 4.552*** |
| | (0.156) | (0.138) | (0.159) | (0.0331) |
| IDO Fixed Effects | Y | Y | Y | Y |
| $R^2$-Within | 0.032 | 0.026 | 0.019 | 0.047 |
| $R^2$-Between | 0.068 | 0.376 | 0.148 | 0.018 |
| Observations | 469 | 178 | 168 | 266 |

Standard errors in parentheses
* $p<0.05$, ** $p<0.01$, *** $p<0.001$

Table 7.2 Navigation by Judgment Systematically Mediates the Relationship between Environmental Predictability and IDO Project Success. Where projects are not likely to be manageable based on outputs without distortions, Navigation by Judgment propensity differentiates IDOs in how environmental unpredictability impacts IDO Project Success. [a]

| DV: Project Success (6-pt scale) | (1) Transportation Management | (2) Agricultural Policy and Administration | (3) Social/Welfare Services (Administration, Capacity Building) | (4) All Administration/ Administration/ Policy Management |
|---|---|---|---|---|
| Environmental Unpredictability | -0.953*** | -0.248*** | -0.379*** | -0.157*** |
| | (0.0195) | (0.0319) | (0.0254) | (0.0144) |
| Env Unpredict*Nav by Judg | 1.580*** | 0.354*** | 0.547*** | 0.199*** |
| | (0.0291) | (0.0543) | (0.0423) | (0.0230) |
| Constant | 3.218*** | 4.315*** | 4.649*** | 4.575*** |
| | (0.0244) | (0.185) | (0.0323) | (0.0238) |
| IDO Fixed Effects | Y | Y | Y | Y |
| $R^2$-Within | 0.206 | 0.013 | 0.055 | 0.023 |
| $R^2$-Between | 0.006 | 0.181 | 0.042 | 0.344 |
| Observations | 47 | 60 | 170 | 1575 |

Standard errors in parentheses
* $p<0.05$,**$p<0.01$,***$p<0.001$
[a] Model 4 is not a formal OECD Development Assistance Committee Sector but is rather created by the author, combining all administrative sectors (all OECD DAC purpose codes with the final two digits "10")

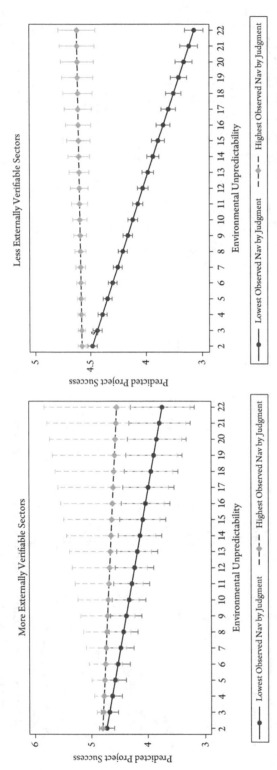

*Figure 7.1* Returns to Navigation by Judgment Differ by Project Verifiability. Whether projects are in sectors where it will likely be possible for projects to be effectively managed using observable outputs plays an important role in explaining the effects of Navigation by Judgment. Box and whiskers around each point estimate represent 95% confidence intervals. The "lowest-observed" Navigation by Judgment propensity score is .56 on a zero to one scale and the "highest-observed" is .80; these represent the extremes of Navigation by Judgment propensity in the PPD. See Appendix Table II.14 for a full list of Navigation by Judgment propensity scores.

sectors, this difference is not what is driving the results. It is simply that, for more externally verifiable sectors, it is not the case that more or less Navigation by Judgment–prone IDOs can be differentiated from one another.

This analysis finds less systematic support than expected for the benefits of more top-down control (and less Navigation by Judgment) in sectors where management based on observable data is likely to yield few distortions. Nonetheless, this analysis suggests that project verifiability plays an important role in explaining IDO performance. The rest of this chapter explores differences in project verifiability and management using the two South Africa case study pairs.

## USAID and DFID Interventions in South Africa

This section uses the four South African case studies to compare the performance of DFID and USAID interventions in South Africa from approximately 2003 to 2013. This section's structure parallels that of the case studies examined in chapter 6. I first provide a brief background on South Africa over the period of the case study projects. I then turn to the case pairs themselves, examining first the health and then the capacity-building case pair. Within each case pair, I first introduce and provide some background on USAID and DFID's interventions. I then compare the navigation strategies of the interventions, and where possible I discuss how the IDOs arrived at the particular project plan and navigation strategy. I then compare the success of DFID and USAID interventions. I close by linking that level of success to navigation strategy.

The health case study pair contains an additional brief comparison between the US Centers for Disease Control (CDC) and the U.S. Agency for International Development (USAID). This comparison takes advantage of CDC and USAID's parallel implementation of projects under the United States President's Emergency Plan for AIDS Relief (PEPFAR). This interagency comparison of two U.S. agencies provides additional analytic leverage on authorizing environments and their role in shaping navigation strategy.

### Background and Context: South Africa, 2004–2013

In 2004 South Africa celebrated ten years since the fall of apartheid. A sluggish economy in the first years following apartheid had transitioned to steady growth, at least until the 2008 financial crisis.[4] South Africa remained a very unequal society; in 2009 the bottom half of the population accounted for just 8 percent of the country's income.[5] While whites comprised less than 10 percent of the population, white farmers owned 85 percent of the agricultural land.[6]

*Table 7.3* **Diagram of South Africa Case Studies. * indicates the end date is the time period discussed in interviews regarding the intervention, rather than the end date of the intervention itself**

|  | *USAID* | *DFID* |
|---|---|---|
| **Capacity Building** | Local Governance Support Program (LGSP) phase 2, 2004–2010; implemented by RTI International | Consolidation of Municipal Transformation Programme (CMTP), 2003–2009; implemented by Deloitte |
| **Health** | President's Emergency Plan For AIDS Relief (PEPFAR), 2003–2013*; various implementers | HIV/AIDS Multisectoral Programme (MSP), 2003–2008; implemented initially by Futures Group, succeeded by HLSP |
|  |  | Rapid Response Health Fund (RRHF), 2008–2009; implemented by HLSP |
|  |  | Strengthening South Africa's Response to HIV and Health (SARRAH), 2010–2013*; implemented by HLSP |

South Africa was, and is, not without political, social, and economic challenges. The legacy of apartheid continues to play a substantial role in South African society and government policy and institutions. That said, during this period South Africa was a stable, growing, legible country; the biggest economy in Africa; host of the 2010 World Cup; and a member of the Group of 20 (G-20) major economies. The case of South Africa allows us to explore IDO navigation strategy and performance in a relatively stable and predictable environment and thus to more directly examine the role of project external verifiability. Table 7.3 presents a diagram of the discrete projects this section will examine.

## A Best-Case Context for Navigation from the Top: DFID and USAID in the South African Health Sector

The South African health cases look largely, though not exclusively, at a realm of health particularly tractable to management by outputs—the Prevention of Mother to Child Transmission (PMTCT) of HIV/AIDS. To prevent HIV transmission, mothers receive antiretroviral drugs while pregnant and breastfeeding; newborns also receive treatment for their first four to six weeks of life.[7] Treatment for PMTCT is bounded in time and place; as one interviewee with a long history in public health put it,

PMTCT is a no brainer because you have got a captive audience, you have got a clear intervention . . . it is fairly quantifiable . . . you can get the results for a particular clinic and demonstrate to people how they are doing, you know you have got a hundred mothers coming, you tested ninety-eight of them, thirty are positive, how many of those did you put on treatment, how many of those did you take a CD 4 [a blood test for the severity of disease] count for . . . it is quite easily understandable in a short period of time, you are not following people for years and years and so it is a once off cohort.[8]

Thus PMTCT is highly tractable to management based on output measurement (and thus highly "verifiable," as I use the term). Agents are unlikely to meet measures at the expense of the development goal, as the measures are excellent summary statistics that are well correlated with the ultimate goal. PMTCT is thus a development goal for which chapter 2 would predict Navigation by Judgment is not appropriate, with tight principal control faring better than relying on fallible agent judgment.

### *Establishing Differences in Navigation Strategy: USAID, CDC, and DFID in South African Health*

USAID's South African health portfolio was largely focused on executing the U.S. President's Emergency Plan for AIDS Relief (PEPFAR), the U.S. government's primary HIV/AIDS funding mechanism.[9] The initial allocation of PEPFAR was USD$15 billion over five years, known as PEPFAR 1; in 2008 PEPFAR was funded for an additional five years and USD$48 billion, known as PEPFAR 2.[10] By the late 2000s PEPFAR was providing over USD$500 million a year to South Africa, with PMTCT spending well over USD$50 million annually and likely far higher.[11] It is unarguable that PEPFAR's scope and ambition was unprecedented. One interviewee described being told by U.S. officials that, had all PEPFAR-supported personnel worked for a single firm, that firm would be the fifth-largest employer in South Africa, with over 60,000 employees.[12] Another interviewee erroneously, but tellingly, described Right to Care—a South African PEPFAR implementer—as the highest-funded U.S. government aid recipient in the world.[13] The prevention of mother-to-child transmission (PMTCT) of HIV/AIDS was a substantial focus of PEPFAR from the beginning; PEPFAR has consistently highlighted PMTCT achievements, including numbers of mothers treated and babies born to HIV+ mothers who are HIV-, in its annual reports.

It is striking the extent to which PEPFAR navigates in a top-down fashion using quantitative targets. Global targets are set by the Office of the Global AIDS

Coordinator in Washington, DC.[14] Those targets then flow through national annual Country Operational Plans (developed by U.S. government agencies in country and submitted via the U.S. ambassador to the country for approval by the Office of the Global AIDS Coordinator) to a series of tenders. In South Africa—as in most countries—PEPFAR worked through multiple U.S. agencies, including USAID and the U.S. Centers for Disease Control, to deliver care; PEPFAR formed the vast majority of the South African activities for these organizations, with one USAID official estimating PEPFAR as 95 percent of USAID's work in South Africa.[15] These IDOs then make competitive awards to primary recipients—initially mostly international firms—who would in turn subcontract to a variety of local partners via whom services are delivered.

Decisions about PEPFAR design and activities "all happen in DC," as one South African government actor put it.[16] This is by design; the original PEPFAR strategy makes clear that "the United States Global AIDS Coordinator will oversee and direct all US Government international HIV/AIDS activities in all departments and all agencies of the Federal Government . . . this will result in more effective and efficient programs."[17] A few lines later, PEPFAR commits to "establish measurable goals for which we will hold ourselves and our partners accountable."[18]

In-country personnel have some role in setting direction,[19] but ultimately country strategies need to address these global targets. One senior DC-based PEPFAR official noted just how structured this top-down target system is, saying that for PEPFAR:

> "Targets" are set from above, i.e., the Global AIDS Coordinator's Office in DC. In PEPFAR 1, the original target was 2—7—10. Put 2 million people on treatment, prevent 7 million new infections, and put 10 million people in care. The targets for PEPFAR 2 are 6—10—10. When targets are set from above, everything then flows down to the agency level, country level, and partner level, so all the funds that we are given, at the different levels, have to add up to meet these arbitrary goals set from above and there is a heavy quarterly, semi-annual, and annual reporting burden and a complex and arduous annual target setting and planning process to try to meet the goal.[20]

What is true of PEPFAR in design is also true in implementation. Interviewee quotes from PEPFAR implementers make this abundantly clear: for example, "PEPFAR is about those targets, and we will fund you if you can demonstrate you can help us with those targets but that's all that it's about, nothing else matters";[21] "[PEPFAR] found much a bigger emphasis on the quantitative outputs";[22] and "[with PEPFAR] you had to measure, quantify; and it is quite rigorous reporting guidelines, requirements, that the budget had to matched against."[23] Thus PEPFAR is about as clear an instance of top-down navigation using quantitative targets as one could imagine.

On PMTCT DFID's key intervention was the Accelerated Plan for PMTCT (A-Plan), a South African National Department of Health plan to focus on PMTCT initially in 18 of South Africa's 52 districts. The A-Plan sought to reduce mother-to-child transmission to less than 5 percent by 2011, with implementation coordinated by the South African government.[24] A-Plan implementation was completed in 2011.[25] Then DFID focused on working through the national government and influencing policymakers.[26]

While the overarching goals of DFID's projects were quite similar to USAID's under PEPFAR, DFID employed methods that are much more difficult to quantify. The empowered judgment of field staff was a hallmark of all three major DFID projects in this period.[27] The first of these was DFID's HIV/AIDS Multisectoral Program (MSP). The MSP was a source of broad support for South Africa's HIV/AIDS response, designed to provide technical assistance (funds, training, and logistical support) to South African government ministries. One part of the MSP added toward the end of the project was a flexible fund to be spent at the direction of the minister of health, the Rapid Results Health Fund (RRHF).[28] It was this fund that supported the A-Plan on PMTCT, with funding for a pilot program in five districts coming from the RRHF. After this funding mechanism closed in 2009, implementation of the A-Plan continued to be funded through DFID's Strengthening South Africa's Response to HIV and Health (SARRAH).[29] During SARRAH, DFID's South African health advisor became an embedded advisor to the South African National Department of Health based at the ministry, with SARRAH flexible funding devoted to the priorities of the minister of health as they evolved.[30]

That DFID's project was primarily guided by the judgment of its field-level agents was noted by a number of actors.[31] Communication with London was only around "the political stuff . . . everything [else] was left to the country office to work it out."[32] Reporting under DFID's interventions involved some measurement of activities, but there didn't seem to be pressure on these figures; narrative accounts of progress and the judgment of DFID supervisors and government counterparts seemed to implementers to matter more than reaching specific targets.[33] As Gugu Ngubane, the lead implementer of the A-Plan under RRHF and SARRAH, put it, DFID "allow[s] you to be the expert in your field and [allows] you [to] do what needs to be done . . . [DFID] were supportive and they just let me inform them, I think they gave me the platform to advise them on what is the reality, what can happen, what cannot happen."

The design of DFID's projects were also much more driven by agents' judgments and networks. The design process of DFID's Rapid Results Health Fund is particularly striking in illustrating Navigation by Judgment. Robin Gorna, then DFID's health advisor resident in South Africa, recalls that having received incoming Minister of Health Barbara Hogan's number from a mutual friend she

> picked up my phone to Barbara [Hogan] one night from my kitchen, I remember it very distinctly and said, "Hello, I'm a friend of Zackie's, could I help you with fifteen million pounds, could you use it, would it help you strengthen things?" Strangely she said yes, and this again is a delightful part of how DFID has been able to work in the past. That's just a little anecdote I cherish but it's also part of how we as health advisers traditionally had been able to work, this was a rather extreme experience, but I think that a quality of DFID health programmes traditionally was that individuals could spot something and then work it up into a bureaucratically acceptable proposal.[34]

Once again, USAID and DFID seem to have inhabited almost entirely different worlds regarding Navigation by Judgment. The DFID projects, with their flexible funding to be deployed according to the judgments of field personnel, could not exist under a PEPFAR-type navigation strategy. As one actor involved in implementing components of both USAID PEPFAR and DFID projects put it, "This [DFID] type of work wouldn't, couldn't happen under a PEPFAR type structure."[35]

### Comparing USAID and CDC's Navigation Strategy

While not originally part of the case study design, the South African health sector provides an opportunity to compare USAID's navigation strategy to that of the other primary U.S. President's Emergency Plan for AIDS Relief (PEPFAR) implementer in South Africa, the U.S. Centers for Disease Control (CDC.) The CDC and USAID both ultimately report to the same U.S. Congress, and in implementing PEPFAR both were supervised by the same Office of the Global AIDS Coordinator. This does not necessarily mean that USAID and the CDC have the same level of authorizing environment insecurity; chapter 4 suggested there can be interagency variation in authorizing environments even when the actual authorizers are the same.

The CDC and USAID are structurally similar; the CDC is a unit of the Department of Health and Human Services just as USAID is a unit of the Department of State. The CDC, however, arguably exudes an aura of reputational authority that USAID lacks. The CDC is also based in relatively distant Georgia rather than in Washington, DC, which may also assist in providing additional operating slack for the agency. I would expect, then, that the CDC would have more organizational autonomy—and thus a greater propensity to Navigate by Judgment—than USAID.

The CDC's implementation of PEPFAR was described as more flexible than USAID's implementation of PEPFAR.[36] One implementer of both CDC and USAID PEPFAR funds described USAID as "2/3 monitoring, 1/3 implementation"; the CDC as "1/3 monitoring, 2/3 implementation."[37] This implementer added that for USAID "everything is by the book . . . there's a lot of legality around USAID—there are more regulations, things are more stringent than CDC."[38] The CDC was described as less formalized, for better[39] or for worse.[40] The CDC's awards were also more hands-on; the CDC tended to be actively involved with implementers in a way USAID was not.[41]

The CDC's more fluid working relationship—closer to DFID's relationship with contractors in some ways than USAID's—allowed, in the view of one respondent, for more responsiveness for contractors when things arose that were not foreseen in the original contract.[42] The CDC was also seen by a number of interviewees to be more responsive to South African government requests and to working through government.[43]

The CDC exhibited a greater degree of Navigation by Judgment than USAID, which CDC used precisely when unpredictable events occurred, and thus there was a need for flexibility and adaptation. The CDC's country directors seemed to have more autonomy than USAID's regarding PEPFAR execution and technical approvals.[44] That said, the CDC's financial systems are not oriented toward overseas operations; as a result the CDC, much more than USAID, needed to route all financial approvals and contracting through headquarters in the United States.[45]

The degree to which they Navigated by Judgment is not the only margin on which CDC and USAID differed. The CDC's staff tended to be doctors, epidemiologists, nurses, and other health professionals. The CDC also put a greater priority on research.[46] USAID was praised for its understanding of community work, an area in which the CDC was seen as less adept; the opposite was true of working with hospitals, where the CDC was seen as more knowledgeable.[47] The CDC resisted credit claiming, not allowing its logo on anything unless it met standards of scientific rigor; USAID, on the other hand, encouraged the use of its logo on reports, vehicles, etc.[48] These differences are suggestive of the differential institutional histories of the two organizations—of the CDC as a disease research institution and USAID as one focused on delivering development assistance. The differential organizational histories of USAID and the CDC seem to have path-dependent consequences.[49]

The greater Navigation by Judgment of the CDC as compared with USAID is what chapter 4's discussion of authorizing environments would imply, following from the CDC's relatively better reputation and lower level of authorizing environment insecurity. The CDC's greater centralization and concentration of approvals in distant headquarters is the opposite of what might be predicted, however. That the CDC is nonetheless the more flexible and more Navigation by Judgment–prone organization suggests that constraints at the top—from political authorizers vis-à-vis headquarters—may be more predictive of realized organizational navigation strategy than the formal structures within the agency itself. Formal decentralization of authority may not be determinative of relative flexibility and organizational navigation strategy.

*Establishing Levels of Success: DFID versus USAID*

To return to the central USAID versus DFID comparison: Which IDO's South African health interventions were more successful? As noted in the preceding discussion, prevention of mother to child transmission (PMTCT) of HIV/AIDS is a relatively easy intervention to monitor and implement. As one South African public health leader put it:

> There was a recognition that this was a relatively solvable problem . . . it is easily measurable, so if we couldn't do this it would be a complete indictment of South Africa's health system, you know, all the elements were in place to do it, you have got a very high attendance at antenatal clinics, you have got an excellent laboratory network which can give you results, you have got the infrastructure around the country, it was just a matter of getting the drugs out, testing them and then getting them [pregnant mothers] to take the drugs.[50]

If PMTCT is the "low-hanging fruit" of HIV/AIDS response, it is nonetheless fruit that was unplucked, and withering on the vine, when DFID and USAID began focusing on PMTCT.

The USAID and DFID interventions over this period aimed toward broadly similar objectives, particularly as regards PMTCT: the reduction of mother-to-child transmission rates and the establishment of a health system capable of sustaining those reductions.[51] In the period when these interventions were operating, there was substantial progress regarding HIV/AIDS treatment in general, and PMTCT in particular, in South Africa. Before 2007, the best available data suggested mother to child transmission rates of 8–9 percent, with a few studies suggesting substantially higher rates.[52] By 2011 the mother-to-child transmission rate had fallen to 2.7 percent.[53] According to the Joint United Nations Programme on HIV/AIDS (UNAIDS), between 2009 and 2013 the likelihood of pregnant and breastfeeding women receiving drugs to prevent transmission rose from 63 to 90 percent; over the same time period, the number of new child infections dropped by a little more than half, while the number of HIV+ women delivering babies remained virtually unchanged.[54] While these clear successes make it easy to conclude that progress was made, it is less clear to what or to whom to attribute this success. Yes, PMTCT treatment has been successful—but what of these aid interventions specifically?

The general view of DFID's early project, the Multi-Sectoral Program (MSP), was overwhelmingly negative. Beset by management challenges, and requiring a change of implementer to avoid a projected eight million british pounds (GBP) overspend on a project with little to show for it,[55] it is hard to ascribe much by way of positive impact to the MSP. This view was echoed by those who led the project; Robin Gorna, the DFID health lead over the MSP's latter period, remarked, "I never felt we really got anything wonderful out of MSP."[56]

By 2008, when President Thabo Mbeki departed and South Africa's denialism came to an end, DFID had little to show for their efforts in the sector. By contrast, 85 percent of pregnant mothers were receiving HIV counseling and testing by 2008 as compared with 46 percent in 2004;[57] this increase is surely attributable in substantial part to PEPFAR's structure and delivery channels, with PEPFAR by 2008 having funded 2,211,000 counseling sessions for pregnant women and drugs for 333,100 HIV+ pregnant women.[58] As one senior member of South Africa's medical community put it, "Had it not been for PEPFAR and government just had the drugs, we would have treated a few patients and we would have carried on, but we would have been, I would say, ten years behind [the scope of treatment we achieved due to PEPFAR]."[59]

DFID's Rapid Results Health Fund and the A-Plan (funded under both RRHF and its successor, SARRAH) were seen as marked successes.[60] The A-Plan was frequently mentioned as key in catalyzing the government's broader PMTCT response as well as providing direct care to PMTCT patients in target districts.[61] DFID's project completion report supports the view of interviewees that the RRHF's success offset the less-than-successful MSP.[62]

That said, even this DFID success required PEPFAR's assistance; DFID's A-Plan required PEPFAR's support for actual delivery to pregnant mothers. As one individual involved in the A-Plan put it, "At the end of the day we all depended on PEPFAR actually to do the implementation support because they [PEPFAR implementers] are the ones that are on the ground and they have all the resources and all the people in each of the districts."[63] South African government officials and non-PEPFAR beneficiaries echoed this, talking about PEPFAR's deep and broad involvement in PMTCT, including in A-Plan implementation.[64]

USAID's health portfolio dwarfed DFID's in size. It also dwarfed DFID's in net impact. Controlling for relative size is less of a challenge to comparing DFID and USAID's interventions than it would be had both been quite successful. While DFID had some modest successes, a substantial portion—arguably

the majority—of its efforts yielded little progress toward broader development goals. By contrast, USAID and PEPFAR's successes are unambiguous.
USAID's PEPFAR was clearly more successful than DFID's health-sector
efforts both in PMTCT and in addressing the broader health challenges of
HIV/AIDS.

### Linking Success with Navigation Strategy

While some of DFID's relative successes seem inextricably linked to Navigation
by Judgment, so too do many of the intervention's shortcomings. Speaking generally about DFID's penchant for flexible and responsive health projects, one
respondent said that, as a result, Project Success

> is based on charisma, it depends who is in the [DFID and South African
> government] positions at the time. If it is somebody who is well mean-
> ing and whose heart is in the right place and who is clear thinking, then
> it [the project's success] is probably going to be good, but if it is some-
> body who is muddled, you know you can get money being dispersed
> and not strategically used.[65]

As actors inside DFID and the government's National Department of Health
changed, so did project focus. When Gorna was replaced as DFID's health advisor, SARRAH was changed substantially by her successor.[66] It seems very possible that a design that provided more rules and less flexibility in revising projects
would have benefited DFID's interventions. It would have avoided what one
respondent viewed as SARRAH's effective capture by a particular South African
government official and consequent loss of coherence.[67] Arguing for the costli-
ness of DFID's flexibility, one interviewee argued, "Sometimes you do want a
funder that will just stick to the contract and say no, boldly, to the [government]
department irrespective of the political relationships; because if it is not in the
contract, it is not in the contract."[68] In the period of HIV denialism, PEPFAR's
existence outside government and ability to directly fund implementers meant
substantial progress in terms of lives saved and services delivered, even as
national government dallied and DFID's project struggled.

The success of the U.S. government's PEPFAR seems quite related to its
navigation strategy. More than one respondent linked PEPFAR's success during
this period to its focus on targets and numbers.[69] One implementer, by way of
praising PEPFAR, said, "PEPFAR's been great in the sense that it's brought the
American obsession with counting things to kind of a fuzzy field full of cud-
dling."[70] Consistent with the discussion in chapter 2, this target setting in the
context of reliable measures did promote some process autonomy and use of

Navigation by Judgment by contractors when implementing. As one implementer put it:

> Whatever your number was ... if you contracted with the private sector, whether you went through a subgrantee, or whether you did it yourself, or whether you went through public health they didn't care they just wanted the fifty thousand circumcisions done. And I think that was useful because as I said different people brought different strengths.[71]

The process autonomy of PEPFAR should not be misconstrued as broader flexibility or adaptability. Top-down target setting had implications for workplan revision; as one implementer put it, "the way PEPFAR is done where you have to plan your work a year ahead of time."[72] In general, revisions to targets or the five-year strategy proceeded very slowly, if at all.[73]

Target setting within PEPFAR was also less effective when dealing with measures more susceptible to distortion, with one interviewee saying, "One of the things I am critical about is the focus on training because . . . it's something like put fifty backsides on the seats for three hours and you can count them . . .. You would count the people training but what you didn't count was what the impact of that training [was]."[74] Even within this highly verifiable sector, different elements of USAID's interventions were differentially tractable to management via output data.

In this case pair, relying on observable output data proved the superior IDO navigation strategy. The now-familiar pattern as to navigation strategy held: USAID engaged in tighter principal control while DFID used Navigation by Judgment, relying on agent judgment and initiative. In this case pair, USAID's top-down control proved more effective; this is largely because for a highly verifiable project the risks of relying on fallible agent judgment were costlier than the distortions borne of top-down control. This dynamic comes forward most clearly in one interviewee's remark that DFID

> changes too much . . . [DFID's success] is very reliant on there being a country team that is able to not just bend in the wind with every gust but to actually hold its course, whereas with [US]AID that is kind of irrelevant, the country team does some initial design but there is, I think, strong Washington control and then it is out of people's sight because it is locked into implementation.[75]

Consistent with the theory articulated primarily in chapter 2, USAID was successfully able to drive performance from above via quantitative target-setting in delivering treatment in the South African health sector. Whether this navigation strategy is compatible with the capacity-building and government systems-building efforts to which PEPFAR was committed to transitioning by mid-2013 is an open question. What is clear is that relying on externally observable and reportable output data helped USAID operate in the face of a denialist government and avoid the lack of focus and direction that DFID's projects sometimes faced.

The next section turns to the other pair of South African cases, examining USAID and DFID's municipal governance capacity-building projects. This case pair looks at comparative success in the fourth "quadrant" of environmental predictability and project verifiability: a relatively unverifiable project in a relatively predictable environment.

## USAID and DFID Capacity-Building Projects

Reliance on externally observable targets to drive service delivery proved the superior strategy in the South African health sector. But municipal governance capacity-building projects are likely to be much less verifiable than PMTCT efforts. Ivor Chipkin, the executive director of South Africa's Public Affairs Research Institute, suggested a focus on externally observable organizational form was a key problem nonlocals faced when trying to understand South African subnational government. He argued that

> to look at the formal organization structures as your end point, as the be all and end all of how the organization works is very, very misleading . . . consultancies in South Africa are failing more often than succeeding partly because their starting point is the formal structure and where power ostensibly lies within that formal structure . . . usually that doesn't work because that is not how these organizations work.[76]

Chapters 2 and 5 predict that even in a relatively predictable recipient-country environment—one with relative stability and legibility—Navigation by Judgment may well prove to be a superior strategy when projects are not verifiable. The South African municipal governance capacity-building case pair allows for a test of this prediction.

### Comparing Interventions and Navigation Strategies

The U.K. Department for International Development (DFID) and U.S. Agency for International Development (USAID)'s efforts to strengthen the ability of South African municipalities to perform basic back-office tasks, such as budgeting, accounting, and billing, were remarkable for their similarities. In this case both USAID and DFID sought not just the same goal—strengthened municipalities—but also to achieve that goal in broadly similar ways. DFID's Consolidated Municipal Transformation Programme (CMTP)[77] and USAID's Local Governance Support Program, Phase 2 (LGSP)[78] both aimed to help municipalities efficiently and effectively deliver services.[79] Both focused on making local government more effective by transferring knowledge to municipal staff. This capacity building was of both a management and a financial nature; both projects aimed to improve municipal accounting and billing systems and municipal debt management. How USAID and DFID delivered their interventions was quite different, however, as was their management, reporting, and design processes.

USAID's municipal governance project sent trainers to visit municipalities to deliver trainings. On a prearranged day, a trainer would arrive and hold a session, often in a conference room, for part or all of the day on a prearranged topic. Many municipalities were served by the project and many training sessions were delivered. To choose one as an illustrative example: debt management trainings were conducted in Makhado municipality, an area of approximately 500,000 people close to South Africa's border with Zimbabwe. USAID did not actually send its own personnel to Makhado. Instead, USAID contracted Research Triangle Institute (RTI); RTI in turn reported back to USAID on training targets, which included how much of the training needed to be delivered by a given month. For example, for debt management, USAID determined that 50 percent of the training needed to be completed by month 20 of the project and 100 percent by month 24.[80] The contractor, RTI, in turn designed a training plan for each municipality. The Makhado plan included as one of six key objectives: "Credit control policies and implementation, and debt policy implementation."[81] The first action for this task was to "train all staff on implementation of policy." [82] The "Success Indicator" associated with this action was to have "All staff trained in Finance Dept and Municipal Secretariat."[83] To achieve this, RTI devised a deployment plan for each municipality with "Hands-on mentoring dates" under a number of categories, including "Debt policy."[84] Following the trainings, trainers— largely independent contractors hired by RTI—verified that trainings had occurred and tracked how many individuals were trained.[85] USAID's project focused on reporting on quantifiable outputs. USAID once again chose a navigation strategy with a greater degree of principal control (and thus a lesser degree of agent initiative).

DFID's project shared the broad focus of USAID's on improving municipal functioning via skills transfer and systems building. Contractors implemented DFID's project, as they did USAID's. The consulting firm Deloitte implemented on behalf of DFID, in turn hiring consultants and contractors to act as the project's agents in the field. Unlike USAID, DFID's project worked primarily by embedding advisors in local municipalities. Advisors resided in the municipalities for extended periods of time to build skills and systems on an ongoing basis. An illustrative example: in Ba-Phalaborwa, some 200 kilometers southeast of Makhado, DFID's project placed a resident service delivery expert, known as an Integrated Service Facilitator (ISF), for two years.[86] DFID also contributed financing to the placement of a South African National Treasury–sponsored financial advisor for three years.[87]

DFID's project documents specify the goals of the project as a whole and the objectives to be accomplished by each subcomponent of the project. The first output for the resident advisors was "advise/mentor [municipal] managers in achieving targets, plan and budget, unblock delivery obstacles and achieve institutional coherence."[88] There were specific reporting requirements; however, in contrast to USAID, DFID's reporting requirements did not rely on reporting on quantifiable outputs. DFID's reporting requirements included "[resident advisor] ISFs conduct an assessment of status quo and prepare a report."[89] This report would include a workplan for the ISF on what he or she planned to do.[90] Then "[resident advisor] ISFs implement their workplans and report on progress monthly and quarterly."[91] DFID's advisors were ultimately in charge of project direction; *they* set the specific goals against which they were reporting. As one implementer put it, DFID's reporting was "more content-rich; it was not a numbers game."[92]

DFID and USAID both had reporting requirements for their respective projects. However, DFID did not rely primarily on externally observable outputs in reporting, unlike USAID. DFID effectively put resident advisors and their soft information–laden judgments in control, something DFID not only condoned but actually explicitly designed into the project. As DFID's March 2007 annual review of the project put it, "The role of the [resident advisor] ISF has varied considerably because of staffing issues at municipalities; their institutional placement; the skills and experience of the ISF; the conditions within the municipality. Municipalities have also utilized [the DFID project's] support in the ways most urgently required."[93] In contrast to USAID trainers, DFID project advisors based in municipalities had relatively free rein to use their judgment and guide the project accordingly. This was from DFID's perspective a feature, not a bug. DFID's incorporation of agent initiative and judgment was an intentional design feature, an organizational choice to Navigate by Judgment to a greater degree than did USAID.

DFID advisors were able to rely on their own judgment and act on their own initiative in the case of DFID's South African municipal governance project. An advisor sitting in a remote municipality could think primarily about what needed to be done without the need to meet prespecified targets at the expense of impact.[94] Advisors principally determined what occurred under the umbrella of the project in individual municipalities.[95]

Use of soft information was also evident for the DFID project in the choice of municipalities in which to place advisors. The DFID design team actually visited the municipalities that they were considering. The perceived but externally unverifiable likelihood of the municipality working well with an advisor was a key consideration in support decisions.[96] One actor described this as designed to avoid the "looks good on paper but won't work in practice problem."[97] Richard Thomas, DFID's governance advisor at the time of the project's design, noted there was a need to figure out "what's really, rather than officially, going on."[98] In Thomas's view, then, South African municipality selection required soft information. DFID's design and basic delivery model included a substantial degree of Navigation by Judgment. DFID was highly sensitive to the importance of learning from the local context, and it achieved this by empowering actors in the field to exercise initiative and make critical decisions.

The South African municipal governance case allows us to see what different navigation strategies look like in practice even more clearly, perhaps, than the prior case pairs. These projects illustrate the Aghion and Tirole trade-off between agent initiative and principal control. USAID and DFID implemented programs with quite similar goals. They did so through rather similar contracting structures. But DFID's project exhibited far greater Navigation by Judgment than did USAID's. USAID settled on an initial model that delivered monitorable and measurable training by visiting trainers.[99] Navigation from the Top—particularly process measurement and reporting via prespecified targets—played a substantial role in USAID's intervention but little in DFID's. USAID was more rule-bound, with substantial process controls and an orientation toward satisfying bureaucratic requirements.[100] Tight principal control for USAID precluded soft information from being incorporated into agent and ultimately organizational decisions.

DFID, by contrast, Navigated by Judgment to a substantial degree. The "price" of DFID's greater degree of agent initiative was a lesser degree of principal control. DFID placed resident advisors in municipalities and designed the project in a manner less tractable to control from above. It created reporting requirements that did not rely on quantifiable, externally observable information. DFID intentionally designed the intervention so that field agents' judgments would navigate and control the project's direction. On any given day, the driver of what the project was doing, how it was being done, and why it was the right thing to do at that time was the judgment of agents. The presence or absence of autonomy and the nature of measurement regimes was critical for DFID's navigation strategy. Notable, too, was DFID's lack of reliance on externally observable and quantifiable information in project design.

*Establishing Levels of Success*

There was little positive said about USAID's trainings, including—somewhat surprisingly—by the USAID and project team personnel who had actually worked on the project.[101] Former LGSP Deputy Chief of Party Bongani Matomela—the deputy supervisor of the overall project—felt "[LGSP] might have not made the most dent or impact."[102] As one interviewee put it, "I don't think [training under USAID's LGSP] contributed much . . . because you go there, you don't have any authority over the people that you [are] training, so if they don't cooperate you cannot say anything, you go there sometimes, they tell you that we have other priorities, we don't have time now, those kinds of things."[103] A USAID official described LGSP as "classroom oriented," as it was hard to see much as a result of LGSP in those municipalities he had visited.[104] There was only a single interviewee among the dozens who commented on the project's success who felt that the trainings were anything other than a total failure; this individual described them as a "mixed success."[105]

Targets and reporting clearly served as a control in USAID's municipal governance project that may not have served the intervention's ultimate goals. Michelle Layte, the head of project implementation toward the end of the project, said indicators were chosen "because it was easier to count . . . but the numbers didn't tell about the impact."[106] Layte went on to say that, while USAID had been better earlier in the project, "It was more a number chasing toward the end especially because we needed to reach our target."[107] This did not go terribly well; one implementer described a clear sense inside the USAID project implementation team that the trainings were failing.[108] Municipalities were not interested in the visits by trainers, and little was changing within the municipalities. The trainers could see with their own eyes how little their time, travel, and effort amounted to. Those being trained would not pay attention to the training, and many participants showed little if any progress over time.[109] There was, however, no way to change the project in response to this reality, at least not in the short term. Those delivering the training had to continue to visit so they could report having done so. Those at RTI to whom they were reporting might know the training wasn't effective. However RTI had a contract to deliver; in a very real sense what RTI had to deliver was valid numbers.

The correlation between measures and ultimate outcomes broke down in USAID's municipal governance project. The training numbers weren't fabricated; trainings were occurring and individuals were attending. One USAID actor described this as counting "bums on seats."[110] Another described implementing the USAID project as "a numbers game . . . [USAID would say] we want the numbers, we want information."[111] These numerical outputs became disconnected from the broader purpose the project had been designed to serve.

These measures may have had little connection to impact, but they certainly affected implementation. Measures constrained the behavior of field agents (in this case, trainers) and their managers (in this case, RTI), precluding alteration of the project. Measurement was clearly one of the key components of USAID project navigation, and it was at odds with Navigation by Judgment.

USAID's project did eventually move to assigning advisors to particular municipalities toward the end of the project. Even these advisors were not resident in municipalities, instead coming in and out of municipalities and working on average three days a week.[112] If these advisors were successful, it was a quiet success, in that there were no signs of improvement in the fiscal indicators of the LGSP municipalities according to South African municipal audit reports.[113] In multiple cases national South African government officials didn't recall the advisory component of USAID's project, and in one case a long-serving municipal manager whose municipality had received both LGSP training and an LGSP advisor had no memory of LGSP's existence.[114] There is no sign of USAID's LGSP having impact on national policy or being cited as an example by others. As one staff person put it, LGSP was "a real disappointment for us at the end of the program."[115]

Being full-time resident there for the long term, DFID's advisors were often—though not always—able to find a way to positively influence municipal systems. Both beneficiaries and project staff reported that CMTP advisors achieved some shifts in municipal practices.[116] Multiple actors noted the permanent status of advisors in the municipality prevented the project from being sidelined in the way USAID's intervention seems to have been.[117] It would be an overstatement, however, to see CMTP as having accomplished all, or even most, of what it set out to do in terms of direct municipal impact; in some municipalities it accomplished very little.[118] The CMTP project completion report prepared by DFID, in giving CMTP a 3 on a 5-point scale, argues, "The achievement of CMTP purpose, although uneven in parts, included some highly positive examples in selected municipalities."[119] DFID's CMTP also acted as a model for future government interventions. The South African government launched a national campaign focused on strengthening municipalities. Called Project Consolidate, this campaign built in part on CMTP's delivery model, placing advisors in municipalities.[120] Indeed, on two interviewees' views, it was Project Consolidate that influenced USAID's LGSP to move to advisors.

DFID's greater Navigation by Judgment was associated, as theory would expect, with greater ability of agents to act in ways undesired by the principal as well. There were some reports that Deloitte, DFID's implementing contractor, took advantage of the freedom DFID afforded it to sometimes focus on profit to the detriment of the project.[121] In one alleged example, Deloitte supplied Deloitte advisors who were less experienced and thus less costly to

municipalities while billing DFID for more costly advisors, pocketing the difference as corporate profit.[122] A flexible reserve fund had been established by the
project at design, and Deloitte more than any other actor guided the direction of
these funds.[123] This included directing procurements to Deloitte itself, a practice
that deservedly raised eyebrows in the independent final evaluation of DFID's
project, which noted that it had led to conflicts of interest and inefficiently spent
funds.[124]

Whatever the shortcomings of DFID's CMTP may have been, not a single
interviewee who had exposure to both projects thought USAID's LGSP intervention the stronger of the two projects. That DFID's CMTP was more successful was also argued by a number of interviewees who could speak to the success
of both projects and would have no obvious reason to speak better of CMTP
than LGSP.[125] DFID's CMTP was clearly the more successful project, but this
was not because of its exceptional level of success; while neither project lived up
to expectations, DFID's project was less of a disappointment. It may be fairer to
think of LGSP as the "bigger failure" rather than CMTP as the "bigger success."

### Linking Relative Success with Navigation Strategy

As suggested above, "numbers chasing" was clearly a problem for USAID.
Training numbers became disconnected from the harder to measure goal of
actually building knowledge or transferring skills. Despite feedback that the
initial trainings weren't working, LGSP also took quite some time to revise the
frequency or targeting of the trainings—it continued on the path that generated numbers.[126] DFID faced no such pull toward generating numbers. DFID's
model also allowed their project to better cope with a common challenge faced
by both DFID and USAID: the turnover of municipal government personnel.[127]
This meant that USAID's trainings didn't "stick"—today's training often needed
to be repeated tomorrow, as personnel had changed in the interim.[128] The long-
term presence of CMTP advisors allowed them to respond more flexibly to
changes at the local level; that said, a number of years after project close, it was
still the case that a substantial proportion of the individuals with whom advisors
worked had left their posts.

In contrast to the experience in the South African health case pair, the closer
working relationship of DFID's project with the national government was nearly
universally framed as positive in the municipal governance cases. Government
links were seen as allowing the DFID project's results to have broader impact and
influence.[129] One USAID LGSP staff member suggested the USAID project's link
to Government "wasn't as solid as it should have been."[130] Bongani Matomela,
former LGSP deputy manager, suggested explicitly that DFID's CMTP was the
stronger project largely due to USAID LGSP's lack of a government link:

My sense was that it [DFID's CMTP] was probably more successful [than USAID's LGSP] . . . one of the success factors is probably the fact that they [CMTP] were closer to the department [the South African National Department of Provincial and Local Governance], they probably did things according to what the department wanted, you know, and they were directly augmenting Project Consolidate whilst I get it that LGSP seems to have been just the programme . . .. Because it [CMTP] was actually anchored within the department and so the chances of certain tools and models that were being developed and tested were then immediately transplanted to the municipality, so I think that probably it's a more sustainable way of doing projects than maybe the LGSP.[131]

The LGSP's relative lack of a government link was at USAID's specific direction. While the DFID project had offices in the South African government's Department of Provincial and Local Government, USAID's project worked from a separate, independent office. USAID specifically insisted that LGSP not be based inside a government building due to what one actor described as "a warranted worry that whoever was managing the project [LGSP] would be pulled up in too many different directions and not be able to focus on the project."[132] Whatever the virtues of such a choice, it is a striking one given that a close connection to government was directly cited by multiple actors as a factor in CMTP's success as compared to LGSP.[133]

One of the most remarkable things about USAID's intervention is that it followed an externally observable and quantifiable training-centered model *despite* the previous failure of that model. In so doing it suggests the inability of USAID to implement a management strategy that did not rely primarily on management by outputs. This USAID municipal governance project was, in fact, phase 2 of USAID's Local Governance Support Program (LGSP). This phase 2 built on a phase 1. Phase 1 was an exploratory project, with one important goal to be the testing of new models. Phase 1 had an explicit focus on and financing for "lessons learned"; for codifying learning so as to inform future phases of the project.[134]

In reflecting on LGSP phase 1, Creative Associates—the contractor who had been managing the project—identified the lack of local knowledge and use of remote trainings as central to phase 1's failure. They argued that

the design for the first round of the LGSP used few service providers who clustered assistance to widely dispersed municipalities with the same local government developmental needs. It did not work. The key reason was that municipal conditions varied and service providers did not necessarily have the local knowledge to adequately deal with implementation issues that arose.[135]

It is striking, then, that USAID pursued the strategy it did in LGSP phase 2. One USAID actor described the phase 2 strategy this way: "LGSP took the approach of choosing municipalities and then trying to work through a program of capacity building with all of them, your standard sort of package."[136] This is nearly identical to the strategy that had so clearly failed in phase 1. The LGSP phase 1 report also foreshadows some of the other key difficulties faced by LGSP—the rotation of municipal personnel and the difficulty of "political situational management" are also mentioned explicitly.[137]

The LGSP's phase 2 did the same things as had LGSP's phase 1, but hoped for different results. This, perhaps unsurprisingly, did not prove a successful strategy. Despite my best efforts I have been unable to understand precisely what drove LGSP phase 2 to repeat the basic strategy of phase 1. Taking USAID's behavior as a whole, it seems likely that the need for legitimacy-seeking measures, and thus for externally verifiable data, played a substantial role. If accurate, this underscores the potentially pernicious effects of political authorizing environment demands for data in pursuit of accountability introduced in chapter 4.

The relative success of DFID's CMTP was not because of some surprise event or unpredictable "shock" that allowed DFID's project to better react to the unexpected. It is, rather, because the nature of the project made a navigation strategy tied to externally observable and quantifiable data less appropriate. DFID's navigation strategy also allowed a closer working relationship with the South African government than did USAID's, a relationship that was critical for a project whose goals involved strengthening government capacity. DFID's Navigation by Judgment also allowed the project to be guided by resident advisors in each municipality who could use their judgment and soft information to guide the project.

The next section briefly brings the two South African case pairs together, discussing project external verifiability and IDO success. This chapter then closes by briefly summarizing the key findings of Part II, which this chapter brings to a close.

## Project Verifiability and IDO Success

This chapter opened with quantitative findings suggesting that verifiability plays an important role in understanding the relationship between Navigation by Judgment and results. Comparing USAID and DFID's projects further supports this conclusion, and offers support for the notion (which the quantitative empirics, contrary to expectations, left ambiguous) that sometimes Navigation by Judgment is indeed associated with lower levels of success. In the context of South Africa's relatively predictable environment, Navigation by Judgment still proved the superior strategy in municipal capacity-building—the sector where external monitoring was more difficult and soft information more critical to success. Navigation by Judgment seems to have been less useful in PMTCT delivery.

Navigation strategy needs to be tailored not just to the environment but also to the nature of the IDO project. Building a road and building up the skills of the Ministry of Transportation call for very different management strategies. To refer once more to the distinction between Lewis and Clark's 1804 journey and that of a modern user of Google Maps, it is not just environment that determines whether a more Google Maps–laden approach is appropriate for IDOs. Some projects can be guided by externally verifiable data, following clear, monitorable, measurable processes as they build toward the achievement of development goals. Others cannot. The tractability of interventions to management based on externally verifiable outputs—the project's verifiability—is an important part of what determines the best navigation strategy. The next section explores variation in intra-IDO choice of navigation strategy by project, or lack thereof.

## The Stickiness of Navigation Strategy in Part II

We have now four cases from USAID and DFID respectively from which to draw. The U.S. Agency for International Development (USAID) uses quantitative targets where that seems perfectly appropriate (e.g., PMTCT in South Africa) and where it seems less appropriate. There is only one case—USAID's Liberia capacity-building intervention, implemented by its more flexible Office of Transitional Initiatives—in which USAID engages in even a modest degree of Navigation by Judgment. Reporting on outputs substantially drove even this project, however.

USAID's lack of deviation from a reliance on quantifiable outputs is, while striking, plausibly consistent with Part I's theory, inasmuch as it can be read as stemming from a need for legitimacy from political authorizing environments. But DFID exhibits little more variation in navigation strategy than does USAID. This is much more directly at odds with Part I's theory. A lack of authorizing environment constraint was theorized to give IDOs the *ability* to Navigate by Judgment, not the need to do so in every case, whether appropriate or not. Part I took the position, and Part II's empirics broadly support the view, that Navigation by Judgment is an important tool in an organization's repertoire, one that will sometimes but by no means always be appropriate. The quantitative scale used in Part II was framed as "propensity to Navigate by Judgment" rather than "level of Navigation by Judgment." This is because Part I's expectation, as laid out most clearly in Table 2.1, is that more autonomous IDOs will use externally verifiable data and engage in greater Navigation from the Top where appropriate. In the case study's modest sample of projects, however, there is not a single example in which DFID does not Navigate by Judgment.

The U.K.'s Department for International Development (DFID) does seem to vary *whose* judgment drives project navigation in a way plausibly consistent with this book's theory. DFID's South African municipal governance intervention delegates effective control in some ways the furthest from headquarters, with the judgment of individual advisors effectively driving the intervention. DFID's Liberia civil service project, by contrast, largely allowed the judgment of the implementing contractor to guide the intervention, although DFID personnel played an important role. For the more verifiable Liberian and South African health interventions, it is DFID staff whose judgment seems most determinative of project direction. DFID projects suggest variation regarding whose judgment counts in ways plausibly driven by the nature and goals of the project. The two cases where the level of judgment is closest to the field—the South African and Liberian capacity-building cases—are in the sector where returns to soft information are predicted to be highest.

It is nonetheless surprising, and potentially troubling, that DFID never decides *not* to Navigate by Judgment. It is possible that this is an artifact of case study sample size; in a sense the case studies provide only one situation (the South African health sector) where it seems that less Navigation by Judgment would have clearly served DFID well. But it feels as if DFID never even considered a more top-down, data-driven approach in the project design phase of any project.

It seems as if DFID's image of itself, and its agents' sense of what "good development" constitutes, augurs for relative Navigation by Judgment even more widely than might be appropriate. This may be due to a well-intentioned form of bureaucratic capture. Empowered bureaucrats may believe Navigation by Judgment the right solution even where an honest ex-ante reading of the environment would suggest otherwise, with DFID's actions during South Africa's HIV/AIDS denialism a possible case in point. If true, this would imply that DFID, no less than USAID, needs to allow its navigation strategy to vary more according to the specifics of development goals, project plans, and recipient-country environments than is currently the case.

This conjecture—and it is no more than a conjecture, to be fair—that more autonomous IDOs *also* may have more "stickiness" in navigation strategy than appropriate calls into question this chapter's quantitative empirics regarding external verifiability. These empirics found no sign that less Navigation by Judgment–prone organizations fared better in sectors where projects were more likely to be verifiable than their more Navigation by Judgment–prone peers. Put more simply, Tables 7.1 and 7.2, and Figure 7.1, do not show the benefits of Navigation from the Top that this book hypothesized they would. If more

Navigation by Judgment–prone organizations are in fact not using top-down controls when appropriate, we should expect to see these organizations' projects fail when top-down controls are called for. The quantitative analysis, then, is "missing" a result which would suggest that more Navigation from the Top is sometimes a better strategy. Part I's theory and the South African health case study are in tension with Part II's quantitative empirics on this point. I have no satisfying answer for this nonfinding, which remains an open question for further empirical exploration.

## Putting Part II Together: Verifiability, Predictability, and Navigation by Judgment

As Part II of the book draws to a close, what have we learned about Navigation by Judgment's relationship with performance? We have strong evidence that Navigation by Judgment is frequently, but not always, useful. We have evidence that at least some of what determines when Navigation by Judgment is useful relates to the nature of the environment and the tractability of the project to top-down controls, which in practice often means reporting against quantitative output targets. We have also seen evidence supporting the hypothesis that political authorizing environments limit IDOs' Navigation by Judgment both through direct process controls and procedures, such as USAID's inability to contribute to Liberia's health pooled fund, and by inducing what appears to be legitimacy-seeking but otherwise unhelpful measurement, such as in USAID's South Africa capacity-building project.

As predicted, econometric analysis drawing on the PPD—the world's largest database of development project outcomes—suggests there are greater returns to Navigation by Judgment in less predictable environments. This is not because Navigation by Judgment actually leads projects to be more successful as predictability falls. Greater propensity to Navigate by Judgment simply cushions the fall, with high Navigation by Judgment–prone IDO performance declining less as environmental predictability rises. The quantitative results suggest project verifiability is important as well, with the overall effect seemingly driven by sectors where projects are likely to be more difficult to verify.

The case studies showed that USAID and DFID, two IDOs which the quantitative analysis identified as of varying propensity to Navigate by Judgment, responded to similar problems with different navigation strategies in contexts of differing predictability and project verifiability. Table 7.4 reports comparative performance of USAID and DFID in each of the four case pairs, estimating a success rating on a scale from "highly successful" (6) to "highly unsuccessful" (1) for each intervention. The estimates in Table 7.4 are entirely my construction

*Table 7.4* **Comparing USAID and DFID Success in Each Case Pair.**
**High = high verifiability and predictability, low = low verifiability**
**and predictability, medium = either high verifiability or high**
**predictability. DFID outperforms USAID in three of the four case**
**pairs; the one exception is in the South African health sector, where**
**returns to Navigation by Judgment were expected to be lowest**

| | Combined Verifiability and Predictability by Case Pair | | | |
|---|---|---|---|---|
| | *High* | *Medium* | | *Low* |
| | South Africa Health | Liberia Health | South Africa Capacity Building | Liberia Capacity Building |
| **DFID** | Moderately Unsuccessful (3) | Highly Successful (6) | Moderately Successful (4) | Moderately Successful (4) |
| **USAID** | Highly Successful (6) | Moderately Successful (4) | Highly Unsuccessful (1) | Unsuccessful (2) |

based on my judgment of the degree to which each intervention was successful in achieving its development goals.

These results provide strong support for the core conjectures regarding the relationship between Navigation by Judgment and performance. In achieving the prevention of mother-to-child transmission of HIV in South Africa Navigation by Judgment performs least well, comparatively speaking. This highly verifiable intervention in a predictable environment is the only case study pair in which Navigation by Judgment seems to have been a weakness rather than a strength. This does not mean performance actually rises for any IDO as environmental predictability falls; both USAID and DFID perform better when environments are relatively predictable than when they are not. DFID's performance is more consistent across contexts, with Navigation by Judgment mediating the impact of greater unpredictability and lower verifiability.

How robust and generalizable are these findings? Appendix II's extensive robustness tests tell us little about how the data of additional IDOs, were it available, might alter the findings of the quantitative analysis. On the qualitative side, the complexity of projects and the number of margins on which they can differ means that a similar analysis of a wider range of projects and IDOs would almost surely produce a fuller picture of IDO behavior. It is certainly possible that such an exploration could lead to substantively different conclusions than those articulated here. As to external validity within the universe of IDOs, it is not unimaginable that more data could lead to the view that these findings are reflective of a particular kind of IDO rather than generalizing to the full universe of IDOs.

That said, Part II's empirics have attempted to utilize mixed methods in such a way as to maximize the internal validity of these findings. Qualitative cases have provided direct evidence of relative IDO success, linking that success to propensity to Navigate by Judgment. Quantitative empirics have provided evidence that the dynamics identified in these qualitative cases are generally present rather than a result of case selection. Navigation by Judgment is not a complete explanation of IDO intervention success or failure; but Part II provides evidence that it is an important piece of the puzzle.

Part III of this book explores the implications of Part II's empirics in light of Part I's theory. The next chapter, chapter 8, revisits the principal-agent problem of Part I's theory in light of Part II's empirics. Chapter 8 carries the argument and the empirics more directly to the relationship between political authorizers, IDO managers, IDO field agents, and implementing contractors. The final chapter, chapter 9, brings this book to a close by exploring how IDOs could change for the better in light of Part II's findings. Chapter 9 also explores implications of these findings for scholars of international development and well beyond and the implications of this book's findings beyond the aid industry.

# PART III

# IMPLICATIONS

# Delegation and Control Revisited

Part II's empirics focused primarily on hypothesis testing, on establishing comparative levels of Navigation by Judgment and the relationship between Navigation by Judgment and Project Success. The discussion in Part II also established that Navigation by Judgment plays an important role in explaining the success and failure of international development organization (IDO) interventions. This chapter steps back a bit, exploring how the empirics speak to the broader dynamics of delegation and control for political authorizers, IDO management, IDO field agents, and implementing contractors.

This chapter first revisits the central principal-agent relationships theorized in Part I, exploring delegation from political authorizers to IDOs and IDOs to their field agents. The chapter then turns its attention to the contractors who implement projects and discusses other explanations of development Project Success that echo this book's argument regarding delegation and control in IDO project implementation.

## Political Authorizing Principals and IDO Field Agents

This section seeks to further explore the connection between political authorizers, IDOs, and field agents. Part II provided opportunities to compare the navigation strategies of U.S. Agency for International Development (USAID) and the U.K's Department for International Development (DFID). This section assembles the case evidence regarding the relationship between political authorizers, IDO management, and field agent behavior and also connects authorizing environment insecurity to field agent initiative and motivation.

Part II provided no evidence of authorizers intervening directly in IDO activities. There is no example of the U.S. Congress or the U.K. Parliament directly inserting themselves into the design or implementation of development projects. Consistent with chapter 4, political authorizers instead cast a shadow that affected IDO project design and navigation strategy. Authorizing environments can directly restrict IDO action by rule setting, as seen in USAID's inability to contribute to Liberia's health-sector pooled fund. But more often it is not a specific rule or regulation but rather the desire to demonstrate quantifiable performance that precludes IDOs' use of Navigation by Judgment.

If it is the shadow of authorizing environments that IDOs are reacting to, it seems that the U.S. Congress casts a longer shadow than does the U.K. Parliament. While only suggestive, in the transcribed interview data from South Africa the word "Congress" appears thirteen times. "Parliament" is mentioned only once, and by way of *contrasting* DFID with USAID, with an interviewee who worked for both DFID and USAID projects noting that Parliament never came up, in contrast to "the Congress [which] wants these numbers because they are providing so much [money] for South Africa and they want to know what it is that we have done with their money."[1]

Authorizing environment insecurity was evoked with regards to USAID's hiring practices, limiting USAID's ability to hire full-time staff and thus the use of contractors in project supervisory roles.[2] It was used to explain USAID budget unpredictability and the constant need for USAID to fight for funding.[3] As one USAID official put it, "Congress doesn't trust us [USAID]. Thinks we're all a bunch of hippies."[4] In perhaps the most vivid depiction, a different USAID senior official described USAID as "under siege" from Congress, saying "[USAID faces] a hostile Congress and an ineffectual president . . . it has been an agency under siege for, I guess it would be going on for over thirty years now."[5] There is a general sense within USAID that USAID is not well regarded by political authorizers; no similar sentiment seems to pervade DFID.

The need for reporting looms large for USAID, a need connected to justifying actions to Congress. An individual with experience at a number of development contractors described this as the pressure from USAID to "document more than do," suggesting that this pressure to document tends to leave projects with "some really beautiful reports" to please funders and authorizers but less impact on the ground than might have occurred if attention had instead focused on implementation.[6] As one employee of a development contractor implementing a USAID project put it, "USAID wanted reports. USAID pushed [contractor] management, and management pushed us."[7] A former senior manager for a USAID contractor summarized a widely echoed view in saying, "USAID's focus was around meeting numbers as opposed to the impact."[8]

The most direct consequence of authorizing environment insecurity theorized in Part I was tighter IDO headquarters' control of field agents, and thus a loss of agent judgment and initiative in favor of principal control and monitoring. Part II's empirics provided data consistent with this hypothesis in a comparative sense; DFID agents took greater levels of initiative and relied substantially more on soft information and their own judgments of the situation. There is also within-organization evidence of agents failing to take initiative because of tight principal control.

One expatriate USAID staffer in Liberia suggested that very few of her colleagues ever learned much about the world just beyond the embassy walls, as there was no way to make use of that information.[9] As another USAID official put it, the effect of the restrictions and constraint from above is to "make you cautious."[10] Insecurity breeds conservatism, the need to ensure that any action taken can be defended. One interviewee very explicitly linked USAID's tight supervision to an inability to take advantage of available soft information:

> When a person provides oversight they must provide oversight and not be part of the day to day management and just trust you with the decision that you do the analysis and the calculations of what is needed and what is not needed . . .. [This tight USAID control hurts project performance because][11] now you always have this voice in your head that you know is going to say, "no not this" because maybe they don't believe in that way and maybe they are not seeing what you are seeing because you are actually managing the programme and your view has maybe deeper areas of focus than the helicopter view and your decision is purely based on that insight which sometimes you cannot translate into words.[12]

Part II illustrated the importance of "that insight which sometimes you cannot translate into words." Principal control, often accomplished via the setting of targets and reporting regimes, moves IDO agents to focus on reporting "up" to principals rather than accomplishing broader development goals.

Chapter 3 argued that an additional consequence of tighter principal control would be more dissatisfied, less intrinsically motivated agents. Comparing USAID's Office of Transitional Initiatives (OTI) with the rest of USAID provides evidence consistent with the notion that motivation can be kindled or squelched by management practice. The Office of Transitional Initiatives, in its management of USAID's Liberian capacity-building intervention (Building Responsive and Democratic Governance, or BRDG), created a remarkably collegial and positive work environment as compared to other USAID interventions. When asked to compare BRDG to other aid projects on which they have worked, a number of individuals remarked how uniquely satisfying the experience of working with BRDG was.[13] One team member described it as "one in a million" with the kind of coworkers and working environment that comes "once in a lifetime."[14] More than one individual described it as the project they were proudest to have been involved in during their careers.[15] At the project's close, the staff prepared a "yearbook"—resembling an American high-school yearbook—of project activities and staff. Two separate interviewees still had this yearbook easily accessible more than five years after the close of the project.[16]

What is true on the project level also seems to be true of OTI as a unit; OTI seems to pair greater autonomy and greater motivation (or, as Chapter 3 put it, a more "Theory Y" equilibrium) than the rest of USAID. In annual Federal Employee Viewpoint surveys, OTI scores higher on morale and satisfaction than the rest of USAID by significant margins.[17] A 2009 Congressional Research Service report notes the unusual (for USAID) "high staff morale at OTI."[18] Multiple OTI and BRDG interviewees noted the exceptional quality of their colleagues as compared to other USAID projects on which they have worked.[19] This is consistent with greater Navigation by Judgment attracting higher-quality staff.

The association of more Navigation by Judgment with greater motivation and job satisfaction is also present in direct comparisons between USAID and DFID. USAID was described as a particularly unenjoyable place to work by some interviewees.[20] A former USAID project employee who took a job with a DFID project described the transition from USAID to DFID as "a breath of fresh air."[21] As Subethri Naidoo, who played management roles with both USAID and DFID projects in South Africa, put it: "It was easier to work in DFID, and I think it was also far more intellectually stimulating for me. You know, USAID was very rules driven, compliance driven, but there wasn't kind of a recognition of the need for personal growth and development of your staff . . . [on the other hand, with DFID] there would be a regular kind of intellectual thinking and strategizing about where we are."[22]

While I was conducting interviews related to one of Part II's case pairs, multiple interviewees singled out a particular USAID project employee for praise multiple times. I was of course keen to meet, and interview, the individual who elicited such praise. When I later interviewed the individual in question, they had shifted jobs; this formerly exceptionally effective USAID project employee described dissatisfaction with USAID management practices and reporting as key in prompting their departure from the USAID project.[23]

In conducting my case study interviews, I often asked interviewees directly how they would compare USAID and DFID; this is often what prompted interviewees to respond with the views I cite and quote in this chapter.[24] But the modal answer was not, in fact, to respond with a direct organizational comparison. By far the most common interviewee response was that the answer to the questions depended on the abilities, orientations, and talents of USAID and DFID's field staff.

This interviewee focus on individuals seemed to suggest that field staff quality is the luck of the draw; that either USAID or DFID might be better depending on the orientation, quality, and motivation of field staff, which was as-if random. But chapter 3 argued, and I believe the case data suggestively support, the notion that there is a systematic component to who populates a given IDOs' cadre of field staff and the orientation and motivation of these staff members.

There are important and systematic links between political authorizing environments, management strategy, agent motivation, and agent quality. Job design and organizational navigation strategy not only affect current employees but also drive selection of employees into and out of organizations. This yields different equilibria of management practice and agent type for different IDOs. That IDO delivery depends on people does not make it random; there are systematic differences between IDOs that affect who IDO field agents are and what they do.

The case studies provide, then, supportive evidence for the core mechanisms theorized in Part I. Political authorizing insecurity trickles down to agent behavior and motivation. The next section explores the next step in the delegation chain. The USAID and DFID do not actually directly implement any of the projects in Part II's case studies; instead they delegate implementation onward to contractors. This is typical; contractors implement a great deal of official development assistance. The role of contractors, then, is critical to understanding what IDO choice of navigation strategy means in practice. The next section explores the use of contractors and their impact on IDO navigation strategy and Project Success.

# Onward Delegation by IDOs: The Role of Contractors

International development organizations have long contracted out the implementation of development projects to private for-profit and nonprofit firms.[25] The use of contractors continues to grow. Between 2003 and 2012 the annual dollar value of USAID contracts issued increased more than 400 percent to over $USD12 billion.[26] In some instances, contractors have displaced IDO staff; between 1980 and 2001 USAID reduced its permanent workforce by 45 percent even as its budget rose.[27] This section first examines how contracting affects Navigation by Judgment in practice; it then addresses whether contractors should be given more power to Navigate by Judgment.

## Contracting and Navigation by Judgment in Tension

The use of contractors plays an important role in limiting Navigation by Judgment. As Robin Gorna, a former DFID health advisor in South Africa, put it:

> DFID advisors tend to have a particular training which makes them really good at spotting opportunity and creativity and getting in behind

exciting new opportunities, when you get caught up in this kind of contracting process of working through consultants, it doesn't always follow through quite as beautifully . . . this talent-spotting type of design
was great if you had an advisor who was going to be able to pick it up
and make it move, but when you contracted out that responsibility, you
sort of, you couldn't contract out the intelligence in the same way.

Ken Sigrist, an experienced DFID contractor, agreed. He provided a complementary view from the contractor's perspective, suggesting contracts limited
flexibility and reduced the free flow of information and ideas between contractors and IDO. As Sigrist put it:

This whole process of packaging up technical assistance and contracting it out in large lumps actually takes away all of the flexibility, all of
that opportunity to pivot quickly and to take advantage of circumstances, you can't build that into the bloody contract . . .. I want to be
able to say to DFID, as your advisor on the ground, I consider us to be
stuck for these reasons, I consider the way to break out of this situation
is the following, this is the strategy I propose, pros and cons and all the
rest of it, I want to be able to have that conversation and that is more
difficult now.[28]

It is striking that Sigrist's examples of what can't be built "into the bloody
contract" are changes in implementation that would, presumably, rely on soft
information.

A similar contracting mechanism—a multiyear implementation contract—
does not seem to have the same result in imposing inflexibility for DFID as it
did for USAID. One long-serving USAID staff member summarized the effects
of contracts on USAID in saying, "Rigidities of the [contracting] mechanism
affect the way we operate, the way we design, etc. . . . the real world requires a lot
of flexibility; the world of procurement requires a lot of certainty."[29] By contrast,
one veteran of numerous development agencies said, "[With DFID] nothing is
set in stone. DFID—of the development partners I've worked for—is the most
flexible to respond to changes, tweaks."[30] DFID contracting seems not to have
the imposed identical rigidities even as DFID employed similar contracting
structures.

As evidenced by Part II's case pairs, DFID's contracting allowed substantially
greater flexibility in implementation than did USAID's. However, when asked to
compare the DFID of the present to the DFID of the past, interviewees report
a decline in Navigation by Judgment due in part to the increasing use of contracting. These are perfectly consistent views, of course. DFID's increasing use of

contractors may be crowding out Navigation by Judgment even as DFID's use of contractors retains more flexibility than does USAID's. It has been said that the United States and United Kingdom are "two nations divided by a common language."[31] This seems true for DFID and USAID as regards the use of contractors.

The existence of a contractor appears to mean different things for these different IDOs, with informal understandings and working procedures playing a substantial role in what "contracting out" means in practice. There is a need to look beyond the simple existence of a contract to understand its implications.[32] While the USAID official quoted above suggested there was a single "world of procurement," the data support the existence of multiple "worlds" of procurement. Contracting imposes inflexibilities. But it imposes inflexibilities differentially.

## Should Contractors be Given Even More Power to Navigate by Judgment?

DFID seems to put more power in the hands of contractors. A strand of the economics literature on incomplete contracting suggests that this grant of greater power to contractors is likely a good idea. As this book has noted, IDOs work in contexts in which it is difficult to specify all the contingencies that may occur. Economics Nobel Laureate Oliver Hart and his coauthors argue that, just because not all contingencies can be foreseen, all is not lost. Contracts that are incomplete can nonetheless allocate renegotiation or bargaining rights such that contractors can still reach efficient outcomes even when the unforeseen occurs.[33] A key feature of optimal incomplete contracts is writing the contract so that the party that needs to make more investments that *cannot* be contracted—in other words, which are not externally verifiable—has the lion's share of the power if and when unforeseen contingencies arise. This gives the party whose investments cannot be contracted the incentive to nonetheless invest appropriately. In other words, those with access to soft information and local contextual knowledge need to hold the power to drive alterations in the contract. Contractors— those that need to collect and act upon nonverifiable soft information—need to be the more empowered actors in incomplete contracting relationships between IDOs and their contractors.

One might wonder if IDOs should go still further, putting an even greater amount of power in contractors' hands than is currently the case. There are risks to such a strategy over and above the risks for an IDO of relying on the judgment of their own agents.[34] Sarah Bush suggests more contractor autonomy is unlikely to be a good idea in the absence of broader institutional changes in her examination of firms implementing IDO democracy assistance programs.[35] Bush finds that contractors are more likely to engage in tamer projects when it is harder for IDOs to monitor them, and that the legitimacy-seeking advantages of

measurement play an important role in allowing contractors to appear successful without in fact challenging undemocratic regimes. The implication is that
giving contractors more autonomy without changing broader measurement and
contract-reporting systems will lead contractors to engage in *less* useful projects.
The same reporting requirements and principal control that constrains IDO
agents is likely to distort the behavior of contractors. Extending the chain of
delegation is likely to exacerbate the distortionary nature of targets, inasmuch
as it requires the writing of formal contracts and (if Navigating by Judgment)
trusting the judgment of agents the IDO itself cannot hire, fire, or individually
evaluate and reward.

There is good reason to think that Navigation by Judgment cannot fully be
contracted out, with Navigation by Judgment most useful where contracting
out is most difficult. But this does not mean that contractors cannot be useful
actors, or that contracts cannot adapt to changing environments. The net effect
of empowering actors down the delegation chain depends critically on the structure of the contract and the incentives contractors and agents face.

The most successful case of relative contractor Navigation by Judgment for
USAID in Part II is the Liberian capacity-building project, BRDG; notably this
is also the only USAID case in which USAID staff were essentially working in
collaboration with contractors rather than by delegating to contractors. When
implementing BRDG, the contractor (DAI) and USAID's Office of Transitional
Initiatives (OTI) staff seemed to operate as a nearly unified, relatively seamless
BRDG administrative team; this "positive, collaborative, and open" working
relationship is also noted in the externally contracted final project evaluation for
BRDG.[36] The project development phase of BRDG is particularly telling; following identification and approval of a project idea by both DAI and OTI, DAI
would develop a budget to be discussed with the beneficiary and approved by
OTI, with the grant then managed by DAI staff.[37] Staff from DAI and OTI staff
met weekly and collaborated on activity development and review;[38] when consultants who were brought in to conduct short pieces of work departed Liberia,
their exit briefing was with both DAI and OTI staff.[39] This is apparently typical
of OTI, the unit of USAID that was responsible for BRDG. As a Congressional
Research Service report on OTI puts it, "OTI staff are actively involved in every
stage of project planning and implementation, in contrast with typical USAID
staff who, some claim, have become more like contract officers than development experts in recent years."[40] Day-to-day collaboration largely resolves the soft
information problem by allowing contractors and their supervisors access to the
same soft information. The IDOs could place IDO personnel alongside contractor staff to better allow Navigation by Judgment to flourish.[41]

The next section of this chapter brings the key explanation of IDO success
and failure proffered in Parts I and II—variation in navigation strategy—into

conversation with other, more conventionally mooted proximal causes of IDO Project Success that also speak to issues of delegation and control. In what ways does this book provide new perspective on these explanations?

# Local Knowledge and Control:
## Country Ownership, IDO Decentralization, and Country Execution

The notion that local knowledge is important for development success is not a new idea in the aid literature or among aid practitioners. Attempts to integrate local knowledge have long led aid thinkers and practitioners to focus on delegation and control in delivering foreign aid. First, proponents of country owner-ship argue that IDOs should ensure projects are desired by recipient-country governments, who should substantially direct the development goals and spe-cific interventions IDOs pursue. Second, proponents of IDO decentralization argue that IDO offices should be put in countries to allow IDOs to access local knowledge. This section discusses each of these arguments in relation to this book's findings.

## Recipient-Country Ownership, Execution, and Political Will

It is often argued that donors should ensure projects are "country-owned." As a recent paper puts it, "the donor pursues country ownership by strengthening the leadership role played by the partner [recipient-country] government regarding the prioritization, financing, and implementation of a development strategy."[42] If indeed country ownership contributes significantly to performance, the ques-tion remains how an IDO achieves country ownership. "Ownership" is often discussed as if it depends solely on recipient countries. The Liberian Office of Financial Management was "shopped" to USAID and only subsequently to DFID; nonetheless it became a DFID project. As a result USAID's Liberia port-folio had a lower degree of country ownership than would have been the case had USAID executed the project.

DFID's Navigation by Judgment allowed recipient-country governments to guide strategic direction more than did USAID's navigation strategy. As one Liberian government senior official put it, "USAID consults on strategy, but it's *their* strategy."[43] The realized level of country ownership is a function not just of the developing country government but also of IDO priorities and process. As a recent Organisation for Economic Coopaeration and Development (OECD) review notes, "the dominance of Washington-based directives and initiatives inevitably hinder the alignment of US development programming with country priorities."[44]

That said, the South African health case also suggests that whether country ownership is in fact good may depend on where a country's leadership is pointed. I would submit, and I believe many readers may agree, that the South African government was simply wrong in resisting public health interventions to address the AIDS crisis under President Thabo Mbeki. DFID's Navigation by Judgment in the South African health sector made DFID intervention success much more conditional on the support and orientation of South Africa's government. During the period of AIDS denialism, DFID floundered. One senior South African government official complimented DFID for being "demand driven";[45] this is a popular buzzword in the world of foreign aid, one with substantial positive connotations. But perhaps it is possible for an IDO to be unduly driven by recipient-government demands to the detriment of intervention effectiveness and impact.

Political will—a government's commitment to a particular reform—is also often put forward as a cause of intervention success or failure.[46] What's true of country ownership is also true of political will—the same government can have different realized political will toward different projects. By working more closely with, and allowing projects to be guided by, recipient-country governments, DFID's interventions examined in Part II had greater realized political will than did USAID's.

Navigation by Judgment begs the question of when to have recipient-country bureaucracies, rather than IDOs, execute projects.[47] States with more autonomous bureaucracies see more rapid improvement in reducing child mortality rates and tuberculosis prevalence.[48] Judith Tendler famously provided examples of a poor Brazilian state getting better results by empowering bureaucrats, including those without formal skills and training.[49]

Frank Fukuyama has posited a linear relationship between the level of state capacity and the productive use of greater bureaucratic autonomy.[50] Fukuyama uses Nigeria as his paradigmatic example of a low-capacity state bureaucracy in need of tight principal control; however, the best evidence available suggests precisely the opposite. In Nigerian public agencies, more bureaucratic autonomy and less use of pay-for-performance schemes that rely on externally verifiable data are associated with higher project completion rates.[51] These findings strongly suggest further study is warranted as to when and whether IDOs would do better by empowering developing country bureaucrats to execute.

Part II's case studies suggest that political will and country ownership are not randomly distributed among interventions. Secure political authorizing environments and Navigation by Judgment are likely to increase the proportion of IDO projects that are country-owned and regarding which recipient-country political leaders demonstrate political will. Navigation by Judgment can also help us think through when recipient countries are likely to be better executors of development projects than IDOs themselves.

## IDO Establishment of Country Offices

Another argument sometimes put forward is that IDOs should place offices and staff in developing countries so they can take advantage of local knowledge. Case study interviewees often highlighted the returns to "being there," the way physical presence changes views and deepens understanding. But while the most successful examples of Navigation by Judgment in the case studies involve an empowered, experienced in-country decision maker, there is also evidence a physical country office is neither necessary nor sufficient for Navigation by Judgment.

The quantitative analysis of the impact of in-country offices, described in chapter 6 and Appendix II, suggests that having an in-country office is useful, but not equally so. Offices only positively impact Project Success for more Navigation by Judgment–prone IDOs. The case studies further underline that having a physical office in-country is not sufficient for an IDO to gain the benefits of soft information. USAID's South African municipal governance project is a particularly strong illustration that physical presence is not sufficient for gathering soft information or responding to context. If an organization cannot make use of soft information, being in a position to collect it has minimal impact for the production process. In part this is because agents will, per the Philippe Aghion and Jean Tirole model, have no incentive to gather data that they cannot use.

It is also not clear that a substantial field office is necessary to utilize soft information and respond to context. The DFID exhibited Navigation by Judgment in Liberia despite the absence of a substantial DFID presence in the country. While there was a DFID country representative—a single individual—present in Liberia for much of the period in which the Liberia projects occurred, project supervision largely involved actors based in Sierra Leone and London who made frequent visits to Liberia. DFID's project instead utilized soft information by providing the space for implementing contractors to Navigate by Judgment. Actual presence in the country does not guarantee that soft information will be used; even de jure formal devolution of authority is the beginning, not the end, of the story. It is critical to soft information incorporation that actors have the de facto space to Navigate by Judgment.

## Conclusion: Delegation and Navigation

This chapter has connected Part II's empirics more tightly to the mechanisms theorized in Part I and their implications for IDO navigation strategy decisions. It has also explored how onward delegation to contractors affects navigation strategy, and how this book's argument interacts with related explanations of development success often put forward within the aid industry. The next chapter, chapter 9, explores how IDOs can change to improve navigation strategy in light of this book's findings. It also discusses the implications of this book for scholars as well as for those beyond the field of development assistance.

# 9

# Conclusion

## *Implications for the Aid Industry and Beyond*

Putting front-line employees in charge is sometimes superior to using top-down controls to manage foreign aid delivery. Navigation by Judgment allows agents, and by extension their organizations, to incorporate soft information—information that field agents can observe but that cannot be easily codified or verified by distant supervisors. Navigation by Judgment also allows international development organization (IDO) projects to be more flexible and adapt to changing circumstances.

The quantitative analysis presented in chapters 6 and 7 examined the performance of nine IDOs with varying degrees of propensity to Navigate by Judgment. More Navigation by Judgment–prone IDOs see their performance decline less as environmental predictability falls than do their less Navigation by Judgment–prone peers. Project verifiability is an important mediator of this relationship. Some projects can be well managed using externally verifiable data, with outputs and targets well aligned with development goals. For other projects the best available output measures are deeply flawed, and a management strategy that focuses on these measures is unlikely to be the best strategy.

The four case study pairs in chapters 6 and 7 compared USAID and DFID projects in contexts of varying environmental predictability and project verifiability, allowing for a direct comparison of project performance by case pair. The case study pairs confirm that the degree to which an IDO Navigates by Judgment is indeed a critical part of Project Success. Whether more reliance on agent judgment to guide interventions helps or hinders Project Success depends on project type and environment. USAID's relative inability to Navigate by Judgment often came at the expense of relative Project Success in Part II's case study pairs. However, Navigation by Judgment also fails, with USAID's relative reliance on top-down output targets successful in driving the delivery of critical HIV/AIDS relief in South Africa. Relying on top-down controls may well be the best strategy when output measures act as effective summary statistics for an intervention (e.g., the prevention of mother-to-child transmission of HIV/AIDS, or PMTCT) and environments are legible and predictable.

More politically insecure IDOs are less inclined to Navigate by Judgment. More insecure IDOs are also more likely to engage in legitimacy-seeking measurement. A need to reach output measures and targets sometimes precludes agent use of initiative and judgment that would benefit IDO Project Success.

Judgment sometimes fails. So, too, do top-down controls. There are flaws both to a navigation strategy favoring principal control and to one favoring agent judgment and initiative. Where top-down controls work best—in predictable environments and with verifiable projects, where soft information is least valuable—there is no need to rely on agents' fallible judgments or worry about agents' potential to engage in actions undesired by supervisors. As environments become more unpredictable and interventions less externally verifiable, however, the flaws of principal control weigh IDO projects down more heavily than do the weaknesses of fallible agent judgment. When the going gets tough, Navigation by Judgment helps cope with the rougher terrain.

The next section presents a series of suggestions to improve aid effectiveness in light of this book's findings. This chapter then explores the implications of this work for academic disciplines and suggests future potential avenues for empirical inquiry. This book then closes by looking beyond IDOs and development assistance, exploring some of the broader implications of this work for both public and private sectors.

## Making IDOs Fit for Purpose

The aid industry has over the past decades developed a keen focus on impact. I believe this laudable focus can be retained, and indeed that greater Navigation by Judgment is, where appropriate, a critical managerial tool that will help to maximize the positive impact of foreign aid. This section discusses three discrete but complementary strategies that might improve navigation strategy fit with projects and thus increase aid's impact. The first of these three strategies is rethinking when measurement is useful, and how to make it more useful—measuring smarter not harder. This book has spent quite a bit of ink attempting to demonstrate the perils of inappropriate measurement. The next section attempts to put this in a broader context and suggest when and for what purposes measurement is likely to be effective in the aid industry.

## Strategy 1: Measure Smarter Not Harder

Trying to prove success sometimes reduces the actual level of IDO Project Success. This book's findings strongly suggest that the demonstration of results to political authorizers is sometimes in tension with the actual accomplishment of results. In subtle but, I would argue, extremely important ways, measurement of results on the one hand, and measurement as a tool for improving results on the other, are often conflated. International development organizations would do well to separate out these distinct components.

For determining project impact, more data and quantification is in my view a substantial step in the right direction. International development organizations, and scholars of development more broadly, are increasingly shifting from a reliance on output measurement to rigorous impact evaluations of longer-term results, including but not limited to randomized control trials. I believe this move toward greater rigor is both laudable and long overdue. But rigorous impact evaluation will never be able to provide clear guidance on how to respond to unanticipated shocks or when precisely to trust agents' judgments. As the phrase "impact evaluation" implies, these methods are designed to evaluate outcomes, not provide data to help implementers better manage projects.

Additionally, researchers themselves seem to have implicitly conceded that some kinds of development interventions are very difficult to evaluate using rigorous methods.[1] A recent paper drawing from the database of the International Initiative for Impact Evaluation (3ie) presents what the authors describe as "the first complete overview" of international development impact evaluation evidence.[2] It finds that from 2000 to 2012, 64.9 percent of all rigorous evaluations focused on the health sector with an additional 23.1 percent of studies focused on the education sector. By contrast, only 3.3 percent of studies focused on attempts to improve public-sector management.[3] This is quite probably because it is very difficult to identify a plausible counterfactual and/or externally verifiable outcome measures for many public-sector management projects. Some of the same factors that make Navigation by Judgment more beneficial for a particular project also make impact evaluations more difficult, precluding an econometrically rigorous examination of a particular project's results. Navigation by Judgment is most helpful where rigorous evaluation is most difficult and where rigorous evaluation is the least likely to build a robust knowledge base.[4]

Where we can do so, measurement of results using rigorous methods is an excellent idea. But rigorous impact evaluations are unlikely to "solve" the essential tension between principal control and agent initiative for IDOs. From a management standpoint, measuring smarter does not mean putting all our hopes in the power of rigorous impact evaluations. The IDO manager who waits for a randomized trial to guide them in response to changing local circumstances or provide rigorous evidence of when precisely to trust the judgments of employees in the field might as well be waiting for Godot; the wait will be indefinite.[5] In some cases, measuring smarter may mean shifting the frequency of measurement; in other cases, it may mean shifting measurement's purpose away from accountability and control. These two "flavors" of measuring smarter are discussed below.

### *Strategy 1A: Shift Measurement's Frequency Where Practicable*

International development organizations themselves are well aware of the difficulty in managing using quantitative measures. In 2013 the Organization for Economic Cooperation and Development's (OECD) Development Assistance Committee published a member survey of twenty-eight IDOs' experience in "Managing and Measuring For Results."[6] The IDOs reported a variety of challenges with management by measurement. All twenty-eight IDOs reported that they sometimes, often, or 100 percent of the time had difficulties in selecting appropriate indicators against which to measure.[7] Three of the twenty-eight IDOs reported this was a problem *100 percent of the time*; that is, that they never felt it was easy or straightforward to choose targets.[8] Twenty-four of twenty-seven responding IDOs reported they sometimes or often had "difficulty in using information on results for accountability purposes".[9] A separate OECD review of USAID underscores USAID's conflict between output monitoring and strategic, thoughtful use of data. As the review puts it, "USAID requires quarterly reporting for almost all interventions . . .. [The reporting system] creates a transaction and compliance-based approach, rather than a results-based approach in which data are strategically collected and used to correct direction or improve decision making."[10] The OECD Development Assistance Committee and IDOs themselves seemingly agree that setting output targets and managing against them can sometimes lead projects astray.

As the USAID review implies, shifting the frequency of measurement may make data more meaningful in addition to lowering transaction costs. The case studies in Part II suggest that there is sometimes a tension between measurement frequency and measurement reliability and quality at the project level. Resolving this tension in favor of quality and reliability would be a substantial step in the right direction for IDO management and aid effectiveness. What constitutes appropriate measurement in practice can only be determined on a case-by-case basis following a careful examination of an intervention's specifics. International development organizations often develop a monitoring and evaluation plan as part of their overall project design process. This planning process could be altered to allow planners to consider how best to avoid the unproductive distortion of agent attention to targets at the expense of development goals and the crowding out of agent initiative and use of soft information. This altered planning process might, where appropriate, lead to less focus on measurement of short-term outputs and more focus on longer-term outcomes.

As noted in chapter 2, the suggestion that aid measurement ought to focus on outcomes is not a novel one. Proponents of cash on delivery aid and results-based financing have long argued that short-term output measurement is meaningless at best and often counterproductive.[11] The most careful analyses to date, however, suggest that a true shift toward outcome rather than output measurement has yet to be implemented in earnest.[12] Focusing on verifiable outcome measures would allow soft information to be incorporated into the process of achieving these outcomes.

Where verifiable outcome measures can serve as summary statistics for intervention success, changing the timing of measurement will allow Navigation by Judgment over means. There will be many IDO interventions for which this is not the case, however. The next section explores what can be done when there are no verifiable outcome measures that will serve as good summary statistics for the achievement of development goals.

### *Strategy 1B: Rethink Measurement as an Accountability Tool*

Rethinking the timing of measurement will be insufficient when project outcomes are difficult to quantify or if they will not properly orient employees in the field toward achieving a project's broader goals. Take for example DFID's Civil Service Capacity Building (CISCAB) project in Liberia, examined in chapter 6. The project's stated goal was "to help to rebuild and improve the Liberian Civil Service's contributions to effective governance and service provision."[13] It is hard to imagine a useful measure, or group of measures, that could have fully summarized this project's goal and thus could have been relied upon for control purposes. The output measures that might have been used to evaluate the performance of the key government partner, Liberia's Civil Service Agency—such as policies passed or number of new hires efficiently processed—are clearly prone to distorting agent effort toward meeting targets at the expense of the project's goals. Some of the seemingly most plausible outcomes—for example, improvements in the quality of management or frequency of corruption—are quite hard to measure. A more measurable long-term outcome might be citizen satisfaction with the civil service. But any improvement on a citizen satisfaction measure would be quite difficult to attribute to the DFID project rather than to another source that might increase satisfaction (e.g., the end of civil war and rapid postwar economic growth). I see no effective way DFID might have used measurement of outputs or outcomes to properly orient agent actions in its Liberia Civil Service Capacity Building project.

The broad measurement choices DFID might have made in this project each have echoes in Part II's case studies. In chapter 7 we saw that USAID chose to use number of people trained as a key success indicator in their South African municipal governance project. This choice distorted agent effort toward meeting the target at the expense of the project's broader goals. In chapter 6 we saw that in DFID's Office of Financial Management project in Liberia, DFID chose to use as its key success indicators reduction in maternal and infant mortality. This indicator was a clear, measurable outcome, one that in no way distorted agent behavior. But "performance" on this measure—whether maternal and infant mortality rose or fell—ultimately had very little to do with financial management systems.

It makes every sense for IDOs to ask themselves the question, "What is the best possible quantitative performance measure for this project?" But if the possible answers to this question boil down to a choice between unattributable outcome measures (e.g., maternal mortality for a financial management project) and distortionary output measures (e.g., number of people trained for a municipal governance project), IDOs may often be better off choosing neither option. One way forward for an IDO attempting to implement a project that is difficult to effectively manage using measurement of either outputs or outcomes is simple, if somewhat radical, for IDOs: Stop using measures for the purpose of evaluating interventions or managing agents.

There is no need to eliminate measurement; measures simply need to be repurposed. Measures can still be used for organizational learning. Learning is often put forward as a primary goal of IDO evaluation.[14] International development organizations could deepen this focus on learning, sometimes putting aside the use of measures as tools of management control. If USAID agents had not felt pressured to meet output targets in the South African municipal governance project, the number of people trained might have been a measure that contained some useful information for the management and understanding of the project. Measures can become more helpful for organizational learning when the incentive to perform against measures is removed.[15] It is when performance pressure is put on a measure that it becomes an unproductive tool of top-down control.

Lurking just outside this book's frame have been issues of accountability. Accountability, or at least use of the term "accountability," is closely linked in many IDOs (and well beyond) to observation and measurement. Changing the role of measures need not mean forgoing accountability; accountability can be much broader than a managerial focus on rewarding agents who meet performance targets and punishing those who do not. Professional reputations among colleagues and peers can provide horizontal peer accountability.[16] There is suggestive evidence that IDO employees may be particularly susceptible to peer accountability, seeing themselves as part of a sector-wide professional community.[17] Agents can also be asked to explain their behavior after the fact, with all information that can be gathered informing holistic performance reviews of agents by managers. This "discursive accountability" can incorporate more nuance than can standard indicators, and thus it puts managers in a better position to assess both agents' motivations and the reliability of their judgments.[18] Broadening the range of accountability tools can also change how agents feel about their organizations, often for the better.[19]

One additional accountability alternative is to hold agents accountable to others who are also present in the same place and who are involved with the same project. Soft information is not *uniquely* held by a given field agent; it is just unavailable to those who are not locally present. Agents who work for organizations that Navigate by Judgment may also need to be evaluated in part by judgment—by subjective assessments in addition to, or rather than, objective assessments. Other individuals who are present in the same environment may be best placed to evaluate an individual's, or a project's, performance.

I suspect some readers may be less than fully satisfied with these alternative accountability suggestions. None of these accountability solutions have the serious, weighty, objective connotation of employing quantitative performance measures as accountability tools. But this sense of reliability, of measurement as a stable foundation on which to build accountability structures, is sometimes a mirage. This book has demonstrated that measures may mislead authorizers about success and make interventions less likely to achieve the long-term development goals that principals have set. Putting weight on measurement to control agents, then, can be in service of principal managerial accountability or a facade that makes true accountability more difficult. To improve perceived accountability at the expense of actual results seems a pyrrhic victory.

Improving management by measuring smarter will sometimes mean changing when measurement occurs or what is measured. It will sometimes mean changing the purposes for which measurement is used. But measurement is just one tool of the Navigation from the Top with which I contrast Navigation by Judgment. As the next section discusses, IDOs can most directly improve performance in light of this book's findings by finding ways to Navigate by Judgment when appropriate.

## Strategy 2: Pilot New Navigation Strategies

An IDO seeking to increase Navigation by Judgment need not transform organizational management practice across the board. International development organizations can experiment with giving some offices, sectors, or particular projects vastly greater control on a pilot basis. Agencies could commit to evaluating the performance of Navigation by Judgment pilots only after a sufficiently long period to allow the long-term impacts of projects in the pilot to be compared to the projects of a plausible comparative country, sector, or set of projects as appropriate.

It is critical that any Navigation by Judgment pilot be done in conjunction with changes in contracting, staff rotation, and promotion and reporting practices that pertain only to the personnel involved in the pilot. In recent years, IDOs have begun to experiment with their own management practices, including attempts to incorporate greater local knowledge and increase flexibility.[20] But merely changing the formal rules may not yield desired results in the absence of broader changes in how agents are evaluated and promoted.[21] Take USAID as an example, given this book's close examination of USAID authorizing environment constraints and agent behavior. So long as USAID continues to put substantial pressure on measures and reporting, I am skeptical that USAID employees will act in ways that might improve outcomes but that will not be reflected in the numbers by which employees and their projects are evaluated. Broader concern for their careers will keep USAID agents from making use of formal rule changes in the absence of broader changes to agents' incentive structures.[22] In the words of a recent paper on World Bank organizational reform, "ultimately institutional reform and real change requires more than new architecture: it requires a change in the plumbing too—the internal systems, processes and behaviours within agencies."[23] Piloting new navigation strategies must involve the "plumbing" to succeed. Flexibility and initiative taking can no more be mandated by top-down instruction than can "better performance." Engaging in the details of staff incentives is the only plausible path to better navigation strategy.

Development interventions often fail, and fail repeatedly, in particular countries and sectors. Agencies may find it easier to attempt comprehensive Navigation by Judgment pilots where current efforts have clearly failed. This might be called a "NUMMI pilot," recalling the abject failure of the status quo in the NUMMI plant's predecessor described in chapter 3. Where little progress has been made, maybe it's time to try something radically different. Inasmuch as previous failure is correlated with the extreme difficulty of the problem, this does not mean that Navigation by Judgment will somehow lead Zimbabwe to good governance. A history of failure simply suggests there's little to be lost in giving a very different strategy a try. The worst-case outcome – continued ineffective aid – is simply a continuation of the current status quo. Of course, Navigation by Judgment pilots are even more likely to show results in less extreme settings. If attempted in civil service reform or municipal governance projects across a wide range of countries, Navigation by Judgment pilots will allow IDOs to better understand whether and when more Navigation by Judgment is indeed improving organizational performance. Organizations will thus be able to learn more from Navigation by Judgment pilots if they do not focus Navigation by Judgment only on the hardest cases, even as NUMMI pilots may be the easiest way forward for IDOs.[24]

It is worth noting, perhaps, that the causal logic of Navigation by Judgment pilots is almost precisely the inverse of "earned autonomy," a management practice increasingly popular in the U.K. public sector.[25] The logic of earned autonomy is that units or individuals who perform well are given greater latitude for independent action. The NUMMI example itself illustrates the difference in the logic between my proposed pilots and earned autonomy; NUMMI did not give agents more scope for independent action as a reward for past performance. Indeed, the history of the plant that became NUMMI was one of unmotivated employees actively seeking to undermine production. Key to NUMMI's success was that managers empowered workers to use greater judgment in their work as an input to improve performance in the future, not as a reward for past success. Chapter 3 argued that IDO agent quality and motivation are improved by Navigation by Judgment. This book's evidence supports this argument, with case study data in chapters 6, 7, and 8 strongly suggesting that navigation strategy impacts agents' motivation as well as agents' entry into, and exit from, IDOs. Under certain conditions, better performance is likely to be a product of greater Navigation by Judgment. Waiting for workers to improve performance to reward workers with greater autonomy is to confuse cause and effect.

International development organizations would be well served by cautiously piloting greater Navigation by Judgment and carefully evaluating the resulting changes both to project performance and to agents themselves. There is every reason to believe that experimental pilots can change IDO practice for the better.[26] Beginning with a small part of the overall portfolio, IDOs can change navigation strategy to see what works, to iterate, and to improve.

Both this strategy (piloting new navigation strategies) and that which preceded it (measuring smarter) involve internal changes to IDOs. But it is also possible for IDOs to make gains collectively without altering any given IDO's navigation strategy and use of measurement as a managerial tool. The next section suggests IDOs can also reallocate projects to create better matches between project type and IDO navigation strategy.

## Strategy 3: Leverage IDO Comparative Advantage

Chapter 7 noted that there is very little within-IDO variation in navigation strategy. If navigation strategy stays relatively constant within an organization, this suggests that so long as IDOs operate across a vast range of tasks and environments, each IDO—those that Navigate by Judgment as well as those that do not—will often "get it wrong" as regards navigation strategy. It may be possible for the aid system as a whole to serve common goals more effectively without substantial change to any IDO's authorizing environment constraint or navigation strategy. International development organizations could recognize their comparative navigational advantages and sort projects as appropriate among themselves. This work provides fairly strong evidence that constrained IDOs would do best focusing on projects and recipient-country environments tractable to measurement—for example, road construction or drug delivery. This would allow organizations that can Navigate by Judgment to focus on less verifiable projects and less predictable environments.

There is little evidence that this kind of specialization is occurring at present. The project selection data presented in chapter 6 and Appendix II strongly suggest that IDOs are not focusing on the projects where their IDO is most likely to succeed. The case studies similarly provide suggestive evidence of the potential gains to be had from leveraging comparative advantage. Chapter 7 showed USAID's impressive effectiveness in delivering antiretroviral drugs to prevent mother-to-child transmission of HIV, while DFID helped the government of South Africa roll out a plan (the "A-Plan") that implemented using U.S. government–funded health delivery infrastructure. I believe this leveraging of IDO comparative advantage was, at least by USAID and DFID headquarters, unintentional. But it shows the gains to be had from strategic collaboration that takes seriously comparative IDO managerial strengths.

The best navigation strategy for a project depends on precisely what projects intend to do, not just the country and sector in which they occur. As in the South African health example, any division of labor among IDOs should focus on specific tasks rather than broad sectoral or country allocations. Designing this change into IDO project approval processes would be difficult but not impossible. Insecure IDOs would need to find some way to frame their increasing focus only on projects that are verifiable in positive terms; for example, a constrained IDO would need to frame their pivot as an "infrastructure strategy" rather than a "we're avoiding things we can't manage well" strategy. Project planning and preparation cycles might need to be harmonized across IDOs, building on commitments to harmonization and alignment to which IDOs have already agreed under the Paris Declaration on Aid Effectiveness. The benefits to leveraging comparative advantage could be substantial.

## Making IDOs Fit for Purpose in Sum

There is much that IDOs can do to improve performance in light of this book's findings. First, IDOs can try new things, experimenting with their managerial approaches. In addition, IDOs can recognize their comparative constraints, taking advantage of each IDO's relative managerial strengths; and IDOs can measure smarter, not harder. Development assistance should focus on actually benefiting recipients and achieving important outcomes. Being outcome-driven need not always mean being driven by measured outcomes. From a management standpoint, this means thinking critically about when target setting and management by measurement is in fact in service of achieving outcomes and when it undermines performance. Change is possible, though by no means easy. Following any of these strategies to change how IDOs manage will necessarily involve experimentation, learning from experience, and adjustment along the way.

The rest of this chapter moves away from the management of IDOs. The next section discusses this book's implications for scholars and future research. The chapter then discusses the broader implications of this book's findings in light of the increasing penetration of technology and quantification into modern life and work.

## Implications for Scholarship and Directions for Future Research

International relations (IR) scholars have arguably fallen behind their peers in public administration, bureaucratic politics, and economics in the sophistication and nuance of principal-agent models, particularly as regards animating agents.[27] This book by no means overturns existing principal-agent theory as it applies to international organizations and IR; discretion and autonomy are key features of models both within and beyond international relations and the study of international organizations.[28] In beginning its analysis with agents in the field, this book highlights costs to principal control that are rarely discussed or theorized in international relations.[29] Asymmetric information is not merely a source of dysfunction or of potential hidden action by agents unwanted by the principal. Asymmetric information is also a critical component of success that can only be effectively used by an organization that lets go of tight principal control.

For scholars of foreign aid, this book suggests that organizational structure may be an important and often overlooked component of aid effectiveness. This book contributes to what Nilima Gulrajani has called "the bureaucratic turn" in studies of foreign aid.[30] My argument supports an emerging literature and community of practice suggesting that traditional "blueprint" ways of doing development are often misguided.[31] This book connects scholar and practitioner concern about best-practice solutions to the "results agenda" and measurement practices via a novel, more systematic empirical analysis than has previously appeared in the literature.[32]

For scholars of public administration and public management, perhaps the most distinct contribution of this work is to highlight a rarely conceptualized class of public-sector organization: a public agency whose clients are not part of the body politic.[33] An IDO's clients are not constituents, resulting in broader scope for distortions—for the appearance of performance without actual delivery—than typically conceived.[34] This book's depiction of IDOs ought to raise concern regarding the potential façade of meaningless metrics in other contexts where clients are not voters and thus typical democratic accountability feedback loops are weak or absent. Possible examples might include military engagement overseas (e.g., the U.S. military's reconstruction role in Iraq and Afghanistan); customs and border patrol treatment of noncitizens; and prison education programs for (voting ineligible) felons. These contexts may have more echoes of the colonial past than the liberal democratic present, with bureaucratic structures likely to manage "up" to authorizing environments at the expense of their ostensible clients.

I believe that the degree of difference between public-sector and private-sector organizations is more a river than an ocean—the two groups are distinct, but not so far from one another that lessons from one side of the divide cannot inform thinking in the other.[35] Scholars with an interest in performance measurement, target setting and goal setting, and hybrid governance may find this work of particular interest. This book connects some of the foundational concerns in organizational behavior regarding the impact of task and environment on management flexibility (as contrasted with standardization) to a more recent strand concerned with the potential distortions of management practices such as goal setting and tight observation.[36] It does so in a relatively novel empirical setting, one that offers a rich data-generating context for cross-organizational empirics and thus rigorous mixed-methods analysis. For more general management scholars, this book perhaps fits most squarely in a strand of the literature that flows from scholarship on environmental uncertainty and differential task routinizability.[37] An IDO's field agents could also be seen as the coalface of organizational sensemaking, with top-down measurement in IDOs precluding the ability of organizations to use field operative perceptions to make sense of ambiguous or uncertain situations.[38]

Virtually all the data that undergird the quantitative component of this book's analysis are now public.[39] The Project Performance Database (PPD) is now available for download on my website, danhonig.info. The success and failure of development interventions stem from many sources, making causal attribution difficult. The size and scope of the PPD—with individual projects nested in different organizations, sectors, recipient countries, and time periods—facilitates better-identified empirical exploration of important questions than has previously been possible.[40] International development organizations are involved in a dizzyingly diverse array of projects in the vast majority of countries in the world. They thus serve as a relatively novel source of empirical data regarding organizational performance across task and environment. Most immediately, this database is of use to scholars studying the determinants or consequences of aid effectiveness. What contributes to the relative success of aid projects? What impacts do more or less successful projects have on economic and political outcomes in developing countries? How does Project Success affect bilateral relations—do more successful projects improve diplomatic relations or recipient country public sentiment toward donors? There is also surely variation in outcomes between projects and countries that could be productively modeled as an outcome variable for further exploration of management practices.[41] New data on agent hiring, review, and promotion practices, agent rotation practices, agent backgrounds, etc. could also be paired with the PPD to explore broader organizational dynamics.[42]

As noted in this book's preface, I believe the central tension this book highlights between principal control and agent judgment is a general phenomenon. While IDOs may face relatively extreme contexts in the extent to which they need to engage in a journey without maps, IDOs are not unique; IDOs differ in degree, not kind, from many other organizations.[43] The next two sections of this chapter explore the broader implications of this book's findings for managers and employees.

## Management in the Broader Public Sector and Beyond

From public schools to multinational firms, many organizations struggle with Philippe Aghion and Jean Tirole's tension between principal control and agent initiative. Aghion himself, in collaboration with a number of illustrious coauthors, has recently applied his model to private firms during the Great Recession.[44] Using data from eleven OECD countries, they find that private firms with more local plant-manager control outperform more centralized firms in the sectors hardest hit by the crisis. As they put it, "Higher turbulence benefits decentralized firms because the value of local information and urgent action increases."[45]

There are a great many private-sector examples of distortions borne of output measurement.[46] Perhaps my favorite comes from the quest for employee fitness. Workplaces are putting pressure on fitness data generated from devices like Fitbits for control purposes. These controls sometimes take the form of links to health care premiums (e.g., walk 10,000 steps a day and pay less for health insurance), though more often they seem to be linked to "challenges" or "competitions" that are often linked to prizes. The result? A rash of Fitbits adorning dogs, hamster wheels, and ceiling fans.[47] The Fitbit can register that motion is taking place, but not that the employee is the one actually moving.

Of much more substantive consequence, the global economy increasingly calls on firms to engage in complex and only dimly understood contexts, for example, as a multinational firm works with a local supplier in an emerging market. As contexts decrease in their tractability to blueprint planning and top-down controls, there is an increased likelihood that management control from above will alter things for the worse if done without due care and attention. Evidence from IDOs—a kind of organization that, quite unusually, does many different kinds of things in many different kinds of places while keeping systematic data on performance—supports this assertion.

Over a century ago, Frederick Taylor described the tension between output measurement and employee use of soft information. The father of scientific measurement, Taylor advocated replacing "traditional or rule-of-thumb knowledge" with scientific measurement, rules, and monitoring.[48] Taylor noted that scientific management would—in his view for the better—shift control from agents to principals, with the benefits of principal control outweighing the loss of agent judgment and initiative. As he put it, "[The current reliance on agent judgment] necessarily leaves the solution of all of these problems in the hands of each individual workman, while the philosophy of scientific management place their solution in the hands of the management."[49]

This book can be read as a claim that Taylor is sometimes wrong when he decries "rule-of-thumb knowledge" and agent control in favor of "scientific management" which places control with managers. Trusting professionals to make their own judgments sometimes leads to better organizational outcomes. This book suggests some ways of systematically thinking through whether Navigation by Judgment is likely to help or hinder in a particular case by considering the predictability and legibility of environments and the tractability of tasks to output controls.

For a multinational firm, this might mean thinking about the management of sales teams in relatively predictable and legible New Jersey quite differently from those in less predictable and legible New Delhi. For the New Jersey production team, it might mean target setting and monitoring with tighter principal control. For the New Delhi sales team, it might mean less principal control in favor of agent initiative. It also might mean managing firm expansion into new markets in light of the verifiability of the firm's activities, the extent to which the tasks employees do can be managed using the best possible externally observable and verifiable data.

# The Creep of Quantification

In 1989 James Wilson's <u>Bureaucracy</u> theorized as to how management strategy was affected by the observability of outputs and outcomes.[50] Wilson's paradigmatic examples of bureaucrats for whom both outputs and outcomes were externally unobservable were teachers and police officers.[51] In the quarter-century since Wilson wrote, much has changed; neither police officers nor teachers labor unobserved today.

Teacher outcome measurement is now an industry of its own, and—as noted in chapter 2—there are efforts, such as those by Bridge International Academy, to tightly observe and control teacher outputs as well. Police officers are observed by both body cameras and via the camera-equipped phones in many of our pockets. The police force is today arguably the paradigmatic example of management based on externally verifiable data in the public sector via the widely used Compstat system.[52] While principals have long desired greater monitoring and control, recent decades have seen a proliferation of tools allowing principals to turn this desire into reality.

The growth of observation and quantification as tools of top-down monitoring and control is not unique to the public sector. A recent episode of a popular U.S. National Public Radio program was titled "The Future of Work Looks Like a UPS Truck."[53] Apparently, the search for efficiency has driven UPS, a parcel delivery service, to an incredibly high degree of technology-enabled process control. Drivers are instructed as to how to load their trucks, what order to deliver packages in, and where to stop the truck on a given street to make multiple deliveries. To save valuable seconds when signing forms, left-handed drivers are required to keep their pens in their right-front pockets; right-handed drivers in their left-front pockets. The central message of the radio story was that "technology means that no matter what kind of job you have, whether you're alone on a truck on an empty road or sitting in a cubicle in front of your computer, your company can now monitor everything you do."[54] Many firms, much like the IDOs this book examines, will have to be vigilant to ensure that the data they use to evaluate their performance does not orient agents toward meeting targets as the expense of the broader purpose quantitative targets were intended to proxy. The growth of technology arguably makes this a more pressing challenge today than ever before in human history.

The rapid penetration of technology in all walks of life has increased the opportunities for observation and quantification. Monitoring technologies pose risks to Navigation by Judgment by removing some of the technological limits that previously allowed agent initiative and judgment to thrive by default. There are fewer and fewer spaces where tight principal observation and control is impossible. We need to think more critically about what we may be losing to the creep of observation, quantification, and codification.

Sometimes soft information and informed judgment remain critical to good outcomes. Where this is true, firms that fail to Navigate by Judgment will be at a comparative disadvantage. A management system that works well for UPS may not work for a banker or a plumber. For foreign aid delivery, quantification as a tool of top-down principal control may lead to the construction of many successful dams but leave recipient countries without the ability to manage and maintain those dams or to put the electricity to use. For a struggling U.S. public school, a focus on what can be quantified may ensure students are in classrooms but not that they are learning. On a factory floor, management technology–enabled observation and quantification may ensure quantitative production targets are met at the expense of quality.[55]

Chapter 2 introduced General Stanley McChrystal's use of Navigation by Judgment, or as he puts it "empowered execution," in the conduct of counterinsurgency (COIN) operations in Iraq.[56] During McChrystal's time in Iraq, technology improved. By 2006, McChrystal reports, "My laptop had special software that enabled me to monitor (and speak to) any part of our force on internal radio nets. In real time I could see what was happening, hear the operators' internal discussions, and read their ongoing reporting. For a closet micromanager, it was a new opportunity to pull the puppet strings from great distances."[57] McChrystal did not take advantage of the opportunity these technologies provided for control. Though not acting was "counterintuitive," telling field agents what to do would have "been a mistake" in his view.[58]

We would do well to follow McChrystal's example in considering the costs, not just the benefits, of technology-enabled managerial "puppet strings." As managers, employees, and citizens, we need to think critically about the reductive seduction of numbers and their patina of objectivity.[59] This requires recognizing that the information that can be displayed on a data dashboard, or even a livestream of real-time activities, is only a representation of reality. When those in power—such as managers or political leaders—act based on this representation, it is likely to alter the behavior of agents in ways that make the data look better. Whether this improvement in the data will be mirrored by an improvement in actual outcomes is a more complicated and subtle question, one that is increasingly important to ask.

## The Future of Foreign Aid Management

International development organizations operate in difficult contexts, and they attempt to do difficult things. They face challenges that are often more like Lewis and Clark's 1804 journey with their Corps of Discovery and less like a 2015 trip using Google Maps.[60] It does not seem that IDOs often accomplish all, or even most, of the development goals they set out to achieve, or that it is realistic to expect that most IDO projects will do so even if management practice were perfect. The mission of IDOs drives these organizations towards arguably some of the most inherently difficult challenges on the planet, in some of the most difficult places to operate. More Navigation by Judgment does not shift IDOs from relatively secure success via tight principal control to risky longshots, but rather from one fallible strategy for undertaking relatively "1804" journeys to another fallible strategy.

Where environments are predictable and projects tractable to top-down controls, tight control by distant principals using externally verifiable data should be used to better deliver vaccines or more efficiently build electricity transmission infrastructure. In the universe of IDO projects, these are the exceptions; when trying to do any of the myriad things for which output management is inappropriate and there is no blueprint to follow, more reliance on agent judgment may be the better strategy.

There are some promising examples of IDOs beginning to change their management systems in pursuit of greater flexibility and adaptability. These efforts face headwinds, however; broader trends in the development industry augur toward less Navigation by Judgment. These challenges include:

- A greater eagerness by some political authorizers to more tightly control development assistance, particularly as a wave of populist leaders has refocused attention on narrower domestic priorities at the expense of foreign aid.
- A laudable concern (voiced by both authorizers and the broader aid industry) regarding aid impact, which induces a sometimes misplaced focus on measurement and reporting.
- The proliferation of technology, which allows the measurement of things that would have been unimaginable a decade ago, without a concomitant increase in our understanding of the managerial distortions measurement may induce.

Navigation by Judgment, and agent initiative at the expense of principal control, is not always the best strategy. Principal control can preclude fraud and corruption or simply eliminate mistakes borne of agents' mistaken judgments. Choosing the right navigation strategy depends on the nature of the project, the technology, the agents, and the environment. A move by IDOs toward more tailoring of navigation strategy by project and environment has the potential for great gains in Project Success.

Those providing foreign aid wholly control the organizational features of their IDOs. This makes IDO organizational structure quite unique among the commonly mooted causes of success or failure in development assistance. Changing IDO navigation strategy is by no means easy or straightforward. Allowing more Navigation by Judgment to drive interventions requires thinking about the complex relationships of agents, contractors, IDO managers, and political authorizers. A move toward Navigation by Judgment is still, I would argue, easier and more straightforward than altering the domestic political settlement upon which a particular developing country government relies for support. Organizational design is the "low-hanging fruit" of international development—the factor in development outcomes arguably most changeable by donor governments and polities.

Navigation by Judgment allows IDOs, where appropriate, to get better performance *for free*. It requires no substantial infusion of capital or high-priced technology. As I write these words the Kentucky Derby, perhaps America's most famous horse race, is on in the background.[61] Horseracing is a competition between sets of managing principals (jockeys) and their agents who do the work (horses). Each jockey must decide when to hold the reins tightly, and when to give their agent more slack. To do the latter, all the jockey must do is loosen his grip.

Horses will sometimes go off-course; agents will sometimes make mistakes or engage in fraud. Whether employing Navigation by Judgment is a good organizational decision depends on the alternative—how well holding tightly to the reins is likely to work. Where a tight grip is highly likely to be successful, releasing them adds unnecessary risk. Where tight control is likely to fail, then releasing the reins may be an organizational risk worth taking.

Political authorizers and IDO managers would be well served by working toward a common understanding of where Navigation by Judgment is in service of political authorizers' and IDOs' goals. Moving toward greater Navigation by Judgment where appropriate is not without challenges; changing organizational management strategy involves risk for those IDO managers and political authorizers who might push for its adoption. But these risks need to be weighed against the benefits of better performance. To do otherwise is to condemn some foreign aid efforts to meaningless numbers and a façade of success that does little for aid's intended beneficiaries. In many contexts, political authorizers and IDOs are likely to achieve better development results by simply letting go.

# Appendix I

## DATA COLLECTION

This appendix provides additional information on the processes via which data were collected. This appendix discusses both the process of assembling the Project Performance Database (PPD) and my case study interview methods. First, I discuss the quantitative data and then turn to the qualitative data.

## The Project Performance Database (PPD)

As described in chapter 5, the Project Success data had to be collected from each international development organization (IDO) in the sample individually as there is no existing cross-IDO database of project outcome data. The PPD, save the European Commission data that cannot be publicly disclosed, is available for download on my website, danhonig.info. The website also contains a codebook describing all the variables in the dataset.

I pursued Project Success data from every Organization for Economic Cooperation and Development (OECD) Development Assistance Committee (DAC) bilateral aid agency ranked in the top ten in terms of the volume of official development assistance aid delivered directly in 2010 (the 2010 data was the most recent OECD data when this data collection commenced in 2012). The top ten OECD DAC donors at the time were the United States, Germany, the United Kingdom, France, Japan, Canada, Norway, Australia, Sweden, and Denmark. I also pursued data from all of the biggest multilateral aid agencies (the European Commission, United Nations [UN] Development Programme, World Bank, African and Asian Development Banks, and Global Fund), as well as other agencies with which I had links (e.g., Irish Aid, International Fund for Agricultural Development, Food and Agriculture Organization, and International Monetary Fund).

As noted in chapter 5, there were two basic reasons to exclude international development organizations (IDOs) from the sample. First, many IDOs do not in fact assign an overall holistic success rating to projects ex post. Second, for some IDOs I could not get access to outcome data that do exist (e.g., the African Development Bank). The IDOs included in this analysis are a convenience sample, raising concerns regarding broader generalizability. To the extent that the willingness to make data public, or an agency's decision to give projects an overall success rating, are plausibly correlated to an agency's propensity to Navigate by Judgment, this is a threat to generalizability that must be considered in examining these quantitative results in isolation (that is, without incorporating the case study findings). Appendix II suggests there is cause for concern as none of the bottom ten IDOs with a propensity to Navigate by Judgment are included in this analysis. It seems plausible that Navigation by Judgment–prone agencies—those with the least stable relationships with their political authorizing environments—are less likely to collect and/or make public information that might cast some of their projects in a less than stellar light.

The most straightforward result of this undersampling would be to reduce the power of the quantitative tests in chapters 6 and 7; it is harder to imagine how this might lead to spurious findings. Spurious findings would result if the "true" shape of the relationship between Navigation by Judgment and Project Success were parabolic. This seems most likely in the sense that the most Navigation by Judgment–prone agencies might engage in "too much" Navigation by Judgment; however, there is a good sampling of the "top" of the IDO distribution as regards Navigation by Judgment. While seemingly unlikely, if those with modest degrees of Navigation by Judgment fared even worse than those with the lowest degrees of Navigation by Judgment as environmental predictability rose, this parabolic relationship (with the extremes of Navigation by Judgment both faring better than the middle) would be missed due to the lack of data availability for the least Navigation by Judgment–prone IDOs.

As noted in chapter 5, of the nine IDOs included, only the World Bank's information is publicly accessible. The Asian Development Bank and UK Department for International Development (DFID) released data following formal public information requests. The European Commission (EC) and the German Government-owned development bank KfW released data under confidentiality agreements that limited their disclosure and further use. KfW later waived its confidentiality provision, allowing its data to be included in the PPD; the EC declined to do so.

The German Corporation for International Cooperation (Gesellschaft für Internationale Zusammenarbeit, or GiZ), the International Fund for Agricultural Development (IFAD), and the Japan International Cooperation Agency (JICA) all maintain publicly accessible archives of individual project evaluation documents. In converting these individual project documents into a usable database, I contracted research assistants using the online job contracting platform Odesk. Research assistants (RAs) speaking the appropriate languages (English, German, or Japanese as appropriate) extracted the relevant data— project names, performance scores, start and completion dates, budgets, etc.— from source documents, with me selectively double-checking their work (in the case of foreign-language documents, with the help of Google Translate). After compilation of each IDO's data, I sent to each IDO an Excel spreadsheet with their agency's data for comment and/or correction. A handful of minor corrections were provided by GiZ; these changes were incorporated into the data. The Japanese International Cooperation Agency (JICA) had no substantive comment on the data itself but wished it to be made clear that the JICA data were generated by me rather than by JICA, which bears no responsibility for errors or omissions. I hereby note that is the case, with all JICA data unofficial and unverified. The International Fund for Agricultural Development's Independent Office of Evaluation never responded to a request for review of the IFAD data assembled from their public source documents and included in the PPD.

## Qualitative Case Study Interview Methods

In both Liberia and South Africa I began with a series of contacts regarding each case drawn from personal networks and official project documents. While I happily accepted referrals from interviewees to other key actors, I made sure to "re-seed" my network several times to minimize the possibility of referral bias; for example, to ensure I was speaking not just to those government actors to which I was referred by donor actors (or vice versa).

At the beginning of interviews, I made clear to each interviewee that the conversation was confidential by default—that no specific content would be linked to their name without their express permission (which was received in all cases of specific quotation/reference). I also made clear that interviewees could request anonymity at any time, either before, during, or at any time after the interview, and I would list them as anonymous rather than include their proper name on the list of interviewees.

In addition to taking notes, I made recordings of interviews where context or the preference of the individual (I asked before each interview) did not preclude same. I also turned off the recording device in the few cases where it became clear that the interviewee was significantly constraining responses due to the recording (e.g., an interviewee frequently glancing at the recorder combined with vague answers containing little substance). In the end, I recorded over 80 percent of interviews, and I relistened to these interviews while writing up full (electronic) notes prior to writing the case studies proper. As noted in chapter 5, I had some interviews transcribed by third parties (with transcribers signing confidentiality agreements).

I thought of each project as involving three phases in which the degree of Navigation by Judgment might be relevant—program design, program implementation, and program revision (or lack thereof). For each case I made sure to interview those responsible for leading the project for the donor; those responsible for coordinating day-to-day implementation (sometimes a donor representative, sometimes that of an international contractor, sometimes a government actor—a data point in itself), and the responsible recipient government representative who was the key point of contact on the project. In many cases, multiple people filled a particular role (e.g., lead responsibility for the project on the donor side) over the course of the project; I tried to interview as many of these individuals as possible.

My primary objects of inquiry were descriptions of how the project was formed and why (including the goals of the interviewee and their agency in preparing the project), what revisions were contemplated and implemented (and why these and not others etc.), and the process/structure of day-to-day management—what was possible for various actors to do, and how this translated into project decisions. In general, I was interested in what features of organizations (recipient government bureaus and IDOs) and the incentives key decision-makers and implementers faced seemed to have causally influenced outcomes.

At the same time, I tried to keep the door open to both conflicting and alternative hypotheses. These included to what extent was country ownership present, and how did it come about? Did recipient governments have an independent vision of what the project looked like, and if so were they successful in engaging in a dialectical back-and-forth with IDOs? What were the results of said process if so, and in what ways do they differ across donors/projects?

The flow and structure of the interviews themselves were quite dependent on whom the interviewee was. I began each interview by asking the interviewee the open-ended question, "How did you first hear of X project?" and then proceeded from there. I always asked about their personal role and that of their organization—their organization's dealings with contractors/government/donors as appropriate. In nearly every interview, toward the end, I asked three specific questions. First, I asked for the interviewee's evaluation of the success of the project; second, what could have made the project better; and third, why the project was as successful as it was. The latter two questions were specifically designed to allow alternative hypotheses to be put forward—other causes of success and failure unrelated to navigation strategy.

Following a few initial interviews in which it proved difficult to get critical responses regarding what might have improved projects, I began to ask for a project rating on a scale of 1 to 10; I would then ask what would have made the project a 10 rather than the number (e.g., 6, or 8.5) at which the interviewee rated the project. Where relevant, I also asked about project reporting and measurement, at both personal and organizational levels—what was being measured, whom it was being reported to, etc., and I also asked for a project timeline/narrative regarding the evolution of projects.

To avoid implicitly encouraging certain types of answers, I asked questions in as open-ended a way as possible, and tried to ensure I made every response sound equally desired. I avoided stating my hypotheses at all, and if pressed, I described the work in the most general and neutral terms (e.g., "I'm interested in the organizational features of development success and to help others learn from this project"), though in a few cases I became more specific after the end of the interview (my promise to do so having been necessary ex ante for the interview to proceed). I asked follow-up questions when things were unclear and additional questions as they were prompted by the project narrative.

In general, I was open to the interview flowing in the direction the interviewee wished to take it to a moderate extent, inasmuch as I suspected (as was proven out by events) that many people wanted to express particular positive or negative things regarding the projects in which they had been involved.

In addition to publicly available information, I was also able to access nonpublic (or in some cases theoretically public, but not publicly available, documents) in concert with interviews or from other individuals. In parallel to the standard employed in interviews, I made it clear that blanket confidentiality applied to document disclosure. I also filed freedom of information requests with both the U.S. Agency for International Development (USAID) (US FOIA) and DFID (UK FOI), which led to the further declassification and disclosure of documents. I have verified the veracity of all referenced documents not from an official source to my satisfaction, and I have not incorporated or referred to documents regarding whose accuracy I remain unsure. In a few cases, documents were shared on the condition they not be referenced or referred to in any way; these documents are thus not listed in the references or referred to in the text.

## Interviewee Data and Numbering Schemes

The following tables indicate all individuals that provided information (mostly by interview, but in a handful of instances by email correspondence) that informs the case studies. I offer a few explanatory notes for these tables. First, the number in the left-hand column does not correspond to the number in the interview citations (e.g., interview 63, 6/25/13). The cited numbers are randomized to maintain the promised confidentiality to interviewees. The dates of the interviews are omitted from the tables below, as including dates would make it much easier to infer the identity of a given speaker, given that I incorporate the date in the in-chapter references. For the same reason, individuals who contributed in more than one domain—for example, speaking to South African interventions in both municipal governance and health—are given a new randomly generated number for use in each country-task (e.g. South African Health, as opposed to South African Capacity Building); to do otherwise would make it exceedingly easy to identify these speakers. As such, although 147 interviews are listed below, there is a degree of overlap; it is small, however. Tables AI.1 and AI.2 provide information on the South African Capacity Building and Health sectors, respectively; Tables AI.3 and AI.4 do the same for the Liberia Health and Capacity Building sectors. Each table includes the interviewees' name, position, and an indication of which interventions within each sector the interviewee discussed. There are more than 135 unique interviews on which these cases collectively draw.

*Table AI.1* **South Africa Capacity-Building Interviews**

| # | Surname | First Name | Position | USAID | DFID |
|---|---------|-----------|----------|-------|------|
| 1 | Anonymous | Anonymous | Cooperative Governance and Traditional Affairs (CoGTA) Senior Official | | |
| 2 | Bester | Angela | Former DFID staff, then Deloitte; also former Director General, Public Service Commission | | |
| 3 | Brooks | Frikkie | Head of KwaZulu-Natal Provincial Planning Department | | |
| 4 | Chipkin | Ivor | Executive Director, Public Affairs Research Instituts | | |
| 5 | Chrystal | Blake | Supervisory Program Officer, USAID South Africa | | |
| 6 | Dei | Colleen | Former USAID South Africa Mission Chief | | |
| 7 | Fortuin | Joe | Director of Aid, CoGTA | | |
| 8 | Francis | Virginia | USAID Health Team, former RTI International South Africa staff | | |

*Table AI.1* **Continued**

| # | Surname | First Name | Position | USAID | DFID |
|---|---------|-----------|----------|-------|------|
| 9 | Glasser | Matt | Former USAID advisor in South Africa on municipal financing | | |
| 10 | Hackner | Allan | USAID South Africa Financial Sector Manager | | |
| 11 | Harding | Joel | DFID Governance Advisor | | |
| 12 | Heymans | Chris | Lead Project Designer, Consolidated Municipal Transformation Program (CMTP) | | |
| 13 | Hofmeyr | Beatie | Head of Education and Training Unit, Local Governance Support Program (LGSP) implementing subcontractor | | |
| 14 | Horn | Steve | Former Chief of Party (CoP) for different (than LGSP) USAID municipal governance project | | |
| 15 | Kolker | Joel | Former USAID staff, municipal program | | |
| 16 | Konig | Ferdie | CMTP Advisor in Phalaborwa, Mpumalanga | | |
| 17 | Layte | Michelle | Former RTI LGSP CoP | | |
| 18 | Madurai | David | Chief Director, Norms, Standards, Policy and Research, CoGTA; former Chief Director, Development Planning & Local Economic Development | | |
| 19 | Mangokwena | Andries | Advisor in Thulamela under CMTP | | |
| 20 | Mathivha | Makonde | Municipal Manager, Thulamela, Limpopo | | |
| 21 | Matomela | Bongani | Former Deputy Project Director, LGSP | | |
| 22 | Naidoo | Subethri | Former Governance Advisor, DFID; former Local Government Sector Manager, USAID; former Deloitte Program Manager on CMTP | | |

*(continued)*

*Table AI.1* **Continued**

| # | Surname | First Name | Position | USAID | DFID |
|---|---------|-----------|----------|-------|------|
| 23 | Olver | Chippy | Former Deputy Director General (DG), Department of Provincial and Local Government (DPLG) | | |
| 24 | Powell | Derek | Former Deputy DG, DPLG | | |
| 25 | Rambulana | Wilson | Former LGSP Revenue Enhancement Advisor (trainer) | | |
| 26 | Sadan | Mastoera | Office of the South African Presidency | | |
| 27 | Savage | David | Former World Bank (WB) staff; when interviewed in 2013, South African Treasury Head of Cities Support Program | | |
| 28 | Snook | Steve | Former USAID Democracy and Governance Deputy Team Leader | | |
| 29 | Tazewell | Littleton | Deputy Mission Director, USAID South Africa Regional Program | | |
| 30 | Thomas | Richard | Former DFID South Africa Governance Advisor on CMTP | | |
| 31 | Timm | Jeremy | Former CMTP; when interviewed in 2013, Treasury municipal government support | | |
| 32 | Toli | Robin | Chief Director, International Development Coordination, South African Treasury | | |
| 33 | TV | Pillay | Head of Municipal Finance, South African Treasury | | |
| 34 | Vaz | Peter | Former RTI LGSP CoP | | |
| 35 | Yako | Pam | Former Municipal Manager, Amathole District; former DG, Environmental Affairs, Water Affairs | | |

*Table AI.2* **South Africa Health Sector Interviews**

| # | Surname | First Name | Position | USAID | DFID | CDC |
|---|---------|-----------|----------|-------|------|-----|
| 1 | Agenbag | Rentia | Government and Civil Society Support Manager, South African National AIDS Council (SANAC) | | | |
| 2 | Anonymous | Anonymous | US Centers for Disease Control (CDC) & USAID President's Emergency Plan for AIDS Relief (PEPFAR) Implementer | | | |
| 3 | Anonymous | Anonymous | Senior DC-based PEPFAR official | | | |
| 4 | Anonymous | Anonymous | Senior CDC official in another Southern African country | | | |
| 5 | Anonymous | Anonymous | USAID and CDC PEPFAR Implementer | | | |
| 6 | Barker | Pierre | Senior Vice President, Institute for Health Care Improvement | | | |
| 7 | Barron | Peter | Public health specialist & advisor to Deputy DG Pillay, National Department of Health (NDOH) | | | |
| 8 | Coovadia | Ashraf | Head of Pediatric HIV, Rahima Moosa Mother and Child Hospital, Johannesburg | | | |
| 9 | Coovadia | Jerry | Director, Maternal Adolescent and Child Health (MatCH) | | | |
| 10 | Dei | Colleen | Former USAID South Africa Mission Chief | | | |
| 11 | Desmond | Chris | Chief Research Specialist, Human Sciences Research Council | | | |

*(continued)*

Table AI.2 **Continued**

| # | Surname | First Name | Position | USAID | DFID | CDC |
|---|---------|-----------|----------|-------|------|-----|
| 12 | Fryatt | Bob | Former DFID Health Advisor, South Africa | X | | |
| 13 | Giddy | Janet | Former HIV Program Coordinator, McCord Hospital, Durban | X | | X |
| 14 | Goga | Ameena | Senior Specialist Scientist, South African Medical Research Council (MRC) | X | X | X |
| 15 | Gorna | Robin | Former Senior Regional Health and AIDS Advisor for DFID Southern Africa | X | X | |
| 16 | Grant | Ken | Health and Life Sciences Partnership (HLSP) Program Director, Strengthening South Africa'S Revitalised Response to AIDS and Health (SARRAH) | X | X | |
| 17 | Harding | Joel | DFID Governance Advisor | X | X | |
| 18 | Holst | Helga | CEO, McCord Hospital, Durban | X | X | X |
| 19 | Kok | Michelle | Advisor to Precious Robinson, NDOH | X | X | |
| 20 | Kumar | Smita | USAID Prevention of Maternal to Child Transmission (PMTCT) Lead | X | | X |
| 21 | Lesole | Lerato | PMTCT Specialist, CDC South Africa; previous NDOH | X | | X |
| 22 | Mahasela | Lusanda | Deputy, Research & Monitoring and Evaluation, Johns Hopkins Health and Education in South Africa | X | X | X |

*Table AI.2* **Continued**

| # | Surname | First Name | Position | USAID | DFID | CDC |
|---|---------|-----------|----------|-------|------|-----|
| 23 | Mazibuko | Ntombi | Right To Care (RTC) PMTCT Project Manager; former NDOH | ■ | | ■ |
| 24 | Ngubane | Gugu | Former HLSP A-Plan Project Manager and Technical Advisor on PMTCT | | ■ | |
| 25 | Nkulu | Hilary | Former DFID South African Program Manager | | ■ | |
| 26 | Pattinson | Robert | Director, MRC Maternal and Infant Health Care Strategies Unit, University of Pretoria | | | |
| 27 | Pillay | Yogan | NDOH Deputy Director General | ■ | | |
| 28 | Robinson | Precious | NDOH Deputy Director in charge of PMTCT | ■ | | |
| 29 | Sanne | Ian | CEO, Right To Care | ■ | | ■ |
| 30 | Schneider | Helen | Director, School of Public Health, University of the Western Cape; former SANAC, MRC | ■ | | |
| 31 | Slingers | Nevilene | Donor Coordination Manager, SANAC | ■ | | |
| 32 | Taback | Rayna | Senior Public Health Advisor, CDC South Africa | | | ■ |
| 33 | Tazewell | Littleton | Deputy Mission Director, USAID South Africa Regional Program | ■ | | |
| 34 | Toledo | Carlos | Chief, HIV Prevention Branch, CDC South Africa | | | ■ |
| 35 | Toli | Robin | Chief Director, International Development Coordination, South AfricanTreasury | ■ | | |

*(continued)*

*Appendix I*

*Table AI.2* **Continued**

| # | Surname | First Name | Position | USAID | DFID | CDC |
|---|---------|-----------|----------|-------|------|-----|
| 36 | Venter | Francois | Deputy Executive Director, Wits Reproductive Health Institute | ■ | | ■ |
| 37 | Vranken | Peter | CDC Senior Technical Advisor, PEPFAR | ■ | | ■ |
| 38 | Wilson | John | HLSP Programme Manager | | ■ | |

*Table AI.3* **Liberia Health Sector Interviews**

| # | Surname | First Name | Position | USAID | DFID |
|---|---------|-----------|----------|-------|------|
| 1 | Anonymous | Anonymous | Former Liberia National AIDS Control Program (NACP) Advisor | ■ | |
| 2 | Anonymous | Anonymous | Liberia Ministry of Health and Social Welfare (MoHSW) senior personnel | | ■ |
| 3 | Anonymous | Anonymous | Senior official, USAID Liberia | ■ | |
| 4 | Anonymous | Anonymous | USAID Liberia international staff | ■ | |
| 5 | Augustin | Randolph | Lead Health Officer, USAID | ■ | |
| 6 | Benson | Angela | Fixed Asset Reimbursement Agreement (FARA) Coordinator, MoHSW | ■ | |
| 7 | Bility | Kalipha | Former Program Coordinator, NACP; in 2013 Deputy Minister, Ministry of Agriculture | ■ | |
| 8 | Bruce | Lwopu | Head of Blood Safety, MoHSW; former Deputy Head, NACP | ■ | |
| 9 | Curran | Desmond | DFID Representative in Liberia 2007–2009 | | ■ |

*Table AI.3* **Continued**

| # | Surname | First Name | Position | USAID | DFID |
|---|---------|-----------|----------|-------|------|
| 10 | Dahn | Eunice | Chief Medical Officer, MoHSW | | |
| 11 | Davis | Natty B. | Chairman and CEO, Liberia National Investment Commission; former Minister without Portfolio and National Coordinator, Liberia Reconstruction and Development Committee (LRDC) | | |
| 12 | Dolopeh | Dr. Eugene | Former Program Manager, NACP | | |
| 13 | Duncan | Julie | Commissioner, National AIDS Commission (NAC); former Assistant Minister for Preventive Services, MoHSW | | |
| 14 | Dworku | Tanu | Former USAID Health Officer, Former NACP Coordinator | | |
| 15 | Dzokoto | Agnes | Senior Technical Officer responsible for Liberia, Action for West Africa Region Project (AWARE) | | |
| 16 | Flomo | Matthew | Deputy Minister for Administration, MoHSW | | |
| 17 | Freeman | Josephine | Former PMTCT Coordinator, NACP | | |
| 18 | Gabelle | Chris | Former lead Liberia Governance Advisor, DFID | | |
| 19 | Gaddis | Beth | Health Officer, USAID | | |
| 20 | Gwenigale | Walter | Minister of Health, MoHSW | | |
| 21 | Hughes | Jacob | Head of Liberia Health Pooled Fund (PF) Management firm | | |
| 22 | Hymowitz | Dan | Advisor to the Monserrado County Ebola Response, African Governance Initiative | | |
| 23 | Jones | Janyaj | Monitoring & Evaluation (M&E) Deputy, NACP | | |

*(continued)*

*Table AI.3* **Continued**

| # | Surname | First Name | Position | USAID | DFID |
|---|---------|-----------|----------|-------|------|
| 24 | Karzon | Toagee | Controller, MoHSW | ■ | |
| 25 | Lippevald | Theo | Rebuilding Basic Health Services (RBHS) Deputy CoP, John Snow International (JSI) | ■ | |
| 26 | Logan | David | Global Fund Coordinator, MoHSW; former Deputy Coordinator, NACP | ■ | |
| 27 | Macaulay | Rose | RBHS/JSI CoP | ■ | |
| 28 | Manuel | Marcus | Former DFID Deputy Director for West Africa | | ■ |
| 29 | Mapleh | Louise | Peformance Based Financing Coordinator, MoHSW | ■ | |
| 30 | Martin | Bill | Former Senior Adviser to the Minister, MoHSW; when interviewed in 2013, PF Manager | ■ | |
| 31 | McDermott | Chris | Former health sector lead, USAID Liberia | ■ | |
| 32 | Nartey | Alex | Former lead of Price Waterhouse Coopers (PwC) team to MoHSW Office of Financial Management (OFM) | | ■ |
| 33 | Niyuhire | Floride | RBHS Advisor on PBF to MoHSW | ■ | |
| 34 | Nyoweh | Moses | Sexually Transmitted Infections (STI) Officer, NACP | ■ | |
| 35 | Sanvee | Dr. Lilly | Head PMTCT implementer, Catholic Hospital, AWARE | ■ | |
| 36 | Scheening | Sarah | Senior Policy and Implementation Advisor, USAID Global Health Bureau | ■ | |
| 37 | Sieh | Sonpon | Program Coordinator (head), NACP; former M&E on HIV, NACP | ■ | |

*Table AI.3* **Continued**

| # | Surname | First Name | Position | USAID | DFID |
|---|---------|-----------|----------|-------|------|
| 38 | Sirleaf | Momolu | Head of Aid Coordination, MoHSW | ■ | |
| 39 | Subah | Pewu | Head of Project Implementation Unit, MoHSW | ■ | |
| 40 | Tamattey | Felix | Senior Partner leading PwC Engagement, MoHSW OFM | | ■ |

*Table AI.4* **Liberia Capacity-Building Interviews**

| # | Surname | First Name | Position | USAID | DFID |
|---|---------|-----------|----------|-------|------|
| 1 | Anonymous | Anonymous | Senior Civil Service Agency (CSA) Official | | ■ |
| 2 | Anonymous | Anonymous | Senior DC-based USAID Official | ■ | |
| 2 | Allen | William | Former Director General, Liberia Civil Service | ■ | |
| 3 | Atuanya | Jenkins | Former Deputy Director General, CSA; when interviewed in 2013, Assistant Minister, Ministry of Lands Mines & Energy | | ■ |
| 4 | Baki | Shadi | Head of Biometrics, CSA | | ■ |
| 5 | Belleh | Willie | Partner Subah Belleh Associates; local implementing partner for DFID Civil Service Capacity Building Project (CISCAB) | | ■ |
| 6 | Callender | Elizabeth | Deputy Head, USAID Office of Transition Initiative (OTI) Liberia | ■ | |
| 7 | Cooper | Lloyd | Grants Manager, USAID OTI Building Recovery and Reform through Democratic Governance – Liberia (BRDG) | ■ | |

*(continued)*

*Table AI.4* **Continued**

| # | Surname | First Name | Position | USAID | DFID |
|---|---------|-----------|----------|-------|------|
| 8 | Cooper | Vicky | Former WB consultant on Civil Service Pay Reform; when interviewed in 2013 Chief of Party, Global Environmental Management Support Project (GEMS) Liberia | | |
| 9 | Curran | Desmond | DFID Representative in Liberia 2007-2009 | | |
| 10 | Davis | Natty B. | Chairman and CEO, NiC; former Minister without Portfolio and National Coordinator, LRDC | | |
| 11 | Drosaye | Alfred | CSA Principal Administrative Officer (PAO) | | |
| 12 | Fahnbulleh | Louise | Former OTI staff, Liberia | | |
| 13 | Fn'Piere | Pat | Consultant, BRDG; OTI Field Advisor | | |
| 14 | Gabelle | Chris | Former DFID Governance Advisor in Liberia | | |
| 15 | Gattorn | John | Former Africa Program Manager, OTI | | |
| 16 | Glentworth | Garth | former senior Governance Advisor, DFID; also member, Order of the British Empire (OBE) | | |
| 17 | Hare | Sam | Former Deputy Minister, Ministry of Youth and Sports | | |
| 18 | Hunter | Rosslyn | M&E team, BRDG | | |
| 19 | Johnson | Mimi | Human Resources team, BRDG | | |
| 20 | Kialain | David | Former Principal Deputy, Governance Reform Commission | | |
| 21 | Lauer | Barb | Former CoP for BRDG | | |
| 22 | Liberty | T. Edward | Director General, Liberia Institute of Statistics and Geo-Information Services (LISGIS) | | |

*Table AI.4* **Continued**

| # | Surname | First Name | Position | USAID | DFID |
|---|---------|------------|----------|-------|------|
| 23 | Logan | James | Former Deputy Minister, Ministry of Agriculture | | |
| 24 | Mayshak | Nellie | Former head, Adam Smith International (ASI) CISCAB team 2007–2009 | | |
| 25 | Muhula | Raymond | Public Sector Specialist, World Bank | | |
| 26 | Neymah | Oblayon | Former Reform Directorate CSA; current head of Liberia Institue of Public Administration (LIPA) | | |
| 27 | O'Neill | Dominic | Head of DFID Sierra Leone 2008–2011 | | |
| 28 | Panton | Richard | Deputy Director General, Training, LIPA | | |
| 29 | Patel | Jalpa | Former Coordinator, ASI CISCAB, 2009–2010 | | |
| 30 | Sigrist | Ken | Former head, ASI CISCAB team 2009–2010 | | |
| 31 | Tarpeh | Dominic | Former CISCAB consultant; when interviewed in 2013, with Governance Commision (GC) | | |
| 32 | Thompson | James | Subah Belleh staff; former member of CISCAB core team | | |
| 33 | Wilson | Mark | Grants Manager, BRDG | | |
| 34 | Wilson | Peter | Program Development Officer, BRDG | | |

# Appendix II

## ADDITIONAL ECONOMETRIC ANALYSIS

This appendix provides additional analysis and robustness checks for the econometric analyses in chapters 5 and 6. It is less a narrative than it is a series of explorations of the data, and it is intended for those with a particular interest in these data and tests.

## Additional Summary Statistics: Project Success

Tables AII.1 and AII.2 provide additional information regarding the key dependent variable, overall Project Success. Project Success is "inflated" to a six-point scale from whatever the Likert-type base scale is for each donor (see chapter 5,

*Table AII.1* **Summary Statistics of Project Success by Donor (6-point scale)**

|  | Count | Mean | SD | Min | Max |
|---|---|---|---|---|---|
| AsianDB | 1572 | 3.892176 | 1.048012 | 1.5 | 6 |
| DFID | 1917 | 4.618466 | .9685305 | 1.2 | 6 |
| EC | 608 | 4.075658 | .9766801 | 1.5 | 6 |
| GFATM | 581 | 4.747849 | 1.227072 | 1.5 | 6 |
| GIZ | 130 | 4.469231 | .8732765 | 2 | 6 |
| IFAD | 33 | 4.181818 | .7269175 | 2 | 5 |
| JICA | 716 | 4.994413 | 1.200803 | 1.5 | 6 |
| KfW | 2021 | 4.16477 | 1.112515 | 1 | 6 |
| WB | 7039 | 4.116068 | 1.27238 | 1 | 6 |
| Total | 14,617 | 4.234439 | 1.203871 | 1 | 6 |

*Table AII.2* **Summary Statistics of Project Success by Donor (Z-scores)**

|  | Count | Mean | SD | Min | Max |
|---|---|---|---|---|---|
| AsianDB | 1572 | −9.69e-08 | 1 | −2.282585 | 2.011261 |
| DFID | 1917 | −4.58e-08 | 1 | −3.528346 | 1.425033 |
| EC | 608 | 1.69e-07 | 1 | −2.637156 | 1.970289 |
| GFATM | 581 | −6.57e-08 | 1 | −2.646827 | 1.020438 |
| GIZ | 130 | 1.25e-07 | 1 | −2.827548 | 1.752903 |
| IFAD | 33 | 2.58e-07 | 1 | −3.001466 | 1.12555 |
| JICA | 716 | 3.86e-08 | 1 | −2.910065 | .8374288 |
| KfW | 2021 | −1.85e-07 | 1 | −2.8447 | 1.649623 |
| WB | 7039 | 1.67e-07 | 1 | −2.449007 | 1.480637 |
| Total | 14,617 | 4.66e-08 | .9997263 | -3.528346 | 2.011261 |

note 5 for more discussion of this process). This has no implication for the econometrics so long as international development organization (IDO) fixed effects are employed, but it makes interpretation of the results more intuitive.

Another way of thinking about these data is to calculate z-scores, comparing each donor's projects to the distribution of that donor's other projects directly. In a few of the robustness checks that follow, I also drop the IDO fixed effect from regression models, employing the z-score as the dependent variable.

# Direct Effect of Propensity to Navigate by Judgment on Outcomes in Primary Analysis

As noted in chapter 5, the models in the tables presented in chapters 5 and 6 do not incorporate a base term for IDO propensity to Navigate by Judgment as it is collinear to IDO fixed effects. Table AII.3 replicates Table 6.1, incorporating the IDO propensity to Navigate by Judgment base term and dropping IDO fixed effects. While we cannot learn much from the coefficient on the base term (as the IDO-specific z-score outcome measure precludes any direct comparison between IDOs), it is worth noting that without IDO fixed effects it becomes much easier to interpret the $R^2$ terms. Model 1 suggests that propensity to Navigate by Judgment and environmental unpredictability (and their interaction) are jointly explaining a remarkably large share ($R^2$-between =.44) of the variance in differential normalized Project Success among IDOs.

Table AII.3 Adding Base Term for Navigation by Judgment to Table 6.1. Running regressions without IDO fixed effects but with the "base" Navigation by Judgment propensity score leaves the key results on the interaction term substantively unchanged

| DV: Project Success (Z-score) | (1) | (2) | (3) | (4) | (5) | (6) |
|---|---|---|---|---|---|---|
| Nav by Judgment Propensity | -1.559* | -2.033*** | -1.725*** | -2.016*** | -0.292 | -0.466 |
| | (0.671) | (0.435) | (0.354) | (0.289) | (0.613) | (0.661) |
| Environmental Unpredictability | -0.127*** | -0.146*** | -0.123*** | -0.132*** | -0.0866*** | -0.0921** |
| | (0.0235) | (0.0206) | (0.0192) | (0.0171) | (0.0261) | (0.0284) |
| Env Unpred*Nav by Judg | 0.148*** | 0.174*** | 0.151*** | 0.161*** | 0.0846* | 0.0910* |
| | (0.0372) | (0.0287) | (0.0277) | (0.0235) | (0.0411) | (0.0438) |
| Project Size (USD Millions) | | 0.000562*** | | 0.000353 | | 0.000468** |
| | | (0.000119) | | (0.000182) | | (0.000143) |
| Constant | 1.383*** | 1.715*** | 1.104* | 1.326** | 1.544 | 1.673 |
| | (0.418) | (0.306) | (0.442) | (0.451) | (0.999) | (1.009) |
| IDO Fixed Effects | N | N | N | N | N | N |
| Recipient Fixed Effects | N | N | Y | Y | N | N |
| Sector Fixed Effects | N | N | N | N | Y | Y |
| R²-Within: Model | .0259 | .0222 | .0777 | .0789 | .0870 | .0936 |
| R²-Between: Model | .4447 | .0859 | .0023 | .0649 | .2156 | .3913 |
| Observations | 9312 | 7247 | 9312 | 7247 | 7370 | 5446 |

Standard errors in parentheses.
$p < 0.05$, ** $p < 0.01$, *** $p < 0.001$.

# Subgroup Analysis

Splitting the sample along the mean of the state fragility index (the measure of environmental unpredictability) suggests that results are being driven by high fragility contexts. Table AII.4 suggests it is differences between fragile and less fragile states (see the difference in the constant—the absolute level of success—particularly comparing Models 3 and 4, with recipient fixed effects), and within high-fragility states, that is driving the results.

*Table AII.4* **Subgroup Analysis by Level of Environmental Unpredictability. Dividing the measure of environmental unpredictability (the State Fragility Index) at the mean suggests that the main effects are driven by more unpredictable environments**

| DV: Project Success (6-pt scale) | (1) | (2) | (3) | (4) | (5) | (6) |
|---|---|---|---|---|---|---|
| Sample by Env Unpredictability | High Unpred | Low Unpred | High Unpred | Low Unpred | High Unpred | Low Unpred |
| Environ Unpredictability | −0.187*** | −0.00727 | −0.149** | 0.0217 | −0.0578 | −0.00761 |
| | (0.0353) | (0.0747) | (0.0401) | (0.0930) | (0.0647) | (0.123) |
| Env Unpredict*Nav by Judg | 0.242** | -0.0222 | 0.190* | −0.0730 | 0.0323 | -0.0165 |
| | (0.0494) | (0.116) | (0.0665) | (0.133) | (0.105) | (0.198) |
| Constant | 4.536*** | 4.643*** | 2.488*** | 4.469*** | 5.973*** | 5.566*** |
| | (0.105) | (0.0555) | (0.185) | (0.178) | (0.150) | (0.0584) |
| IDO Fixed Effects | Y | Y | Y | Y | Y | Y |
| Recipient Fixed Effects | N | N | Y | Y | N | N |
| Sector Fixed Effects | N | N | N | N | Y | Y |
| $R^2$-Within | 0.006 | 0.004 | 0.053 | 0.070 | 0.077 | 0.086 |
| $R^2$-Between | 0.188 | 0.025 | 0.164 | 0.001 | 0.457 | 0.100 |
| Observations | 4668 | 4644 | 4668 | 4644 | 3586 | 3784 |

Standard errors in parentheses.

* $p < 0.05$, ** $p < 0.01$, *** $p < 0.001$.

## Evaluation Bias

A primary concern—certainly one of my primary concerns—was that these data rely on evaluations of Project Success made by the agencies themselves. One might worry that an agency with a fragile relationship with its political authorizing environment would be less autonomous and thus would have a greater incentive to self-evaluate projects as successes. This is not a threat to validity inasmuch as a consistent bias would be absorbed by the IDO fixed effect; of greater concern would be bias that moves with the interaction of Navigation by Judgment and environmental predictability. If, for example, more autonomous IDOs both Navigate by Judgment to a greater degree and give their agents more leeway in self-evaluations, which those agents differentially exercise to a greater degree as environmental unpredictability rises, this would be a threat to the validity of the main findings.

The involvement of independent evaluation units provides suggestive insight into this problem, as independent evaluation units should not have the same degree of incentive as agents themselves to give favorable evaluations. Table AII.5 controls for the type of evaluation; that is, whether the data source is an internal review by project staff, a review conducted by an IDO's own independent evaluation unit, or a review conducted by an externally contracted evaluator. The relationship between propensity to Navigate by Judgment and environmental unpredictability remains unchanged, suggesting that differential evaluation bias by different IDOs is not driving the results.

## Time Fixed Effects and Selection Issues

Table AII.6 adds a series of fixed effects to the main findings. Inclusion of time fixed effects (either yearly or in five-year periods) does nothing to diminish the association between propensity to Navigate by Judgment and recipient unpredictability. The result remains robust to including time*IDO fixed effects and time*recipient fixed effects.[1] These results, in conjunction with the selection analysis in chapter 6, should allay any concerns that the primary results are driven by heterogeneous IDO project performance over time or by heterogeneous entry of IDOs into and out of recipient countries over time.[2]

## Principal Components Analysis

Chapter 5 explained the construction of the primary Navigation by Judgment propensity measure and the basis of my decision to use a simple average

*Table AII.5*  **Controlling for Evaluation Type. There are very few IDOs who use externally contracted evaluators (the third, omitted category); as such, when using IDO fixed effects, internal evaluations become the omitted category**

|  | (1) | (2) | (3) | (4) |
|---|---|---|---|---|
|  | *6pt scale* | *Z-score* | *6pt scale* | *Z-score* |
| Environmental Unpredictability | −0.165** | −0.132*** | −0.145** | −0.119*** |
|  | (0.0289) | (0.0185) | (0.0260) | (0.0175) |
| Env Unpred*Nav by Judg | 0.199** | 0.159*** | 0.177** | 0.143*** |
|  | (0.0416) | (0.0271) | (0.0356) | (0.0174) |
| Internal Evaluator | 0.209*** | 0.788 | 0.251** | −0.174 |
|  | (0.00389) | (0.658) | (0.0501) | (0.601) |
| Independent Eval Office | 13.17*** | 0.334 | 12.83*** | 0.337 |
|  | (0.0750) | (0.473) | (0.569) | (0.701) |
| Internal Eval*NbJ |  | −1.222 |  | 0.254 |
|  |  | (0.935) |  | (0.955) |
| Independent Eval*NbJ | −20.06*** | −0.617 | −19.54*** | −0.587 |
|  | (0.111) | (0.850) | (0.847) | (1.190) |
| Propensity to Nav by Judgment |  | −0.950 |  | −1.811 |
|  |  | (0.972) |  | (1.103) |
| Constant | 4.855*** | 1.066*** | 5.074*** | 0.609 |
|  | (0.180) | (0.202) | (0.0626) | (0.336) |
| IDO Fixed Effects | Y | N | Y | N |
| Recipient Fixed Effects | N | N | Y | Y |
| Observations | 7722 | 7722 | 7722 | 7722 |

Standard errors in parentheses.
$^{*} p < 0.05, ^{**} p < 0.01, ^{***} p < 0.001.$

*Table AII.6* **Expanding Fixed Effects for Robustness. Controlling for time, or time interacted with recipients or IDOs, does little to change the main effects**

| DV: Project Success (6-pt scale) | (1) | (2) | (3) | (4) |
|---|---|---|---|---|
| Environmental Unpredictability | −0.169*** | −0.167*** | −0.0904* | −0.0843* |
|  | (0.0262) | (0.0277) | (0.0327) | (0.0337) |
| Env Unpred*Nav by Judg | 0.204*** | 0.200** | 0.145** | 0.137** |
|  | (0.0379) | (0.0406) | (0.0302) | (0.0316) |
| Constant | 4.707*** | 4.303*** | 3.333*** | 3.068*** |
|  | (0.0853) | (0.0377) | (0.445) | (0.477) |
| IDO Fixed Effects | Y | Y | Y | Y |
| Year Fixed Effects | Y | Y | N | N |
| Year*IDO Fixed Effects | N | Y | N | N |
| 5-yr bin Fixed Effects | N | N | Y | Y |
| Recipient Fixed Effects | N | N | Y | Y |
| Recipient* 5-yr bin FEs | N | N | Y | Y |
| IDO*5-yr bin FEs | N | N | N | Y |
| $R^2$-Within | 0.031 | 0.048 | 0.145 | 0.149 |
| $R^2$-Between | 0.063 | 0.014 | 0.073 | 0.128 |
| Observations | 9312 | 9312 | 9312 | 9312 |

Standard errors in parentheses.

* $p < 0.05$, ** $p < 0.01$, *** $p < 0.001$.

of five component measures drawn from the Paris Declaration Monitoring Surveys rather than a principal components approach. A principal components analysis of these five measures—aid predictability, untied aid, use of parallel implementation units, use of country public financial management systems, and use of country procurement systems—yields a first principal component with an eigenvalue of 3.09, thus explaining 62 percent of the variance in the five measures. This first principal component has quite even loading across the five constituent measures. The second component has an eigenvalue of 1.08, just barely above the traditional cutoff of 1. Figure AII.1 presents the scree plot.

The second principal component, then, is quite marginal to begin with. Table AII.7 examines the loading of the variables onto the first three principal components. The loading makes clear that the second component is picking up

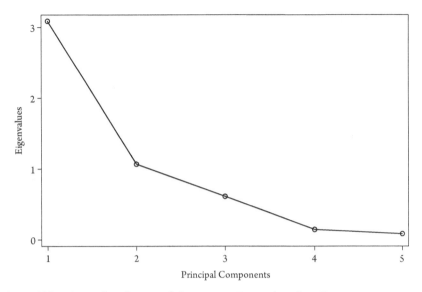

*Figure AII.1* Scree Plot of Principal Component Eigenvalues from Propensity to Navigate by Judgment Scale Measures.

*Table AII.7* **Loading of Propensity to Navigate by Judgment Measures onto Principal Components**

| Variable | Component 1 | Component 2 | Component 3 |
|---|---|---|---|
| Use of PIUs | .2796 | .6668 | .6767 |
| Aid Predictability | .5254 | −.1996 | .1177 |
| Use of Country PFM | .5339 | .1003 | −.2800 |
| Use of Country Procurement | .4980 | .1905 | −.5030 |
| Untied Aid | .3358 | -.6849 | .4436 |

devolution propensity (with all three of the measures that form part of that sub-scale positive) where it does not overlap with authorizing environment insecurity (with both the measures that form that subscale negative). Thus, combining the two principal components will lead to an overemphasis on devolution propensity relative to authorizing environment.

Using only the first principal component struck me as quite similar, but much less intuitive, than simply averaging the five measures. A cluster analysis (via Stata's clv command) suggests, as implied by both the principal components analysis and intuition, that a single cluster with all five measures—that is, a single scale—is most appropriate here. As such I construct a simple average; the

*Table AII.8* **Robustness to Use of Principal Components. A principal components approach does not alter the primary results**

|  | *(1)* | *(2)* | *(3)* | *(4)* |
|---|---|---|---|---|
| **DV:** | *6pt scale* | *Z-score* | *6pt scale* | *Z-score* |
| Environmental | −0.0587*** | −0.0456*** | −0.0466*** | −0.0393*** |
| Unpredictability | (0.00435) | (0.00377) | (0.00894) | (0.00737) |
| Env Unpred*Nav by Judg | 0.0199*** | 0.0142*** | 0.0171*** | 0.0125*** |
| (Principal Component) |  |  |  |  |
|  | (0.00312) | (0.00269) | (0.00363) | (0.00315) |
| Nav by Judgment |  | −0.146*** |  | −0.129** |
| (Principal Component) |  | (0.0399) |  | (0.0451) |
| Constant | 4.733*** | 0.530*** | 4.213*** | 0.141 |
|  | (0.0313) | (0.0507) | (0.178) | (0.157) |
| IDO Fixed Effects | Y | N | Y | N |
| Recipient Fixed Effects | N | N | Y | Y |
| Observations | 9312 | 9312 | 9312 | 9312 |

Standard errors in parentheses.
* $p < 0.05$, ** $p < 0.01$, *** $p < 0.001$.

Cronbach's alpha of this scale (.825) suggests to me that this simple averaging is reasonable.

Nonetheless, I do retain the first principal component in the data to allow it to be used in robustness checks. Table AII.8 displays the results, which show the same effect as does my primary construction of the Paris Declaration monitoring survey–derived scale.

## Using my Alternate Field Survey Measure Of Navigation by Judgment Propensity

One might be concerned that the Paris Declaration monitoring survey–derived propensity to Navigate by Judgment measure is not actually mapping the propensity to Navigate by Judgment. As noted in chapter 5, I conducted a small survey of aid experts in the field who come into contact with a wide range of IDOs (largely as consultants or as employees of developing country governments) and thus can make expert inter-IDO assessments. The

*Table AII.9*  **Robustness to Use of My (Rather than Paris Declaration Monitoring) Survey Measure. Using the results of the survey I conducted as the measure of IDO propensity to Navigate by Judgment does not alter the primary results**

|  | *(1)* | *(2)* | *(3)* | *(4)* |
|---|---|---|---|---|
| *DV:* | *6pt scale* | *Z-score* | *6pt scale* | *Z-score* |
| Environmental | −0.102*** | −0.0852*** | −0.0760*** | −0.0724*** |
| Unpredictability | (0.0170) | (0.0144) | (0.0205) | (0.0173) |
| Env Unpred*Nav by Judg | 0.0170*** | 0.0146*** | 0.0123** | 0.0119** |
|  | (0.00417) | (0.00352) | (0.00467) | (0.00401) |
| Nav by Judgment (Survey) |  | −0.142** |  | −0.132* |
|  |  | (0.0478) |  | (0.0535) |
| Constant | 4.744*** | 0.892*** | 4.248*** | 0.526* |
|  | (0.0326) | (0.193) | (0.189) | (0.263) |
| IDO Fixed Effects | Y | N | Y | N |
| Recipient Fixed Effects | N | N | Y | Y |
| $R^2$-Within | 0.025 | 0.022 | 0.076 | 0.073 |
| $R^2$-Between | 0.129 | 0.449 | 0.228 | 0.213 |
| Observations | 8313 | 8313 | 8313 | 8313 |

Standard errors in parentheses.
* $p < 0.05$, ** $p < 0.01$, *** $p < 0.001$.

correlation between this survey measure and the propensity to Navigate by Judgment scale drawn from the Paris Declaration surveys is .71. Table AII.9 substitutes the survey measure of propensity to Navigate by Judgment for that of the Paris Declaration–derived measure, otherwise paralleling the analysis of Table 6.1; the results are similar, which should increase confidence in the primary analysis.

# Placebo Tests

One might be concerned that, despite the survey of aid experts, what this paper calls the absence of political constraint on propensity to Navigate by Judgment is in fact mapping a more general construct of good donor practice. If this were accurate, the results presented here might provide reassurance that the consensus wisdom on what constitutes good development—articulated, in part, by the very Paris Declaration from whose monitoring surveys the propensity to Navigate by Judgment measure employed above is constructed—is on point. These results would not, however, suggest that organizational propensity to Navigate by Judgment is an important factor in project success, nor necessarily that soft information is critical in aid delivery.

To address this concern I ran a series of placebo tests examining whether other measures of good donor conduct yield the same relationship with the data observed for the propensity to Navigate by Judgment measure. These placebo tests employ the Commitment to Development Index (CDI) and the Quality of Official Development Assistance (QuODA) measure.[3] The CDI is an annual product of the Center for Global Development; the QuODA is an occasional product of the Brookings Institution in collaboration with the Center for Global Development (the last wave was in 2009). The CDI has a number of components (Aid, Investment, Migration, Environment, Security, and Technology) that assess the commitment of nations (multilateral organizations such as the World Bank are not included) to assisting the developing world. The QuODA has four components: Maximizing Efficiency, Transparency and Learning, Reducing Burden, and Fostering Institutions. All components of both the CDI and the QuODA involve a variety of submeasures. There is some overlap between these measures and my propensity to Navigate by Judgment scale (which is repeated below for ease of reference). The CDI aid index penalizes tied aid (a component of the propensity to Navigate by Judgment scale); untied aid is also a component of QuODA's Maximizing Efficiency measure. The QuODA's Fostering Institutions component draws from the Paris Declaration monitoring surveys as well, incorporating avoidance of project implementation units and use of recipient-country systems (this last measure combines the procurement and public financial management measures I use in the propensity to Navigate by Judgment scale).

Table AII.10 provides summary statistics of the CDI and QuODA scales in the sample data, conditional on the State Fragility Index (SFI)—the key measure of environmental predictability with which they will be interacted below—being present. For both measures I also examine the subscales that seem most relevant—CDI's Aid subscale and QuODA's Maximizing Efficiency and Fostering Institutions subscales.

Table AII.11 reruns the primary model employed in Table 6.1, substituting each of these measures in turn for the propensity to Navigate by Judgment scale; scales are standardized using Stata's "std" command to allow for direct comparison across scales.

Navigation by Judgment has a unique relationship with Project Success in interaction with environmental predictability. In interaction with

*Table AII.10* **Summary Statistics for Alternate Scales**

| Variable | Obs | Mean | SD | Min | Max |
|---|---|---|---|---|---|
| Propensity to Navigate by Judgment (from Paris Declaration Monitoring Survey) | 9312 | .659 | .075 | .559 | .799 |
| Commitment to Development Index (CDI) 2012 Overall | 3627 | 5.178 | .858 | 3.4 | 5.7 |
| Commitment to Development Index (CDI) 2012 Aid | 3627 | 4.909 | 2.031 | 1.6 | 6.8 |
| Quality of Development Assistance (QuODA) 2009 Overall | 9204 | .502 | .143 | .043 | .655 |
| Quality of Development Assistance (QuODA) 2009 Maximizing Efficiency | 9204 | .1 | .314 | −.89 | .51 |
| Quality of Development Assistance (QuODA) 2009 Fostering Institutions | 9204 | .426 | .285 | −.1 | .93 |

environmental predictability, a better QuODA overall score and a better score on QuODA's Maximizing Efficiency subscale move in the opposite direction to that of propensity to Navigate by Judgment, with higher scores associated with greater environmental unpredictability being more detrimental to Project Success relative to the IDO's performance on average. The Maximizing Efficiency subscale contains measures such as the ratio of project administrative costs to total project costs, which one could think of as a sign of greater monitoring; it is therefore not entirely surprising that this scale moves in the opposite direction, with higher scores on Maximizing Efficiency associated with greater declines in performance in more fragile states. The QuODA's Fostering Institutions measure and the CDI's Aid measure—the two measures below whose indicators most overlap with those of the Paris Declaration–based Navigation by Judgment propensity scale—move in the same direction as propensity to Navigate by Judgment but with very small point estimates that are not statistically significant. None of the other measures have anywhere near the strength of association of the propensity to Navigate by Judgment scale. Taken as a whole, this analysis should give reassurance regarding the uniqueness of the propensity to Navigate by Judgment measure's relationship with Project Success in conditions of differential environmental unpredictability, and thus the importance of soft information in the development production process.

Table AII.11 Placebo Tests. Navigation by Judgment has a unique relationship with Project Success in interaction with environmental predictability

| | (1) | (2) | (3) | (4) | (5) | (6) |
| --- | --- | --- | --- | --- | --- | --- |
| | Nav by Judg | CDI Overall | CDI Aid | QuODA Overall | QuODA Max Eff | QuODA Foster Inst |
| Environmental Unpredictability | −0.0372*** | −0.0167 | −0.0205* | −0.0359*** | −0.0378*** | −0.0345*** |
| | (0.00313) | (0.00928) | (0.00574) | (0.00589) | (0.00644) | (0.00621) |
| Scale in Column Title*Nav by Judg | 0.0134*** | 0.00804 | 0.0146 | −0.0110 | −0.0112 | 0.0121 |
| | (0.00261) | (0.00514) | (0.00545) | (0.00544) | (0.00699) | (0.00645) |
| Constant | 4.724*** | 4.782*** | 4.795*** | 4.718*** | 4.749*** | 4.707*** |
| | (0.0367) | (0.127) | (0.0640) | (0.0901) | (0.0882) | (0.0918) |
| IDO Fixed Effects | Y | Y | Y | Y | Y | Y |
| $R^2$-Within | 0.03 | 0.01 | 0.00 | 0.02 | 0.02 | 0.02 |
| $R^2$-Between | 0.06 | 0.03 | 0.03 | 0.03 | 0.14 | 0.17 |
| Observations | 9312 | 3627 | 3627 | 9204 | 9204 | 9204 |

Standard errors in parentheses.

* $p < 0.05$, ** $p < 0.01$, *** $p < 0.001$.

# Outcome Variance

One might be worried that results are driven by quirks in the variance of outcomes. Table AII.12 examines this concern in a simple nonparametric manner, by dividing environmental predictability and propensity to Navigate by Judgment scores at their respective means and then examining the variance in Project Success z-score by propensity to Navigate by Judgment and environmental predictability quadrant, and finds no substantively large differences. Table AII.12 also shows another nonparametric way of testing the intuition underlying the core findings. Both low- and high-propensity to Navigate by Judgment IDOs do better in contexts of lower environmental unpredictability; the gap between low- and high-SFI contexts is larger for low-propensity to Navigate by Judgment IDOs (approximately .26 SD) than for high-propensity to Navigate by Judgment IDOs (.1 SD). This should give further confidence that the main results are not driven by idiosyncratic features of the modeling.

By calculation, the z-score outcome measure has mean 0 and standard deviation 1 for each IDO. Table AII.12 allows us to examine if the variance in this measure differs systematically along Navigation by Judgment propensity and environmental predictability axes, thus potentially distorting the interpretation of Ordinary Least Squares (OLS) results. The question, then, is whether any of the quadrants deviate substantially enough from 1 to cause concern. Given the large N, the analysis can of course confirm that these variances are not equal; the question is whether they are substantively different enough to potentially bias results. I would argue the answer to this is in the negative.

*Table AII.12* **Analysis by Navigation by Judgment and Environmental Unpredictability Quadrant**

|  | *Low Propensity to Navigate by Judgment* | *High Propensity to Navigate by Judgment* |
| --- | --- | --- |
| High Environmental Predictability | .163 (.863) | .123 (.969) |
| Low Environmental Predictability | −.073 (1.047) | −.060 (1.010) |

# Features of the Modeling (e.g., Overfitting) and Parameterization of the Interaction Term

One might also worry, particularly given the small number of IDOs in this multilevel model, if results are driven by features of the modeling. To address this concern, Table AII.13 below examines the relationship between propensity to Navigate by Judgment and Project Success nonparametrically, summarizing the relationship between environmental unpredictability and overall Project

Table AII.13 **IDO-by-IDO Regressions. This table allows a direct examination of the 2nd-level N that drives results. The IDOs with lower propensities to Navigate by Judgment see a greater negative correlation between environmental unpredictability and Project Success**

| IDO | *Navigation by Judgment Score* | *Correlation between Env Unpred and Success for this donor with only this donor's (Z-score) data in regression* |
|---|---|---|
| EC | .559 | −0.0246*** |
| | | (0.0088) |
| Global Fund | .594 | −0.0471*** |
| | | (0.0087) |
| World Bank | .608 | −0.0365*** |
| | | (0.0029) |
| Asian DB | .669 | −0.0671*** |
| | | (0.0098) |
| JICA | .667 | −0.0221* |
| | | (0.0111) |
| GIZ | .666 | −0.0525*** |
| | | (0.0199) |
| KfW | .666 | −0.0331*** |
| | | (0.0063) |
| IFAD | .681 | −0.0183 |
| | | (0.0363) |
| DFID | .799 | −0.0019 |
| | | (0.0046) |

Standard errors in parentheses.
* $p < 0.05$, ** $p < 0.01$, *** $p < 0.001$.

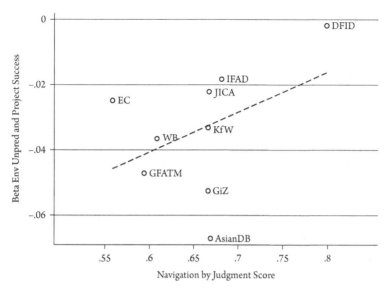

*Figure AII.2* Graph of IDO-by-IDO Slopes.

Success for each donor in isolation; that is, using only data from one donor at a time and implementing nine different regressions.[4] Table AII.13 thus allows a direct examination of the 2nd-level N that drives results. In each case, the model is of the form

$$\text{Project Success}_{i,j} = \beta_1 \text{ * Environmental Unpredictability (State Fragility Index)}_j + \varepsilon_i$$

As expected, greater environmental predictability has a more negative and statistically significant relationship with overall Project Success for less autonomous donors. This confirms—using an approach that does not rely on the parameterization of the interaction term—that higher levels of propensity to Navigate by Judgment mitigate the inverse relationship between the environmental unpredictability measure (the State Fragility Index) and overall Project Success. A figure presenting the data underlying Table AII.13 is presented as Figure AII.2.[5]

## Additional Robustness Tests

In addition to the robustness checks discussed here, the results above are robust to:

- Using ordered logit models rather than OLS
- Using z-scores as outcomes (rather than the six-point scale where employed)

- Compressing success and failure to a binary outcome and employing ordinary logit models
- Employing quantile regression (were results to be driven by only part of the distribution)
- Restricting SFI to common support; that is, only the range of SFI realized in all donors' data (2–22, rather than 0–25 in the main analysis)
- Dropping the latter two waves of the Paris Declaration survey in generating the propensity to Navigate by Judgment measure (to allay concerns that donors responded to measurement by changing their practices)
- Double-clustering standard errors at the IDO-recipient level,[6] or clustering at either the IDO or recipient-country level
- Dropping either subscale of the SFI (legitimacy or effectiveness)
- Using any of the four domains of the SFI (security, political, economic, or social)

## Propensity to Navigate by Judgment Measure in Full

Table AII.14 provides a full list of all organizations for which propensity to Navigate by Judgment scores were generated, along with those scores, for full transparency regarding the measure.[7]

*Table AII.14* **Full List of Propensity to Navigate by Judgment Score**

| IDO | NbJ Score | Rank |
| --- | --- | --- |
| Ireland | 0.878579795 | 1 |
| UK (DFID) | 0.798823953 | 2 |
| Norway | 0.796352506 | 3 |
| Netherlands | 0.773272038 | 4 |
| Sweden | 0.719851851 | 5 |
| IMF | 0.714166641 | 6 |
| Finland | 0.689640522 | 7 |
| IFAD | 0.681465507 | 8 |
| Denmark | 0.678942561 | 9 |
| Canada | 0.677956104 | 10 |
| AsianDB | 0.669080436 | 11 |
| Japan (JICA) | 0.667425275 | 12 |

*Table AII.14* **Continued**

| IDO | NbJ Score | Rank |
|-----|-----------|------|
| Germany (GIZ/KfW) | 0.666281819 | 13 |
| France | 0.628306508 | 14 |
| WB | 0.608462632 | 15 |
| Switzerland | 0.605228841 | 16 |
| GFATM | 0.593850553 | 17 |
| New Zealand | 0.593333304 | 18 |
| EC | 0.558577597 | 19 |
| Austria | 0.535915732 | 20 |
| Spain | 0.533711374 | 21 |
| Belgium | 0.501379311 | 22 |
| Luxembourg | 0.492137939 | 23 |
| African DB | 0.488045961 | 24 |
| Australia | 0.480275869 | 25 |
| Portugal | 0.476367801 | 26 |
| Italy | 0.459770113 | 27 |
| IADB | 0.392873555 | 28 |
| Korea | 0.375316083 | 29 |
| United States | 0.36240229 | 30 |
| GAVI Alliance | 0.330833346 | 31 |
| Turkey | 0.285268188 | 32 |
| United Nations | 0.234992817 | 33 |

## Environmental Legibility

At the risk of tautology, the degree of environmental legibility—that is, the extent to which a context is hard to understand—is itself difficult to evaluate systematically. That said, we can use some rough proxies that seem to isolate environmental legibility—the difficulty of understanding a context from afar. One factor that may decrease legibility is the extent to which the formal de jure rules do not reflect de facto reality. In the language of one prominent piece of recent research: Is business done using informal deals or rather by formal rules?[8] Another factor is the extent to which a society is divided among different groups—the extent to which distinctions between people, which may be difficult to perceive or navigate from afar, affect actions.

Table AII.15 uses the same basic econometric models as those employed above, but substitutes for the environmental unpredictability index a nation's ethnolinguistic fractionalization and the World Bank's International Development Association (IDA) Resource Allocation Index measure on property rights and rule-based governance. More ethnolinguistic fragmentation implies a greater number of groups in the society who may have conflicting interests, and thus an environment harder to understand from afar. The World Bank's rule-based governance measure assesses "the extent to which private economic activity is facilitated by an effective legal system and rule-based governance structure."[9] These measures speak to legibility directly rather than conflating legibility and

*Table AII.15* **Environmental Legibility and Navigation by Judgment**

|  | *(1)* | *(2)* | *(3)* | *(4)* |
|---|---|---|---|---|
|  | *Outcome 6pt scale* | *Outcome 6pt scale* | *Outcome 6pt scale* | *Outcome 6pt scale* |
| Ethnolinguistic fractionalization (ELF) | −1.485** | −2.052** |  |  |
|  | (0.399) | (0.516) |  |  |
| Nav by Judg*ELF | 1.696* | 1.776* |  |  |
|  | (0.637) | (0.684) |  |  |
| Property Rights and Rule-Based Governance (PRRG) |  |  | −0.830 | −0.701 |
|  |  |  | (0.366) | (0.308) |
| Nav by Judg*PRRG |  |  | 0.916 | 0.902* |
|  |  |  | (0.490) | (0.386) |
| Constant | 4.427*** | 4.496*** | 4.782*** | 4.748*** |
|  | (0.0292) | (0.0495) | (0.0884) | (0.212) |
| IDO Fixed Effects | Y | Y | Y | Y |
| Recipient Fixed Effects | N | Y | N | Y |
| $R^2$-Within | 0.009 | 0.065 | 0.014 | 0.073 |
| $R^2$-Between | 0.014 | 0.047 | 0.055 | 0.062 |
| Observations | 13297 | 13297 | 2940 | 2940 |

Standard errors in parentheses.
* $p < 0.05$, ** $p < 0.01$, *** $p < 0.001$.

unpredictability; they also provide suggestive evidence of the relevance of the legibility channel.

## Environmental Unpredictability

Table AII.16 looks at political stability as evaluated by the World Bank's World Governance Indicators (which includes propensity for violence and regime change) as well as the EM-DAT International Disasters database. These variables speak to the likely (political stability) and actual (disaster database) occurrence of rapid change that would require adaptation—that is, that would operate through the flexibility channel hypothesized in Part 1. As noted in chapter 6, point estimates are in the hypothesized direction but none of the variables have a relationship with Project Success that is statistically significant at the 95 percent level.

## The Effect of Having an Office In-Country

The theory articulated in Part I argues that the gathering and incorporation of soft information is one of the channels through which propensity to Navigate by Judgment impacts project performance. As discussed in chapter 5, we might expect, then, that the returns to having an in-country office will be higher for IDOs more likely to Navigate by Judgment, who are thus better able to incorporate soft information into decisions. Table AII.17 interrogates this hypothesis using a subset of six IDOs for which country office data is available. The six IDOs are the AsDB, DFID, IFAD, JICA, KfW, and GIZ. These data are quite messy, and it is frequently difficult to determine when precisely in-country offices opened or closed. The analysis presented in Table AII.17 assumes that where opening or closing dates are unknown, offices presently open always existed. This is surely inaccurate in many cases, and thus adds additional noise.

The triple interaction between Navigation by Judgment, the presence of an office, and environmental unpredictability with recipient-country fixed effects is suggestive of increasing returns to having an office present for more Navigation by Judgment–prone IDOs in more unpredictable environments. It is also notable that the mere existence of an office is not, in and of itself, a predictor of greater Project Success, or an increasing benefit as environmental unpredictability rises. It is only more Navigation by Judgment–prone IDOs that see a return to having an office, and only as environmental unpredictability rises (and when controlling for recipient-country fixed effects).

Table AII.16 Environmental Unpredictability and Navigation by Judgment

| DV: Project Success (6-pt scale) | (1) | (2) | (3) | (4) | (5) | (6) |
|---|---|---|---|---|---|---|
| WGI Political Stability | 0.529 | 0.306 | | | | |
| | (0.294) | (0.269) | | | | |
| Nav by Judg*Pol Stability | −0.641 | −0.209 | | | | |
| | (0.403) | (0.375) | | | | |
| Total Disaster Deaths | | | −0.00000287 | 0.00000912 | | |
| | | | (0.00000771) | (0.00000563) | | |
| Nav by Judg*Disaster Deaths | | | 0.00000716 | −0.0000140 | | |
| | | | (0.0000112) | (0.00000827) | | |
| Disaster Damage | | | | | 1.61e-08 | 1.92e-09 |
| | | | | | (8.20e-09) | (1.06e-08) |
| Nav by Judg*Disaster Damage | | | | | −9.23e-09 | −2.89e-09 |
| | | | | | (1.20e-08) | (1.52e-08) |
| Constant | 4.402*** | 4.942*** | 4.233*** | 5.414*** | 4.226*** | 5.414*** |
| | (0.0202) | (0.0260) | (0.00109) | (0.0169) | (0.000551) | (0.0181) |
| IDO Fixed Effects | Y | Y | Y | Y | Y | Y |
| Recipient Fixed Effects | N | Y | N | Y | N | Y |
| $R^2$-Within | 0.007 | 0.079 | 0.000 | 0.066 | 0.003 | 0.066 |
| $R^2$-Between | 0.048 | 0.019 | 0.006 | 0.027 | 0.035 | 0.028 |
| Observations | 7502 | 7502 | 14610 | 14610 | 14610 | 14610 |

Standard errors in parentheses.
* $p < 0.05$, ** $p < 0.01$, *** $p < 0.001$.

*Table AII.17* **Presence of a Country Office**

| | (1) | (2) | (3) | (4) |
|---|---|---|---|---|
| | Project Success (Z-score) | Project Success (Z-score) | Outcome 6pt scale | Outcome 6pt scale |
| Nav by Judg*Env Unpred*Office | −0.0536 | 0.162* | −0.0991 | 0.203* |
| | (0.0596) | (0.0804) | (0.0728) | (0.0779) |
| Nav by Judg*Office | 1.659 | −0.909 | 1.333 | −2.692 |
| | (0.943) | (1.203) | (1.092) | (1.293) |
| Nav by Judg*Env Unpred | 0.185*** | 0.0527 | 0.299*** | 0.0850 |
| | (0.0121) | (0.0528) | (0.0391) | (0.0463) |
| Office*Env Unpred | 0.0316 | −0.110 | 0.0680 | −0.139 |
| | (0.0387) | (0.0572) | (0.0512) | (0.0551) |
| Environmental Unpredictability | −0.149*** | −0.0534 | −0.238*** | −0.0770* |
| | (0.0108) | (0.0368) | (0.0294) | (0.0282) |
| Nav by Judgment | −2.748*** | −1.353 | | |
| | (0.249) | (0.801) | | |
| Office | −1.066 | 0.632 | −0.816 | 2.004 |
| | (0.598) | (0.853) | (0.755) | (0.975) |
| Constant | 2.170*** | 0.906 | 4.658*** | 4.640*** |
| | (0.223) | (0.727) | (0.0676) | (0.184) |
| IDO Fixed Effects | N | N | Y | Y |
| Recipient Fixed Effects | N | Y | N | Y |
| Observations | 7992 | 7992 | 7992 | 7992 |

Standard errors in parentheses.
* $p < 0.05$, ** $p < 0.01$, *** $p < 0.001$.

A thread of recent scholarship has argued that IDO support stimulates isomorphic mimicry in recipient-country governments, with the result of de jure reform but little de facto progress and a divorcing of formal organizational form from function.[10] One could interpret this finding as suggestive evidence that the same is true of the IDOs themselves—that while many IDOs open offices, it is only for the more autonomous IDOs that offices actually lead to improved project performance, presumably via better incorporation of soft information by properly placed field agents. It also suggests that formal opening of an office may be less important to Navigation by Judgment than de facto empowerment of field agents, which may happen in the absence of a formal office presence.

# NOTES

## Prelims

1. Pritchett and Sandefur 2013, 162.
2. Many thanks to Nils Hagerdal for this insight. In an effort to coin a name for this consensus, I looked up the geographic midpoint between the University of Chicago (for Hayek) and the University of Wisconsin (a broadly liberal institution where Scott spent many years). The midpoint between the two is Harvard, Illinois. Both Hayek and Scott might appreciate Harvard, Illinois' motto: "Success Comes Naturally Here."
3. Polanyi 1966, 4.
4. Many thanks to Andrews, Pritchett, and Woolcock 2017, and Michael Woolcock, for reminding me of this eloquent quote.

## Chapter 1

1. This account comes from an individual working on the project who asked that he and the contractor for which he worked remain anonymous. In my judgment, this required anonymizing either the country in which the project took place or the proper name of the IDO; I chose to anonymize the IDO.
2. International Monetary Fund 2003, 263. This definition of official development assistance is widely used by the Organization for Economic Cooperation and Development's (OECD) Development Assistance Committee and its members.
3. Deaton 2013. Deaton's view is that foreign aid is a net hindrance to developing countries, something that interferes with their economic and social development.
4. See Radelet 2007, chap. 9, for an accessible description of some of development's successes.
5. See Roser 2017 for a broad summary of the available data on long-term trends in living conditions.
6. While there are a number of sources that note aid's failure, a particularly nice and well-cited summary of aid's failures, broken out by category (harmful, ineffective, poorly executed, etc.), is GiveWell 2017.
7. An incomplete list of wise pieces on aid effectiveness and allocative strategies includes Andrews, Pritchett, and Woolcock 2012; Andrews 2014; Bermeo 2016; Booth 2012; Buntaine 2016; Buntaine, Parks, and Buch 2017; Bush 2015; Chandy, Seidel, and Zhang 2016; Cruz and Schneider 2016; Dietrich 2013; Dietrich 2016; Easterly 2002; Easterly 2006; Gibson et al. 2005; Girod and Tobin 2016; Israel 1989; Johnson 2016; Levy 2014; Pritchett and Woolcock 2004; Woods 2007; Wright and Winters 2010.
8. The OECD estimates over USD$210 billion in concessional development financing was disbursed by members of the OECD Development Assistance Committee in 2013 (OECD

2015, 101). This number is almost certainly a massive underestimate; it excludes multilateral and regional banks (e.g., the World Bank and African Development Bank), who in combination with the UN OECD estimates spent an additional $41.5 billion in 2013. This figure also excludes all non-OECD bilateral aid—perhaps most notably Chinese aid.

9.  This is not to suggest that a focus on the organization of foreign aid as an important driver of results is a new idea; far from it. Distinguished scholars have long argued that the organization matters in foreign aid: e.g., Hirschman 1967; Tendler 1975; Ostrom, Gibson, and Shivakumar 2002.

10. See, e.g., Derbyshire and Donovan 2016; DFID 2014; USAID 2014a.

11. See, e.g., Gulrajani 2011. This push for data fits deep historic echoes for IDO; development assistance was originally conceived as part of a broader modernization theory, a doctrine with a deep faith in technology and the power of numbers to drive societal transformation (see, e.g., Ekbladh 2010 on U.S. development assistance). Robert McNamara, after his tenures managing Ford Motor Company and the U.S. war effort in Vietnam using numbers as a central part of his management strategy, became the World Bank president, often credited with bringing more rigorous measurement practices to international development assistance.

12. Ramalingam 2013, 265. In development literature the urban planning and complexity theory notion of "wicked problems" is sometimes confounded with Hogarth's notion of "wicked environments" (e.g., Hogarth, Lejarraga, and Soyer 2015), though not by Ramalingam. Avoiding this confusion is the primary reason I don't make broader use of "wickedness" language in this book. "Wicked environments" refers to learning environments, arguing that what makes environments wicked is that an agent cannot learn from them—that intuition cannot be usefully educated by experience. I believe IDO agents often *can* learn effectively and that IDOs face wicked problems, but not particularly wicked (or particularly kind) learning environments.

13. Barnett and Finnemore 2003 provide a particularly compelling account of international organization dysfunction caused by too much agent control.

14. I consider these costs underappreciated as I do not believe they are in fact incompatible with principal-agent models, only rarely considered in conventional models. E.g., in a recent piece titled "Why Organizations Fail," two distinguished organizational economists write, "Incentive problems arise due to the presence of asymmetric information or imperfect commitment, which lead agents to act according to their own biases or preferences rather than in the interest of the organization" (Garicano and Rayo 2016, 138–39). Miller and Whitford 2016 is a recent, and excellent, piece of public administration scholarship that similarly sees "too much" control as a potential source of dysfunction.

15. The U.S. Congressional Research Service has framed this as the tension between "Too Little" and "Too Much" accountability for USAID. Tarnoff 2015, 38–40.

16. Natsios 2010, 8.

17. Andrews, Pritchett, and Woolcock 2017, chap. 6.

18. Smalley 2017.

19. Hawes 2016.

20. In the interests of full disclosure, I own no car; this is thus an aspirational Chevy Traverse. As a native Detroiter, I have chosen as my aspirational car the vehicle produced by a Detroit-headquartered automaker that scores highest in 2016's Cars.com American-Made Index, which includes the labor and parts content of cars in its calculation of "American-ness." (Mays 2016).

21. USAID 2016b, 7.

22. World Bank Project nos. P163049, P160512, P160029, and P155303, respectively. April 2017 is chosen as the most recent available data from the public World Bank Projects & Operations database on date of access (World Bank 2017).

23. Sectors as defined by OECD Development Assistance Committee five-digit purpose codes. These codes group five-digit "purposes" (e.g., 12262, Malaria Control) under three-digit "sectors" (e.g., 122, Basic Health). Except where noted otherwise, when I use the term "sector" I mean the more precise five-digit codes. "Countries" as described here includes countries no longer in existence (e.g., Yugoslavia, Zanzibar) and some noncountry geographic units (e.g., Tristan da Cunha).

24. While the movement for aid information transparency has made impressive strides in the past few years, most of the progress to date has been on inputs—on spending data and financial flows. No other public source (e.g., the International Aid Transparency Initiative, the OECD Development Assistance Committee's Creditor Reporting System, and the AidData archive) includes systematic information on the results of projects in a way tractable to quantitative analysis for any donor other than the World Bank.

25. The PPD available online does not perfectly replicate the project performance data used in this book, as my data agreement with the European Commission (EC) does not allow for disclosure of the EC data.

## Chapter 2

1. This account draws from Ross 2014 and Pilling 2017.

2. I am not drawing on any particular account in painting this contrast; while Mombasa schools have not historically seen very much top-down control (see, e.g., Anderson and Nedithu 2002), this account may very well overstate the Navigation by Judgment of Mombasa schools at present. I have witnessed schools that seem to operate in the manner described here, e.g., in Liberia and East Timor.

3. This definition appears in the context of 29 CFR 541, which in Subpart C (541.200), in the context of determining whether a job is exempt from overtime pay standards, defines nonadministrative employees as those "whose primary duty includes the exercise of discretion and independent judgment."

4. This description comes from the U.S. Department of Labor's online glossary of terms as regards overtime and employment law, https://webapps.dol.gov/elaws/whd/flsa/overtime/glossary.htm?wd=discretion_and_judgment, retrieved September 13, 2016.

5. Including Carpenter 2001; Huber and Shipan 2002.

6. Aghion and Tirole 1997.

7. This is an implication of Gailmard and Patty's expertise model (Gailmard and Patty 2007; Gailmard and Patty 2012). Andersen and Moynihan 2016 provide empirical evidence consistent with this; Bertelli and Lewis 2013 connect the retention of expertise to employee turnover, paralleling some of chapter 3's discussion of agents.

8. See, e.g., Grant 1996. Tacit knowledge from Polanyi 1966. These are far from the only echoes of the management literature in this chapter; management scholars may see echoes in foundation management literature on the connection of optimal organizational structure to environmental uncertainty and task routinizability. See, e.g., Lawrence and Lorsch 1967; Perrow 1967; Thompson 1967; March and Simon 1958.

9. Scott 1998. Definition of "metis" from ibid., 311. Scott continues, "metis is most applicable to broadly similar but never precisely identical situations requiring a quick and practiced adaptation that becomes almost second nature to the practitioner. The skills of metis may well involve rules of thumb, but such rules are largely acquired through practice (often in formal apprenticeship) and a developed feel or knack for strategy. Metis resists simplification into deductive principles which can successfully be transmitted through book learning, because the environments in which it is exercised are so complex and non-repeatable that formal procedures of rational decision making are impossible to apply" (ibid., 316).

10. Other alternatives more within organizational economics and contract theory to Aghion and Tirole include Melumad, Mookherjee, and Reichelstein 1992; their model uses private information in much the same way I employ soft information, connecting private information transmission to delegation. There are also echoes here of Baker, Gibbons, and Murphy 1999. As Garicano and Rayo 2016 point out, this also echoes Jensen and Meckling 1990, who focus on agent information in organizational adaptation to local circumstance. I prefer to focus on the credible commitment rather than costly communication or coordination frames, as I believe the problem cannot be solved via making communication and coordination costless; indeed, as I suggest in the concluding chapter 9, I believe the growth of technology may exacerbate the underlying tension.

11. Aghion and Tirole 1997.

12. Stein 2002, 1892.

13. Tacit information is the idea that "we can know more than we can tell" (Polanyi 1966); that there are actions that can be done by agents but cannot be fully explained, codified for onwards transmission. Examples of tacit knowledge in daily life include how to jiggle the key "just right" to open your door, how to facilitate a meeting, or how to cook a perfect steak.

14. This is put in simple terms for its illustrative value. More realistically, Steve's IDO may ask him to report only on how many students enroll in school, making a meeting focused on teacher quality less important. This is not so far-fetched, as Part II will demonstrate. The U.S. government's standard foreign assistance indicators include many "counts" in the education sector, including "number of learners in primary schools or equivalent non-school based settings reached with USG education assistance" (U.S. Department of State Office of Foreign Assistance Resources 2016, 3.2.1-14) and "number of laws, policies, regulations, or guidelines developed or modified to improve primary grade reading programs or increase equitable access" (ibid., 3.2.1-38).

15. McChrystal et al. 2015.

16. Subtitle of ibid.

17. Ibid., 7.

18. Ibid., 216.

19. Ibid., chap. 10. McChrystal's view is by no means unique. While by no means an area of my particular expertise, discussions of field control, decision making, and unit autonomy are quite developed in the military context. See, e.g., Russell 2011; Ucko 2009; Biddle 2004; Pollack 2002.

20. This discussion of the relationship between Navigation by Judgment and measurement owes a special debt to Israel's 1989 gem, *Institutional Development* (Israel 1989). Israel anticipates the tension between measurement and Navigation by Judgment, noting that for a development agency like the World Bank quantification can diminish flexibility and distort incentives (ibid., 162). Israel also is one of the few to note that not all international development tasks are created equal; that there are scope conditions under which different organizational arrangements are likely to thrive that go beyond the nature of the developing country and incorporate features of the task or service via this focus on task specificity and complexity. Andrews, Pritchett, and Woolcock 2013 and Pritchett and Woolcock 2004 provide a more contemporary version of this insight, focusing on the "discretionary-ness" of tasks (2004) and the extent to which "logistical" solutions are possible (2013) in describing differential success and the need for different strategies.

21. See, e.g., Natsios 2010; Gulrajani 2011.

22. OECD 2016, 82.

23. Heisenberg's principle states that determining the position of a particle changes its momentum (and vice versa); the act of observation affects what is observed. That the act of observation can be a form of control dates at least to Foucault's Panopticon (Foucault 1978). This is perhaps most eloquently put by Foucault: "Hence the major effect of the Panopticon: to induce in the inmate a state of conscious and permanent visibility that assures the automatic functioning of power. So to arrange things that the surveillance is permanent in its effects, even if it is discontinuous in its action; that the perfection of power should tend to render its actual exercise unnecessary; that this architectural apparatus should be a machine for creating and sustaining a power relation independent of the person who exercises it; in short, that the inmates should be caught up in a power situation of which they are themselves the bearers" (ibid., 201).

24. Performance management issues are also discussed in the context of IDOs in Clist 2016.

25. See, e.g., Gelb and Hashmi 2014 and Perakis and Savedoff 2015 on how IDOs find it difficult to move beyond output measurement.

26. Kerr 1975.

27. There is substantial work that suggests that if a job is "multitask"—having both measurable and unmeasurable components—measurement will be distortionary. Dewatripont, Jewitt, and Tirole 2000; Holmstrom and Milgrom 1991.

28. Another way of thinking about this susceptibility to a breakdown of the correlation between outputs and project goals is via Goodhart's Law, the observation that "any observed statistical

regularity will tend to collapse once pressure is placed upon it for control purposes." Goodhart 1981, 116.

29. Pritchett 2013.

30. Robinson et al. 2014, 63.

31. Tirole 1994.

32. In standard economics models the concern is regulatory capture, with regulators unduly influenced by the firms with which they interact. E.g., Dal Bo 2006; Laffont and Tirole 1991; Levine and Forrence 1990.

33. See, e.g., Woods 2006, 56. Woods frames the concern as one of staff "going native," a phrase that can still sometimes be heard in the corridors of aid organizations.

34. E.g., in Niskanen's foundational model of bureaucratic behavior bureaucrats wish to maximize their budgets irrespective of what organizational superiors or political authorizers might wish to see transpire (Niskanen 1968). While Niskanen himself has somewhat fallen out of favor—in the words of Barnett and Finnemore 2003, "Adopting the rather battered Niskanen hypothesis seems less than promising given the glaring anomalies" (706)—the more general point that agents may want quite different things from their principals remains. See, e.g., Prendergast 2007.

35. In my view, policing is the context where this issue is most contested. Relying on police judgment clearly gives rise to disparate treatment, e.g., by race; however, it is unclear if tight control of police officers is likely to lead to better outcomes. See, e.g., Brehm and Gates 1999; Prendergast 2001.

36. See, e.g., Chandler 1977; Williamson 1983 on the tension between flexibility and standardization on organizational management and structure.

37. "After two years studying at Bridge in Kenya, pupils passed the national exam at a 59% rate, 15 points above the public school pass rate. For those who'd studied at Bridge for at least 4 years, the pass rate was 74%." http://www.bridgeinternationalacademies.com/results/academic/; accessed April 28, 2017.

38. Drawn from Bridge International Academies' website, http://www.bridgeinternationalacademies.com/company/investors/; accessed April 28, 2017.

39. That is, when free-riding problems can be avoided. Prendergast 1999 provides a nice, if quite lengthy, overview of the incentives literature; Prendergast notes the tension of high-powered incentives with verifiability as well. He argues "pay-for-performance is constrained by the noisiness of the measures used to reward agents" (ibid., 8).

40. See, e.g., Birdsall and Savedoff 2011. This excellent and thought-provoking book is on cash on delivery but parallels in this regard the general results-based financing literature. These aid-specific tools share much with social impact bonds, which promote socially beneficial ends by paying for long-term success (see, e.g., Liebman and Sellman 2013).

41. Focusing on long-term impact while allowing implementers to determine how to achieve them is a core piece of a broader public management philosophy known as New Public Management. See, e.g., Christensen and Laegreid 2011. An organization employing New Public Management certainly exhibits more Navigation by Judgment than an organization such as Bridge Academies. Critics of New Public Management often point to a number of the issues this book raises including overinvestment in the measurable, a loss of initiative, and agent wisdom. See, e.g., Hood and Dixon 2015; Lorenz 2012; Belle and Ongaro 2014. One additional difficulty in applying New Public Management to IDOs is that IDOs are funded by a different public than the public IDO activities are meant to benefit; there is no feedback loop to beneficiaries for IDOs. See Easterly 2012 and De Renzio 2016 for a discussion of this problem.

42. This follows from contract theory's multitask models, e.g., Holmstrom and Milgrom 1991.

43. The concern here is how to respond to exogenous shocks. Chapter 6 provides a discussion of contracts' response to the 2014 Ebola crisis that speaks to this directly.

44. My view is these conditions do sometimes pertain and thus results-based financing is sometimes an excellent idea, albeit in a more limited set of cases than those envisaged by many of its champions. Among the potential constraints, it will only be possible when we know what "success" will look like ahead of time and when we have verifiable outcomes that we can specify in advance. Albert Hirschman once noted that this is rarely true in the world of

international development; that much of both the good and bad results of development projects are not just unanticipated but incapable of being anticipated. As he put it, "The indirect effects [of foreign aid projects] are so varied as to escape detection by one or even several criteria *uniformly applied to all projects*. Upon inspection, each project turns out to represent a *unique constellation* of experiences and consequences, of direct and indirect effects" (Hirschman 1967, 186; italics in original).

45. See Clist 2016 for an excellent summary of many of these issues in a development context. More broadly, pay-for-performance remains a contentious issue in public administration, with some arguing that the effect of pay-for-performance schemes is likely contingent on dimensions of the task, environment, and agent (thus paralleling some of the theoretical architecture in this book). See, e.g., Weibel, Rost, and Osterloh 2009.

46. Guerrero, Woodhead, and Hounjet 2013.

47. Drawn from ibid., figure 3. The full data: Process, 51%; output, 24%; input, 6%; target, 6%; outcome, 12%; impact, 1%.

48. There are also a number of prominent international development thinkers who would echo my view, as articulated in chapter 9, that there are many aid interventions for which there is no good measurement solution, in part because of the inflexibility even outcome measures induce for IDOs—that not just IDO tactics but broader strategy need iterated revision during implementation. This arguably includes elements of the "Doing Development Differently" (DDD) movement and adherents to "Problem Driven Iterative Adaptation" (PDIA). See, e.g., Algoso and Hudson 2016; Green 2016 for overviews of these schools of thought and many others. Many of these aid thinkers build on similar intellectual foundations as does this book; e.g., Lindblom 1959; Perrow 1967; Thompson 1967; Lawrence and Lorsch 1967; March and Simon 1958; Scott 1998.

49. Control is not the only possible purpose of measurement and reporting, of course. Measurement can be used for learning or improving rather than control; see, e.g., Behn 2003. When there is no pressure upon measures for control purposes, the possibilities for distortion are reduced. While rarely observed in practice, collecting externally verifiable data but not using that data for control purposes will also resolve the tension between measurement and Navigation by Judgment. Chapter 9 discusses this at greater length.

50. This was at a press conference on February 12, 2002 regarding the link between the government of Iraq and weapons of mass destruction. The full quote states, "Reports that say that something hasn't happened are always interesting to me, because as we know, there are known knowns; there are things we know we know. We also know there are known unknowns; that is to say we know there are some things we do not know. But there are also unknown unknowns—the ones we don't know we don't know." (Rumsfeld 2002)

51. Another way of framing this point is via the economics literature on incomplete contracting (e.g., Grossman and Hart 1986; Hart and Moore 1988; Hart and Moore 1990), which argues that decision rights for unforeseen contingencies need to rest with the party who needs to make uncontractible investments. In the sense of Gailmard and Patty 2012, it is the agents who need to invest in their expertise; in the sense of Aghion and Tirole 1997, these agents need to invest in gathering contextual asymmetric information.

52. Legibility is a key element of Jim Scott's framework for thinking about top-down planning in *Seeing Like a State* (Scott 1998).

53. This argument draws from the work of James Q. Wilson. In *Bureaucracy*, Wilson draws a distinction between types of tasks, sorting them according to the answer to two simple questions: "Can the activities of their operators be observed? Can the results of those activities be observed?" (Wilson 1989, 158). Wilson argues that if both outputs (the activities of operators) and outcomes (results) can be observed, then it is possible to design a "compliance system to produce an efficient outcome" (ibid., 160). When outcomes cannot be observed, Wilson predicts management will "focus their efforts [to control agents] on the most easily measured (and thus most easily controlled) activities of their operators" (ibid., 170). This in turn will cause agents to focus on producing what can be measured and reported on (e.g., short-term outputs) rather than longer-term outcomes. Wilson uses the word "observed" in the context of compliance—the ability of an outsider to confirm that a job has been done.

I call this "verifiability," to differentiate this compliance sense of observation from things that can be observed by agents in the field but not distant principals (i.e., soft information).

54. Highly verifiable projects also have reduced tension between principal control and agent use of asymmetric information, including soft information; agents will use soft information to the extent that it leads to better performance on monitored outputs. Some soft information about how to deliver HIV drugs more effectively (e.g., knowledge of local community practices) will likely be incorporated into IDO agents' decisions about how to best deliver drugs.

55. Huber and Shipan 2002 also suggest that delegation strategies should vary depending on the nature of tasks. The private-sector management control systems literature also suggests differential measurement challenges are critical to optimal control, an idea that has made its way into the literature on the contracting of government services to private providers (e.g., Brown and Potoski 2005; Brown and Potoski 2003).

## *Chapter 3*

1. Denizer, Kaufmann, and Kraay 2013.
2. Niskanen 1968; Niskanen 1974.
3. Gibson et al. 2005; Natsios 2010.
4. McGregor 1960.
5. Mansbridge 2014.
6. Ibid., 55.
7. Ibid.
8. This section title is inspired by then U.S. Secretary of War Henry Stimson, who in 1945 wrote to President Harry Truman, "The chief lesson I have learned in a long life is that the only way you can make a man trustworthy is to trust him; and the surest way to make him untrustworthy is to distrust him and show your distrust." Stimson 1945, 2.
9. *This American Life* 2010. The quote is from Bruce Lee, then regional manager for the United Automobile Workers, the union that represented the Fremont plant.
10. Adler 1993.
11. Shook 2010.
12. Adler 1993.
13. Shook 2010; Adler 1993; *This American Life* 2010.
14. Gibbons and Henderson 2012, 30.
15. Adler 1993.
16. Shook 2010.
17. Deci 1971. See Ryan and Deci 2000 for an overview of Self-Determination Theory.
18. On extrinsic vs. intrinsic motivation see, e.g., Gneezy and Rustichini 2000; Gneezy, Meier, and Rey-Biel 2011; Lepper, Greene, and Nisbett 1973. On inappropriate monitoring and evaluation see Belle and Ongaro 2014; Hoey 2015.
19. Bertelli 2006; Frey and Jegen 1999; Frey 1994; Gneezy, Meier, and Rey-Biel 2011; Gneezy and Rustichini 2000; Wrzesniewski et al. 2014. A number of these scholars note that, properly designed, measurement and pay-for-performance are consistent with intrinsic motivation; Bertelli suggests that in some cases pay-for-performance can actually crowd in intrinsic motivation.
20. See Grant and Berg 2010 for an overview of this literature; and Grant 2013 for a (*New York Times* best-selling) accessible overview of Grant's research.
21. Aghion and Tirole 1997.
22. Gailmard and Patty 2007; Gailmard and Patty 2012. Gailmard and Patty do not employ the term "Navigation by Judgment," of course; they discuss "grants of discretion" to bureaucrats.
23. Chapter 9 discusses accountability in more detail. On professional accountability see Jackson 2009; Brehm and Gates 1999; Mulgan 2000. Jackson 2009 is an overview of the Friedrich-Finer debate, a historic debate between an advocate of central control (Finer) on the one hand and professionalism and autonomy (Friedrich) on the other, of which this chapter has many echoes.
24. Lammers et al. 2016.

25. On motivation, see, e.g., Hackman and Oldham 1980; Lopes, Lagoa, and Calapez 2014; Spector 1986. On job satisfaction, see Blegen 1993; Mortimer and Lorence 1989; Nguyen, Taylor, and Bradley 2003. Dan Pink's *Drive* includes a readable and accessible summary of the motivation literature (Pink 2011).
26. Sparks and Malkus 2015.
27. The IMF's focus on economists means these numbers are likely higher than they would be for other IDOs; nonetheless IDO employees as a whole are a very well-educated workforce. Data from International Monetary Fund 2015. Degree numbers taken from tables 14 (Masters) and 15 (PhDs); professional staff from table 9. It is possible this is a slight undercount of total staff, with tables 14 and 15 drawing from a wider base than table 9.
28. See, e.g., Perry and Wise 1990.
29. See Hawkins et al. 2006 for a treatment of these issues in the context of international organizations.
30. Hafliger and Hug 2015.
31. UN International Civil Service Commission 2008.
32. Anderfuhren-Biget, Hafliger, and Hug 2013.
33. Pigni 2016. As discussed in Tiny Spark 2017.
34. Hannay and Northam 2000; Mitchell et al. 2001; Samuel and Chipunza 2009.
35. Moynihan and Pandey 2007, 44, as quoted in Harari et al. 2017. The original quote is a reference to Romzek and Hendricks 1982.
36. Bertelli and Lewis 2013.
37. Cameron, Figueiredo, and Lewis 2015.
38. Giauque, Anderfuhren-Biget, and Varone 2016.
39. USAID Africa Bureau cable of April 13, 1985 as quoted in Snook 1999, 99. This may be the beginning of New Public Management–style reforms within USAID.
40. Ibid., 98. Reported as part of a quote, but with the implication that this reflects the author's view of USAID's general direction of motion—i.e., that the quote is accurate.
41. Ibid., 99.
42. Ibid.
43. Those eight organizations are the World Bank; IMF; Asian Development Bank; Belgian Technical Cooperation; DFID; International Fund for Agricultural Development (IFAD); New Zealand Aid; and German Development Bank (KfW)'s DEG division, which focuses on developing countries. In all cases the most recent year publicly available was taken, which ranged in practice from 2008 to 2015. These statistics are taken variously from KfW Group 2015; Independent Commission for Aid Impact (UK) 2014; World Bank 2016; International Monetary Fund 2015; International Fund for Agricultural Development 2009; NZAid and Williams 2012; Belgian Technical Cooperation 2008; Asian Development Bank 2011. Figure 3 of Das, Joubert, and Tordoir 2017 suggests the World Bank number may be accurate, but from an unusually turnover-prone year; taking the average of recent years would not substantially change the overall interpretation, however. Many thanks to Grace Chao for her assistance in compiling these data.
44. Among the threats to the validity of these findings is selection bias (who reports turnover is likely not unrelated to their organizational navigation strategy); different IDO calculation methods of turnover statistics; and heterogeneous IDO involvement in difficult settings (e.g., conflict environments) that might induce more rapid turnover. This is in addition, of course, to the small sample size, lack of panel data, and reliance on self-reporting of the numbers by IDOs.
45. Tendler 1997. See also Tendler and Freedheim 1994.
46. Rasul and Rogger 2016; Rasul, Rogger, and Williams 2017.
47. In private-sector contexts MIT's Zeynep Ton has described something like these equilibria as a firm's choice between a "Good Jobs" strategy that empowers employees to make decisions and compensates them well and a "Bad Jobs" strategy that does not (Ton 2014).
48. Gailmard and Patty 2007; Gailmard and Patty 2012; Andersen and Moynihan 2016; Bertelli and Lewis 2013.
49. Credit to Dan Nielson, and to a lesser extent the TV show *House*, for this enlightening avenue of inquiry.

50. Groopman 2007, 268.
51. Singh, Meyer, and Thomas 2014. Graber 2013 suggests this 5% rate may be low in reviewing a variety of error rates, with autopsy discrepancies in the 10–20% range, for example.
52. See, e.g., Gigerenzer 2015.

## Chapter 4

1. See, e.g., Resource Dependence Theory, and the long literature following Pfeffer and Salancik 1978.
2. This thus takes the intuition of Axelrod's famous "shadow of the future" (Axelrod 1984) but operates not through a probabilistic chance of repeated interaction but rather through a probabilistic chance of future sanction.
3. King 2015.
4. The notion that development organizations' delegation and control strategies are powerfully affected by the preferences and orientation of powerful principals builds from standard principal-agent models. Mark Buntaine has recently explored these relationships with regards to environmental project performance at multilateral development banks (Buntaine 2016).
5. Hawkins et al. 2006b; Hawkins and Jacoby 2006; Nielson and Tierney 2003b.
6. De Mesquita and Smith 2009; Barnett and Finnemore 2003.
7. Exploring the reasons for authorizing environment differences are beyond the scope of this book, which will largely take authorizing environments as a given. I focus instead on the consequences of differential authorizing environment insecurity. That said, exploring the antecedents of authorizing environment differences seems an important and understudied component of understanding IDO behavior and outcomes.
8. One example of recent cross-national differences in support for foreign aid can be found in IPSOS 2015: http://www.ipsos-na.com/news-polls/pressrelease.aspx?id=6983.
9. Huber and Shipan 2002; Carpenter 2001; Gilardi 2002.
10. United States aid expenditures still flow through the Foreign Assistance Act of 1961. This act, including amendments, runs 384 pages. U.S. Congress Committee on International Relations and U.S. Congress Committee on Foreign Relations 2003. For the United Kingdom there are a number of short pieces of legislation; these are Government of the United Kingdom 2002; Government of the United Kingdom 2006; Government of the United Kingdom 2014; Government of the United Kingdom 2015.
11. OECD 2017.
12. Anderson 2015.
13. Congressional Research Service 2006, 19. This 2006 survey is the most recent comprehensive review of earmarks; this figure is an estimate of earmarks in the Foreign Operations Appropriations Act of 2005, and combines "soft" (19.8%) and "hard" (53.4%) earmarks. Foreign operations budgets are put forward by a number of entities, including notably the State Department. However, as USAID tends to have more earmarks than others (interviews), this estimate is more likely to be low than high.
14. Biden-Palin Debate, October 2, 2008. In the debate the moderator, the late Gwen Ifill, asked "What promises—given the events of the week, the bailout plan, all of this, what promises have you and your campaigns made to the American people that you're not going to be able to keep?" Vice presidential candidate Joe Biden replied, "Well, the one thing we might have to slow down is a commitment we made to double foreign assistance. We'll probably have to slow that down."
15. Anderson 2015.
16. Elgot and Walker 2017.
17. Harris, Gramer, and Tamkin 2017.
18. The .18 percent number is OECD's official statistic for the U.S. government's official development assistance as of May 2017. OECD 2017. The .11 percent estimate here is the estimate of a 37 percent cut to .18 percent, as the Trump budget was reported to include a 37 percent cut to U.S. development assistance. Adams and Sokolsky 2017. This is likely a slight overstatement of the projected level of aid, as the cut is in absolute dollar rather than GNI terms (and

the economy, and thus the denominator, will likely to continue to grow while the numerator shrinks).

19. Since U.S. Freedom of Information Act and U.K. Freedom of Information requests are themselves public, this account could presumably be confirmed with USAID and DFID. For USAID the original FOIA request was F-00268-13; on appeal in 2015 (October 28, 2015) this became appeal A-00002-16. Upon USAID's granting the appeal (August 23, 2017) and reopening the case the remaining portion of F-00268-13 became F-00217-17. The U.K. FOI request was F2013-198 (this was a revision of F2013-165). I did request one additional document from DFID in 2016; this request (F2016-407) was filed on December 21, 2016 and the document delivered on February 7, 2017. Once again DFID's response was efficient and seemingly complete, in contrast to USAID's.

20. Wood and Lewis 2017.

21. Ibid., abstract.

22. Bozeman and Kingsley 1998; Singh 1986.

23. This concern is raised in the context of fragile states in OECD 2014.

24. This commonly takes the form of trading prospects—young players of great, but unproven, potential—for veteran players nearing the end of their peak years of productivity. Insecure general managers may effectively "sell low" on prospects while "buying high" on proven talent, the inverse of a sound investment strategy. See, e.g., Martinez 2013.

25. DFID 2013, 2.

26. OECD 2014, 13.

27. Meyer and Rowan 1977.

28. Dunleavy and Hood 1994; Hood 2004; Lynn 1998; Modell 2004; Oliver 1991.

29. US Government 1993, 2.b.1.

30. Authorizing environments are not the only source of legitimacy-seeking measurement; Buntaine, Parks, and Buch 2017 suggest that recipient countries play a key role in choosing less substantial, easier to monitor targets. This effect as they theorize it should not differentially affect different IDOs after controlling for recipient-country fixed effects (as the empirical models in Part II do), however.

31. E.g., Wynen and Verhoest 2016.

32. Clist 2016 makes a somewhat parallel point about pay-for-performance schemes.

33. DFID 2010b, 6; USAID 2014b, 16.

34. USAID Office of Inspector General 2016, 5.

35. OECD 2016, 59.

36. Ibid., 82.

37. Natsios 2010, 4.

38. Ibid. The MCC is the Millennium Challenge Corporation, another channel via which the U.S. government delivers foreign assistance. Natsios also notes that different development interventions are differentially tractable to management by measurement, arguing that "those development programs that are most transformational are the least measurable" (ibid.).

39. Noted in a casual conversation with a senior USAID staff member.

40. DFID has for many years had a central evaluation department and devoted substantial resources to project evaluation; rigorous evaluations available on DFID's website date from the mid-2000s: https://www.gov.uk/government/collections/evaluation-reports#evaluations-by-country. The USAID, by contrast, historically has had very little rigorous evaluation, though this has changed for the better in recent years (see, e.g., USAID 2016c).

41. These ratings are not publicly disclosed as a matter of course, but they were released by DFID in response to a Freedom of Information request. In any case, U.K. political authorizers have access to these ratings (or can easily get access for any project they might wish to examine).

42. USAID 2017; this is USAID and the U.S. Department of State's current "performance report" spreadsheet.

43. Ibid. The quoted statistic is row 41 (of 4,206).

44. US Office of Personnel Management 2016. Calculation by author from "Global Satisfaction Index" ratings, available online from https://www.fedview.opm.gov/2016/Ranking/.

45. UK Civil Service 2016. Calculation by author from "Civil Service People Survey 2016: All Organisation Scores," available online at https://www.gov.uk/government/uploads/system/

uploads/attachment_data/file/569034/civil_servcie_people_survey_2016_all_organisation_scores.xlsx.

46. Rose 2017. Rose also provides links to the Heritage Foundation and Republican 2015 ("Ryan budget") proposals.

47. Carpenter 2010; Carpenter 2001; Busuioc and Lodge 2015.

48. Interestingly, the MCC's reputation is often linked to the so-called MCC Effect; as the MCC uses quantitative metrics of eligibility, the MCC effect refers to the effort the MCC induces in developing countries to qualify for MCC funds. The MCC's reputation, and relative legitimacy, is thus linked to the use of metrics in the selection of recipients rather than the success of projects. The MCC Effect is defined by the MCC itself as "the incentives created by MCC's selection criteria and captured on its annual country scorecards." Millennium Challenge Corporation n.d.

49. This is Section 491 of the Foreign Assistance Act of 1961, as described in Lawson 2009. Lawson's Congressional Research Service report is a highly readable account of the Office of Transitional Initiatives (OTI), one of whose projects will be examined in chapter 6.

50. See, e.g., Adams and Sokolsky 2017, which argues that the Office of Foreign Disaster Assistance (OFDA), which operates under more flexible rules, is exceptionally effective relative to USAID's Bureau of Population, Refugees, and Migration.

51. More formally these are known as the multiple principals problem on the one hand and collective principals on the other. See Tirole 1994; Dewatripont, Jewitt, and Tirole 1999; Nielson and Tierney 2003; Dixit, Grossman, and Helpman 1997; Dixit 2002; Easterly 2002.

52. This basic insight from the principal-agent literature undergirds many of the pieces in Hawkins et al. 2006a.

53. Moe 1989 describes a series of U.S. cases where bureaucracies are intentionally designed to fail.

54. See, e.g., Alesina and Dollar 2000; Faye and Niehaus 2012; Kuziemko and Werker 2006; Tingley 2010; Fuchs, Dreher, and Nunnenkamp 2014; Dreher, Nunnenkamp, and Schmaljohann 2015.

55. Some aid is given as budget support, such as direct transfers to partner governments. Normally budget support also flows through discrete projects with particular ends; there are exceptions, however. In any case, any aid that is not delivered via a discrete project is by definition not included in the PPD.

56. See, e.g., Congressman Ted Poe's statements related to the Foreign Aid Transparency and Accountability Act of 2015 (HR 3766), which he sponsored.

57. Tendler 1975, 40.

## Chapter 5

1. As noted in the acknowledgments, I thank the European Commission, the United Kingdom's Department for International Development, the Asian Development Bank, the Global Fund for AIDS, Tuberculosis, and Malaria, and the German Development Bank for providing data. The number of recipients includes countries no longer in existence (e.g., Yugoslavia) and subnational units when they are specified as the recipient "country" (e.g., Tristan da Cunha).

2. The GFATM did not require a data agreement to release data; KfW and the EC did. KfW subsequently was kind enough to waive the provision requiring these evaluations remain confidential; the EC declined to do so. As such the PPD publicly available online excludes the EC and thus includes eight rather than nine IDOs.

3. GIZ was kind enough to respond with corrections, which were incorporated; JICA wished it to be made clear that these data were generated by me rather than by JICA and that JICA is not responsible for them.

4. Some IDOs report additional ratings for project success beyond overall success (e.g., sustainability, impact, performance of recipient country government in executing, etc.); these variables are included in the PPD where available.

5. This example is drawn from the World Bank's six-point rating system, as it is perhaps the best known. Some organizations evaluate projects on alternative Likert-type scales (such as a four-point scale, with 4 being best); I transform all scales to be on a consistent six-point scale and

employ IDO fixed effects in all models that use this six-point scale. I also employ a z-transformed version of this variable in the analysis when IDO fixed effects are absent. This process effectively de-means overall project success, just as employing IDO fixed effects would do. The generation of z-scores and the use of IDO fixed effects helps to avoid spurious interpretations by putting each IDO's project results on an identical parallel scale.

6. For more on these terms see OECD 2000; OECD 1991.
7. There is no reason to suspect that this variation would be along the axis of inquiry (the interaction of Navigation by Judgment and environmental predictability), however; as such we might expect this to add noise to the sample but not to directly bias results. The qualitative analysis provides an additional source of data on project success, one that allows for direct comparison of projects against a common standard.
8. Documents were accessed by making requests under the World Bank's Access to Information policy. Following an extended vetting and declassification process I was allowed to view physical documents in the reading room of the World Bank Group Archives, located in the basement of the World Bank's HQ building in Washington, DC.
9. The Paris Declaration on Aid Effectiveness 2005.
10. These data were coded from Appendix C of the published 2011 monitoring survey (OECD 2012), which summarized performance on all three waves. They are indicators 5a (PFM), 5b (procurement), 6 (PIU), 7 (predictability), and 8 (tied aid). The three waves of Paris Declaration surveys (2005, 2007, 2010) are averaged, in keeping with expert advice that these were effectively multiple mappings of the same facts, with insufficient time for organizations to change significantly between the first wave in 2005 and the last wave in 2010. As a result this measure is time-invariant. Empirical results in chapters 6 and 7 and Appendix II are robust to using any wave and dropping any wave of the survey.
11. This is a slight simplification; the indicator also penalizes overdisbursement, in fact calculating something like the absolute value of the deviation from prediction. In addition, disbursements are as-reported by partner government, adding inaccuracy borne of partner government data systems. See OECD 2012, 73–74 for more detail.
12. Celasun and Walliser 2008; Desai and Kharas 2010.
13. Parallel implementation units are separate operating units established at donors' insistence. These units use donor standards and thus give donors more control than would the routing of funds fully through recipient-country government systems.
14. For multilaterals (AsDB, WB, IFAD, EC), tied aid is not reported in the Paris Declaration monitoring surveys; in these cases the scale is an average of the remaining four measures. For those who may be troubled by some element above—e.g., a particular variable used in constructing the overall propensity to Navigate by Judgment scale—note that the empirical results in chapters 6 and 7 and Appendix II are robust to dropping either the authorizing environment constraint or devolution propensity components as well as to dropping any single variable used in constructing the scale.
15. This is for the full scale with all IDOs.
16. The survey has a concentration of nationals and internationals with expertise in Liberia and South Africa (as these are case study countries for my related qualitative work). The small number of individuals in any given country who can make expert interdonor comparisons limits the number of survey respondents.
17. This is the remaining N after removing surveys that were not substantively responsive or gave indications of nonsense answers; the two largest reasons for exclusion were (a) rating the Asian Development Bank despite stating that all relevant development-related work experience was in an African country (where the Asian Development Bank does not function); or (b) rating the survey's anchoring vignettes such that the text that indicated the greatest degree of Navigation by Judgment was evaluated as showing the same or less Navigation by Judgment than the vignette that indicated the greatest degree of Navigation by Judgment.
18. Leuffen, Shikano, and Walter 2012.
19. Correlation in the sample data, thus contracting only on the nine IDOs with results data in the PPD.
20. Weijer 2012; Institute of Development Studies 2014; Ghani, Lockhart, and Carnahan 2005.
21. World Bank 2006, 55.

22. Center for Systemic Peace 2014.
23. In the sample data.
24. In a small number (fewer than 5%) of cases, codes are assigned by me or by research assistants whom I supervised, based on the detailed contents of project reports. The full list of codes can be found at http://www.oecd.org/dac/stats/dacandcrscodelists.htm.
25. As a result, the mismatch between the periodicity of this data and the Paris Declaration monitoring surveys from which the propensity to Navigate by Judgment scale is drawn, which were conducted from 2005–2011, is also reduced.
26. Note that this 4.2 is for illustrative/intuitive purposes only, as not all donors in fact rate their projects on a six-point scale. If, e.g., a donor uses a five-point scale, I am "converting" these to a six-point scale; 1=1.2, 2=2.4, etc. Econometrically the use of IDO fixed effects and (where no fixed effect is taken) z-scores makes this transformation irrelevant, as a scalar transformation does not affect the shape of the distribution. It is much harder to discuss success in any meaningful, even semiintuitive way in the absence of a common scale; I transform all donor data to a six-point scale for this purpose.
27. The time-invariance of the Navigation by Judgment measure is not addressed directly in the tables below but considered (via, e.g., the use of time fixed effects) in Appendix II; see Appendix Table II.6.
28. The allusion is to Churchill in the U.K. House of Commons in November 1947; Churchill said in part, "it has been said that democracy is the worst form of Government except for all those other forms that have been tried from time to time." As quoted in Churchill and Langworth 2008, 573. Churchill is thus the popularizer, if by his own admission not the originator, of the expression.
29. See Appendix Table II.14 for a full list of scores by IDO.
30. The year 2012 was the most recent year available when the case study selection took place.
31. From 2007 to 2008 I served as Special Assistant to Liberia's then minister of finance (and subsequently the Africa Region for the International Monetary Fund), Antoinette Sayeh, playing a chief-of-staff-like role; from 2008 to 2009 I served as aid management advisor to her successor as Minister of Finance Augustine Ngafuan. I remained occasionally engaged with government business for a few years following the close of my full-time engagement in August 2009, and returned to Liberia a few times as a result.
32. This reporting occurs in part because the OECD Development Assistance Committee is the official "scorekeeper" of how much each nation spends in Official Development Assistance (ODA), a number that is calculated by summing all of a country's projects that are reported to the database. See http://www.oecd.org/dac/financing-sustainable-development/development-finance-data/ for the data itself.
33. Transcribers were contracted via a South African transcription service; all transcribers signed confidentiality agreements. This was not practicable for Liberia interviews, as Liberian English is difficult to understand for someone without substantial experience in Liberia. While it might have been possible to contract a Liberian or Liberian American, it is a relatively small pool of relatively elite Liberians who might be able to transcribe interviews; I was worried about the interconnectedness of elite Liberians with Liberian government and donor officials, and thus retaining confidentiality. A few Liberia interviews with expatriates were transcribed by the South African transcribers.
34. A small handful of individuals wished not to be recorded; there were occasional technical or logistical challenges that precluded recording; and in one or two cases it became clear that recording the interview was interfering with an interviewee's candor and I thus turned off the recorder. In all these cases I took copious written notes, which I then relied on in analyzing the data.
35. Dixit 2002, 724.

## Chapter 6

1. This chapter title is inspired by Graham Greene's book on Liberia of the same name, inasmuch as Liberia is my case study example selected because of its 1804-ness, or lack of tractability to a Google Maps–like solution. Greene 1936.

2. The models in Table 6.1 do not incorporate a base term for IDO propensity to Navigate by Judgment. As a time-invariant measure at the IDO level, Navigation by Judgment is collinear to—that is, varies in tandem with—IDO fixed effects. Appendix Table II.3 demonstrates the robustness of the results on the interaction term and on the primary effect of environmental unpredictability to adding the base term and dropping IDO fixed effects.

3. E.g., Chauvet, Collier, and Duponchel 2010.

4. Quote from Corder 2012. An unelected interim chairman ran Liberia for three years between Taylor and Johnson Sirleaf; Johnson Sirleaf thus was Taylor's immediate successor as president, but not as head of state. Taylor won the 1997 Liberian general election using one of most attention-grabbing, honest, and content-rich campaign slogans I'm aware of: "He Killed my Ma, He Killed my Pa, I'll Vote for Him"—making clear that were he not to be elected, active conflict would resume. Polgreen 2006.

5. Challoner and Forget 2011.

6. Liberia Institute of Statistics and Geo-Information Services (LISGIS) 2008, iii.

7. Radelet 2007.

8. International Monetary Fund 2013.

9. Interview 36, 6/25/13; interview 11, 6/10/13; interview 21, 6/4/13. The interview numbering scheme and list of interviewees can be found in Appendix I.

10. Kay 2014.

11. Interview 23, 6/11/13; interview 29, 6/7/13.

12. Interview 29, 6/7/13.

13. Interview 29, 6/7/13; interview 23, 6/11/13. Further underscoring the greater politicization of USAID than DFID, while USAID staff are accountable to (politically appointed) U.S. ambassadors, DFID personnel are not directly accountable to (politically appointed) U.K. ambassadors.

14. Interview 29, 6/7/13; interview 23, 6/11/13.

15. Interview 29, 6/7/13; interview 24, 6/4/13.

16. Interview 29, 6/7/13; interview 23, 6/11/13.

17. Interview 2, 6/25/13; interview 21, 6/4/13; interview 36, 6/25/13.

18. Interview 29, 6/7/13; interview 23, 6/11/13; interview 24, 6/4/13.

19. Interview 21, 6/4/13; interview 2, 6/25/13.

20. Interview 29, 6/7/13; interview 24, 6/4/13; interview 21, 6/4/13.

21. Amount from USAID 2008. The precise amount of the award is USD$51,999,318.

22. Interview 5, 6/6/13; also supported by, e.g., John Snow International (JSI) documents. Johns Hopkins University Center for Communication Programs and Management Sciences for Health 2010.

23. Interview 31, 6/2/13; interview 13, 6/1/13; Interview 5, 6/6/13; interview 11, 6/10/13.

24. USAID and JSI 2009, 5. Released under Freedom of Information Act request #F-00268-13, 4th interim response, March 18, 2015. This report is typical of RBHS reports as a whole.

25. Ibid., 53.

26. Interview 25, 6/6/13. This focus on the quantitative is also supported by RBHS annual reports, e.g., Barh et al. 2011.

27. Barh et al. 2011, 9

28. DFID 2007a, confirmed in DFID 2010a. DFID FOI Disclosure F2-13-198, disclosure 10 and 12 respectively. The project's logical framework (DFID 2007a) is in fact undated, but is assigned a 2007 date here because of the project's formal start in July 2007, according to DFID 2009c.

29. DFID 2007a. To be specific, in the logical framework it was projected that by 2010 the project would be considered a "success" if there were a 10% reduction in maternal mortality and a 5–10% reduction in child mortality relative to 2007 baselines. By the time of the project completion report (DFID 2010a) these numbers had risen to a 15% reduction in maternal mortality and a 10% reduction in child mortality.

30. Interview 24, 6/4/13; interview 29, 6/7/13.

31. This was USD$8 million; Interview 24, 6/4/13.

32. Interview 2, 6/25/13; interview 24, 6/4/13; interview 29, 6/7/13.

33. Interview 23, 6/11/13; interview 34, 6/13/13.
34. Interview 11, 6/10/13.
35. Quote from interview 150, 12/28/15; supported by interview 10, 6/11/13; interview 24, 6/4/13.
36. Interview 11, 6/10/13; interview 24, 6/4/13; interview 34, 6/13/13; interview 15, 6/13/13.
37. Interview 15, 6/13/13; while I have seen the FARA agreement(s) they are not publicly available.
38. USAID 2013. The FARA payment triggers are not public; however, they are alluded to (or rather, FARA targets are alluded to, which I am inferring are payment targets) in public reports, e.g., the public midterm review of FARA cited here.
39. USAID 2011, sec. 317.6.
40. Interview 15, 6/13/13; interview 11, 6/10/13. Revisions have indeed occurred, though the process for doing so has been somewhat lengthy.
41. While external support to the OFM had continued beyond the DFID-funded project, the DFID project was instrumental in getting the OFM up and running. E.g., interview 11, 6/10/13; interview 34, 6/13/13; interview 24, 6/4/13; interview 23, 6/11/13; interview 22, 6/11/13.
42. E.g., interview 21, 6/4/13
43. Sirleaf 2009.
44. Interview 6, 6/7/13.
45. Interview 24, 6/4/13.
46. Interview 5, 6/6/13; interview 35, 6/11/13.
47. Interview 11, 6/10/13; interview 24, 6/4/13; interview 23, 6/11/13.
48. Interview 24, 6/4/13.
49. Interview 29, 6/7/13.
50. Interview 34, 6/13/13; interview 8, 6/9/13.
51. Interview 5, 6/6/13; interview 25, 6/6/13; interview 34, 6/13/13.
52. Interview 37, 5/27/13.
53. Author interview with Dahn, 2013. Dahn was Minister as of December 2017. Dahn became minister of health in 2015.
54. Hughes, Glassman, and Gwenigale 2012, 7.
55. Interview 34, 6/13/13; interview 24, 6/4/13.
56. Interview 24, 6/4/13; interview 29, 6/7/13.
57. Interview 34, 6/4/13.
58. Interview 23, 6/11/13; interview 34, 6/4/13; interview 24, 6/4/13.
59. Interview 34, 6/13/13; interview 23, 6/11/13; interview 37, 5/27/13; interview 11, 6/10/13.
60. Interview 11, 6/10/13; interview 34, 6/13/13.
61. Interview 11, 6/10/13.
62. Interview 34, 6/13/13; interview 11, 6/10/13.
63. Interview 11, 6/10/13; interview 19, 6/11/13; interview 37, 5/27/13.
64. Interview 24, 6/4/13.
65. Interview 15, 6/13/13; interview 11, 6/10/13; interview 34, 6/13/13.
66. Interview 34, 6/13/13.
67. Interview 23, 6/11/13; interview 34, 6/13/13.
68. This statement by Gwenigale in a summer 2013 interview was in response to a question by me asking him to compare the Pooled Fund and FARA.
69. Response to Ebola is a case in which my theory would predict the gap in performance would be relatively small inasmuch as the existence of Ebola was externally observable "hard" information to which the need to adjust was clear; it could be seen by HQ and political authorizers, not just field personnel. As such it is a case where response from above is possible, unlike the perhaps more common case in which the stimulus to which the program need adapt is soft information that can only be perceived by field-level personnel. Nonetheless it allows for illustration of differences between the mechanisms, which evolved in the shadow of differential political authorizing environment constraint.
70. Interview 150, 12/28/15.

71. Interview 153, 1/28/16. In an email subsequent to the interview, the interviewee described two missed targets and confirmed that at least one was while the government of Liberia was grappling with Ebola. This during-Ebola missed payment was related to conducting maternal death audits, a way of investigating the causes of maternal mortality. In the interview itself, interviewee 153 suggested that Ebola response shifted the government's attention from other health matters, a view echoed by others (e.g., interview 152, 1/26/16; interview 151, 1/22/16) This was also true of a related pay-for-performance mechanism that came online in 2014, a Sector Performance Agreement. All the quantitative outcome targets in the agreement were missed in 2015; rather than improve, many of the contracted outcomes actually declined from 2014 and 2015. USAID responded by "re-baselining" the indicators and extending the period over which performance needed to take place but made no payments. Interview 153, 1/28/16.

72. Interview 153, 1/28/16.

73. Interview 152, 1/26/16; interview 153, 1/28/16

74. This includes, but is not limited to, the World Bank's Ebola Trust Fund, the single largest Ebola funding mechanism. Interview 151, 1/22/16; interview 152, 1/26/16.

75. Interview 24, 6/4/13; interview 29, 6/7/13; interview 21, 6/4/13.

76. Tony Blair Africa Governance Initiative 2011, 1.

77. Contract #DFD-I-00-05-00220, Task Order #3, awarded by USAID OTI to Development Alternatives International (DAI), the implementing contractor; signed September 12, 2005.

78. This was not the sole focus of the project, but rather one of three objectives, the one to receive the bulk of funding. The formal objective was to "Assist the Government of Liberia and other key actors to improve capacity in such areas as effective planning, budgeting, communication, and coordination with relevant counterparts," accomplishing this through "(1) short-term technical assistance (STTA) to key GOL [Government of Liberia] ministries and civil society organizations, and (2) small grants to ministries and local partners." Nicolls and Kupperstein 2007, 2.

79. Interview 70, 5/31/13.

80. These are DAIM 102 and DAIM 7, respectively. As reported by the BRDG "Yearbook" list of Liberia grant activities. BRDG 2008.

81. Interview 52, 6/4/13; interview 55, 5/29/13; interview 64, 6/19/13.

82. Interview 52, 6/4/13.

83. Interview 70, 5/31/13; interview 60, 6/27/13.

84. Interview 52, 6/4/13; interview 47, 6/4/13; interview 41, 6/10/13.

85. Interview 44, 6/6/13; interview 57, 6/5/13; interview 62, 6/10/13; interview 58, 6/10/13.

86. Interview 45, 6/10/13.

87. Interview 58, 6/10/13; interview 41, 6/10/13.

88. Interview 47, 6/4/13; interview 41, 6/10/13; interview 48, 6/12/13; interview 44, 6/6/13; interview 45, 6/10/13; interview 64, 6/19/13.

89. Interview 41, 6/10/13.

90. Interview 58, 6/10/13; interview 48, 6/12/13; interview 44, 6/6/13.

91. Interview 60, 6/27/13; interview 70, 5/31/13; interview 64, 6/19/13.

92. Interview 60, 6/3/13.

93. Interview 60, 6/3/13.

94. I have seen a number of these grant files, though they were shared on the condition that I not make specific attribution to them. The general process is described in BRDG's public Grants Administration and Procurement Guide Handbook. Development Alternatives Inc. and USAID 2006.

95. I do not have access to the activity reports of DAIM 102 and DAIM 7, but I am describing what likely would have been in these reports based on general structure outlined by and a reading of the project's administrative manual. Ibid.

96. Interview 45, 6/25/13; interview 41, 6/19/13.

97. In order to develop the strategy, CISCAB brought in a series of short-term consultants to focus on problem analysis and strategy development. Following the strategy's completion, CISCAB shifted formally from a capacity-building program (CISCAB) to a program focused on the implementation of the project (CISREP) until its close in May 2010.

98. DFID 2006, 5. Formally CISCAB's goal was "to help to rebuild and improve the Liberian Civil Service's contributions to effective governance and service provision."
99. Government of Liberia 2008.
100. Adam Smith International 2007, 68.
101. See, e.g., Adam Smith International 2009.
102. Interview 54, 6/5/13; Interview 67, 6/24/13; interview 43, 6/25/13.
103. The roots of DFID's CISCAB went back to 2004, when DFID personnel participated in the design of the EU's institutional support program; a seconded DFID employee, Chris Gabelle, went on to manage the EU's program. Interview 56, 6/4/13; interview 43, 6/25/13. Seeing problems in Sierra Leone as growing out of Liberia, DFID staff began to conceive of supporting reform of the civil service in Liberia as they were doing in Sierra Leone; DFID also saw civil service reform as an area of comparative advantage. Interview 56, 6/4/13; interview 43,6/25/13. Design work began in earnest after the election of 2005 led by Gabelle and a senior DFID governance advisor (Garth Glentworth OBE). This was a long process, involving what both government and DFID actors saw as extensive consultations; Gabelle's substantial Liberia experience played a significant role in the project design. Interview 56, 6/4/13; interview 67, 6/24/13; interview 43, 6/25/13; interview 54, 6/5/13. An initial focus on capacity building was broadened into a more systematic reform program.
104. Interview 54, 6/5/13; interview 38, 6/7/13; interview 56, 6/4/13. The core implementation team was the team formed by Adam Smith International (ASI) and Subah Belleh, the local partner, to implement the project. Following the award to ASI there was a three-month inception period in which the CISCAB core team revisited the project design in conversation with the main project beneficiaries. Interview 54, 6/5/13.
105. Interview 67, 6/2/13; interview 54, 6/5/13.
106. Most notably, revision of the project from CISCAB to CISREP and the replacement of the ATI project team lead. The team leader left of her own accord, and in such a way that it is not clear she was fully aware that this was by popular consensus. Interview 67, 6/24/13; interview 54, 6/5/13.
107. Interview 54, 6/5/13; interview 38, 6/7/13; interview 56, 6/4/13.
108. The DFID's intervention cost approximately USD$4.3 million at the exchange rates of the time (2.73 million GBP), whereas USAID spent just over USD$4 million in support of government; this latter figure is a back-of-the-envelope calculation. A little under 65% of BRDG's funded activities went to the government sector, based on my calculations drawn from the almost-final project database (the last version I could locate). Thus, assigning overheads proportional to spending, a bit over USD$4 million of BRDG's USD$6.4 million total budget is attributable to supporting the government of Liberia in its activities and capacity building. This proportionality is needed because I could identify only USD$3.2 million of actual activity-by-activity spending; according to one interviewee (interview 64, 6/19/13) it's entirely plausible that the remaining monies were consumed by overheads—that is, costs over and above the fees and expenses of consultants and activities (e.g., OTI and DAI salaries, indirect overheads/fees, etc.). While I lack the detailed information to compare this to CISCAB overheads—and thus cannot say with certainty whether BRDG and CISCAB were grossly different in this regard—this strikes me as a surprisingly large percentage of "foreign aid" to not substantially actually benefit the country in any direct fiscal sense.
109. Interview 38, 6/7/13; interview 54, 6/5/13; interview 55, 5/29/13. See also Government of Liberia 2008.
110. That is, mid-2013; I cannot speak to what happened to the plan afterward, but I am not aware of it having been abandoned (that is, I have an absence of evidence rather than evidence of absence). On the relevance of the plan to continued activities: Interview 65, 6/10/13; interview 55, 5/29/13; interview 50, 6/6/13; interview 40, 6/5/13.
111. Interview 53, 10/3/13; interview 55, 5/29/13; interview 42, 5/31/13; interview 49, 5/30/13; interview 67, 6/24/13.
112. Interview 61, 6/7/13. This reform would have limited the number of layers of each ministry's senior leadership that would be staffed with political appointees rather than career civil servants. The proposal was essentially to move Liberia from its "American" system with

many layers of appointments to a "British" system with permanent secretaries and fewer political appointees.

113. Interview 59, 6/12/13; interview 61, 6/7/13; interview 38, 6/7/13; interview 50, 6/5/13; interview 66, 6/7/13; interview 51, 6/11/13.

114. Among these were tensions between Liberian beneficiaries (interview 39, 6/12/13; interview 61, 6/7/13; interview 43, 6/25/13; interview 59, 6/12/13; interview 51, 6/11/13), particularly the Civil Service Administration and Governance Reform Commission, as well as tensions within the contractor Adam Smith International's team (interview 38, 6/7/13; interview 67, 6/24/13; interview 39, 6/12/13), particularly between international and local consultants who were both part of the team. This latter set of tensions eventually led to the replacement of the head of the implementing team.

115. Interview 55, 5/29/13; interview 56, 6/4/13. I have seen, but do not have a copy of, this letter, which is dated November 13, 2009 (before CISCAB closed in March 2010, but after the announcement that it would not be continued).

116. Interview 56, 6/4/13.

117. Interview 50, 6/5/13; interview 43, 6/25/13; interview 56, 6/4/13; interview 55, 5/29/13.

118. Interview 39, 6/12/13.

119. Interview 46, 6/11/13.

120. Indeed, it's somewhat surprising that—five years after the project ended—a number of beneficiaries *could* specifically recall BRDG and, unprompted, name personnel involved, despite the modest size of the support each individual beneficiary received.

121. Interview 55, 5/29/13; interview 58, 6/10/13; interview 57, 6/5/13; interview 62, 6/10/13; interview 65, 5/31/13. The general impression was that it was the government equivalent of a PhD student's $300 travel grant; appreciated, but modest in impact.

122. Interview 57, 6/5/13.

123. Interview 58, 6/10/13.

124. Interview 64, 6/19/13; interview 70, 5/31/13; interview 68, 6/19/13.

125. Interview 57, 6/25/13; interview 55, 6/12/13; interview 40, 6/5/13. The only example of a BRDG program or process (rather than equipment or supplies) that I could identify which continued to operate following the project's end is the Songhai agricultural center, which was initially supported by BRDG funding.

126. Interview 56, 6/4/13.

127. DFID 2006, 27.

128. Interview 38, 6/7/13; interview 67, 6/24/13; interview 49, 5/30/13; interview 53, 10/3/13.

129. Interview 10, 5/29/13. The interviewee was speaking about a different USAID intervention, not one of the projects examined in this book.

130. Interview 56, 6/4/13.

## Chapter 7

1. For the purposes of these analyses by "sector" I mean the OECD CRS's 5-digit "purpose" codes, rather than the 3-digit codes, commonly referred to as sector codes. Purpose codes are nested in 3-digit sectors, which are in turn nested in the 2-digit "broad sectors." For example, all Health codes begin with 12, including both "Health, general" (121) and "Basic Health" (122). Within "Health, general" is both "Medical research" (12182) and "Medical services" (12191). The full list of codes can be found at http://www.oecd.org/dac/stats/dacandcrscodelists.htm.

2. See, e.g., Olken 2007.

3. For the less externally verifiable sectors panel, this is the same as model 4 of Table 7.2, which includes all administration and management sectors and thus the sectors examined in models 1, 2, and 3 of Table 7.2. As was the case for Figure 6.1 in chapter 6, Figure 7.1 can be used for the limited purpose of comparing the slopes of the lines in both graphs rather than comparing the y-intercepts (as the direct effect of Navigation by Judgment is collinear to IDO fixed effects).

4. World Bank 2013.

5. Statistics South Africa 2012.
6. Ibid. on population; World Bank 2013 on land ownership.
7. If breastfeeding, mothers and/or children may also receive treatment for the duration of breastfeeding. This was, and is, standard practice under the treatment protocols commonly referred to as "Plan A" and "Plan B" for PMTCT, which was South African policy throughout the period examined here. In 2013 South Africa shifted to "Plan B+," which has pregnant women continue on treatment indefinitely. One particularly clear explanation of the differences between these three treatment protocols can be found in UNICEF 2012, 3.
8. Interview 117, 7/25/13. The prevention of mother-to-child transmission of HIV is less and less one-off these days, with longer-term tracking; see, e.g., Radin et al. 2017. That said, this "short period of time" statement was broadly accurate during the period in question.
9. The interview comments regarding PEPFAR focus largely on PEPFAR implemented via USAID; however, in some cases it was not clear whether interviewees' references to PEPFAR were as implemented by CDC, USAID, other U.S. agencies, or a combination. As such I use the generic PEPFAR moniker.
10. Kaiser Family Foundation 2014.
11. USD$500 million from Katz, Bassett, and Wright 2013. The PMTCT funding number comes from reviewing PEPFAR annual country operational plans over the period.
12. Interview 117, 7/25/13.
13. Interview 118, 7/18/13.
14. Interview 142, 6/14/13; interview 130, 7/26/13.
15. Interview 134, 7/17/13.
16. Interview 107, 8/2/13.
17. PEPFAR 2004, sec. I.1.
18. Ibid.
19. Interview 122, 8/5/13; interview 130, 7/26/13.
20. Email communication further to interview 142, 6/14/13.
21. Interview 125, 7/31/13; under PEPFAR 1 these targets were in fact different than those of the National Department of Health, further underscoring the parallel nature of the health system. Interview 124, 8/5/13.
22. Interview 128, 7/24/13.
23. Interview 112, 7/23/13.
24. Republic of South Africa National Department of Health 2011.
25. Interview 124, 8/5/13; interview 123, 8/15/13; interview 125, 7/31/13; also supported by the independent mid-term review of SARRAH. Griffiths et al. 2014.
26. Interview 141, 7/16/13.
27. The first such project (DFID Project Reference #104938) began in 2003. The MSP (DFID Project Reference #104938) was designed with the goal of "strengthening South Africa's national HIV and AIDS response and reducing the impacts of the epidemic" (DFID 2008, 6). It aimed to do this by providing technical assistance to the South African federal ministries (departments) of Health, Social Development, and Defence. DFID 2008. The project additionally funded a range of NGOs implementing services and advocating for a change in national policy, as well as research around PMTCT among other matters.
28. Shortly after Hogan became minister of health in 2008, DFID added 15 million GBP to the MSP project in the form of the RRHF. Interview 127, 9/24/13; interview 125, 7/31/13. While the RRHF was not technically a separate project, it is often viewed and discussed as if it was by South African government and donor representatives alike.
29. DFID Project Reference #200325.
30. Interview 123, 8/15/13.
31. E.g., Interview 126, 9/4/13; interview 133, 10/25/13; interview 123, 8/15/13; interview 107, 8/2/13; interview 121, 8/5/13.
32. Interview 133, 10/25/13; this view was echoed by interview 123, 8/15/13.
33. Interview 139, 7/31/13; interview 125, 7/31/13; interview 123, 8/15/13; interview 124, 8/5/13; interview 126, 9/4/13.
34. Author interview with Gorna, 2013. The mutual friend was Zackie Achmat, head of the Treatment Action Campaign (TAC); an advocacy nonprofit, the TAC famously sued the

government of South Africa to force government initiation of PMTCT treatment, winning their case in 2002.

35. Interview 125, 7/31/13.
36. Interview 112, 7/23/13; interview 117, 7/25/13; interview 116, 8/16/13.
37. Interview 116, 8/16/13.
38. Interview 116, 8/16/13.
39. Interview 122, 8/5/13.
40. Interview 111, 8/12/13.
41. Interview 122, 8/5/13; interview 121, 8/5/13.
42. Interview 122, 8/5/13.
43. Interview 121, 8/5/13; interview 137, 8/12/13; interview 123, 8/15/13.
44. Interview 143, 7/10/13; interview 116, 8/16/13.
45. Interview 116, 8/16/13; interview 117, 7/25/13; interview 143, 7/10/13; interview 122, 8/5/13.
46. Interview 130, 7/26/13; interview 116, 8/16/13; interview 122, 8/5/13.
47. Interview 116, 8/16/13.
48. Interview 129, 8/1/13; interview 121, 8/5/13; interview 122, 8/5/13.
49. A similar point was occasionally made about contracting firms, with those from academic origins described as weaker on systems and financial management but better on understanding data. Interview 143, 7/10/13; interview 142, 6/14/13.
50. Interview 117, 7/25/13.
51. PEPFAR arguably was concerned with national health systems only starting with PEPFAR 2.
52. Goga, Dinh, and Jackson 2010.
53. Barron et al. 2013.
54. New child infections fell from 33,000 to 16,000 while births to HIV+ women fell from 270,000 to 260,000. UNAIDS 2013.
55. Interview 133, 10/25/13; interview 127, 9/24/13; interview 123, 8/15/13. Overspend projection from UK Department for International Development (DFID) 2009b.
56. Author interview with Gorna, 2013. Gorna did feel there were some satisfactory elements of the project, though the project as a whole was a disappointment.
57. PEPFAR 2008b. These numbers are for counseling and testing and thus are measuring something distinct from the UNAIDS statistics quoted above, which focus on drug delivery.
58. PEPFAR 2008a. It is possible this 333,100 is not all unique women; some women had multiple pregnancies during the period and are thus counted twice.
59. Interview 128, 7/24/13.
60. Interview 120, 8/14/13; interview 123, 8/15/13; interview 133, 10/25/13; interview 125, 7/31/13.
61. Interview 125, 7/31/13; interview 120, 8/14/13; interview 117, 7/25/13; interview 124, 8/5/13. There is a dissenting view here from some South African National Department of Health actors, who feel the A-Plan was "siloed" and ineffective. Interview 137, 8/12/13; interview 131, 8/12/13.
62. The RRHF was administratively technically a part of the MSP, though all existing MSP activities ceased by December 2008, with separate RRHF activities commencing (DFID 2008). DFID's project completion report argues that "while the outcomes of Outputs 1–4 [those focused on the MSP proper] were mixed in their levels of success, Output 5 in the last year of the programme—which almost exclusively focused on the RRHF—shifted the programme's total impact." DFID 2009b, 5.
63. Interview 124, 8/5/13.
64. E.g., interview 137, 8/12/13; interview 117, 7/25/13; interview 125, 7/31/13.
65. Interview 117, 7/25/13.
66. Interview 132, 7/31/13; interview 117, 7/25/13; interview 127, 9/24/13; interview 123, 8/15/13.
67. Interview 117, 7/25/13.
68. Interview 124, 8/5/13.
69. Interview 109, 9/12/13; interview 111, 8/12/13; interview 128, 7/24/13.
70. Interview 111, 8/12/13.

71. Interview 111, 8/12/13.
72. Interview 125, 7/31/13.
73. Interview 137, 8/12/13; interview 122, 8/5/13; interview 130, 7/26/13; interview 121, 8/5/13.
74. Interview 111, 8/12/13.
75. Interview 93, 7/18/13.
76. Author interview with Chipkin, 2013. PARI is a Johannesburg-based independent research institute—what in the United States might be called a think tank.
77. DFID Project Reference #104886.
78. USAID Contract #674-C-00-05-00001-00.
79. DFID's CMTP stated its goal as to "consolidate accountable local democracy and pro-poor service delivery." The purpose is to promote the development of effective and efficient municipalities." DFID 2003, 1. USAID LGSP's Phase 2 focused on efforts to "improve municipal planning skills and operating systems to increase effectiveness, transparency and accountability; and increase the revenue stream of selected municipalities ensuring that citizens meet their obligations" (RTI and LGSP 2006).
80. USAID 2004, F-2. Acquired via Freedom of Information Act Request.
81. LGSP Makhado municipality action plan (AP220905) as approved June 17, 2005, p. 3. Acquired via anonymous source but producible on request.
82. Ibid.
83. Ibid.
84. Makhado (NP344) Deployment Plan, undated but likely 2006. Makhado's specific dates for debt management are 5/31/06 and 3/16/06. Acquired via anonymous source but producible on request.
85. Reports from contractors (various), acquired via anonymous source but producible (with redacted names) on request. Confirmed via interview 88, 8/1/13.
86. Linkd 2009, 18. Acquired via DFID FOI F2016-407.
87. The South African government program referred to is (to quote the report) the "Municipal Finance Management and Technical Assistance Programme (MFMTAP) which was run by National Treasury and managed by the Development Bank of Southern Africa (DBSA). The bulk of MFMTAP financing came from the World Bank ($15 million U.S.) and GTZ. The purpose of the mostly international Financial Advisors (FA) was to provide technical advice and support in the implementation of the then newly promulgated Municipal Finance Management Act (MFMA)" (Linkd 2009, 20).
88. DFID 2004; Output 2, page 5. Acquired via anonymous source but producible on request. This becomes "policy and implementation capacities established and Municipal Manager offices operational within the municipalities" by DFID 2005; see the November 2005 CMTP annual review (v 1.3; acquired via Freedom of Information request; F2013-198 Disclosure 16).
89. Ibid., 7.
90. Ibid.
91. Ibid., 7–8.
92. Interview 82, 8/1/13. The interviewee was contrasting their experiences with DFID's municipal governance project with their experiences working for a variety of other organizations, not USAID specifically.
93. DFID 2007b, 8–9. Acquired via Freedom of Information request; F2013-198 Disclosure 17.
94. Interview 72, 7/31/13; interview 74, 7/30/13.
95. Interview 72, 7/31/13; interview 74, 7/30/13.
96. Interview 77, 9/17/13.
97. Interview 77, 9/17/13.
98. Author interview with Thomas, 2013.
99. USAID's intervention eventually did place advisors briefly in municipalities; on some accounts this was in response to pressure from South African officials observing the relative success of the two projects. Interview 97, 8/15/13. These USAID advisors still faced quite specific reporting regimes based on externally observable and quantifiable outputs and were far less able to employ metis or use soft information than their DFID project cousins.

100. Interview 103, 7/30/13.
101. E.g., interview 93, 7/18/13; interview 73, 7/19/13.
102. Author interview with Matomela, 2013.
103. Interview 88, 8/1/13.
104. Interview 86, 7/30/13. This official specifically ascribed LGSP's failing in part to tackling of things like anticorruption via remote training, thus threatening entrenched local interests.
105. Interview 85, 11/12/13.
106. Author interview with Layte, 2013.
107. This continued in the later phases of LGSP, which did involve placing some trainers in municipalities after many years of largely fruitless training. In the later phases of the project, resident advisors would report on meetings held, guidelines drafted, and other such externally observable and verifiable indicators. Interview 82, 8/1/13.
108. Interview 88, 8/1/13.
109. Ibid.
110. Interview 86, 7/30/13.
111. Interview 82, 8/1/13.
112. Interview 81, 8/1/13. There is one additional minor exception—multiple actors thought LGSP's support for municipal HIV/AIDS strategies, which was added late in the project, had a positive impact. Interview 80, 7/22/13; interview 84, 7/22/13; interview 79, 8/5/13; interview 103, 7/30/13. This fairly minor element of the program had overlaps with USAID (and the broader U.S. government's) PEPFAR funds, and thus is less about municipal governance and capacity building along the lines of the program's original intent. Given that this small component of LGSP was effectively adopted and directed by PEPFAR, it seems inappropriate to think of it as a part of LGSP's success or failure.
113. This stylized conclusion comes from an analysis of the panel data to emerge from the series of "General Report of the Auditor-General on Local Government," issued by the office of the South African Auditor General annually.
114. Interview 102, 8/13/13; interview 97, 8/15/13; interview 98, 8/14/13. The municipal manager in question had been in his current role when the advisor was present in the municipality.
115. Interview 81, 8/1/13.
116. Interview 103, 7/30/13; interview 72, 7/31/13; interview 98, 8/14/13; interview 75, 7/25/13; interview 76, 7/29/13.
117. Interview 74, 7/30/13; interview 72, 7/31/13. These actors didn't make the comparison to LGSP, only the statement about the importance of being resident.
118. Interview 92, 7/24/13; interview 102, 8/13/13.
119. DFID 2009a.
120. Interview 103, 7/30/13; interview 75, 7/25/13; interview 76, 7/29/13; 97, 8/15/13; interview 103, 7/30/13. Both DFID and South African government interviewees noted the influence of DFID's model. Indeed, on two interviewees' views it was Project Consolidate that influenced USAID's LGSP to move to resident advisors. Interview 81, 8/1/13; interview 102, 8/13/13. In a sense, then, the alteration of USAID's project to shift toward advisors near the end of the project was influenced by DFID's project.
121. Interview 92, 7/24/13; interview 103, 7/30/13.
122. Interview 103, 7/30/13.
123. Interview 75, 7/25/13; interview 103, 7/30/13. While these funds were technically administered by a steering committee, these interviewees claimed Deloitte effectively managed the allocation, with the committee acting as a rubber stamp.
124. Linkd 2009, 38. DFID Freedom of Information disclosure F2016-407.
125. Interview 93, 7/18/13; interview 103, 7/30/13; interview 90, 8/2/13.
126. Interview 88, 8/1/13.
127. This turnover was mentioned by almost every individual interviewed. A partial list: interview 79, 8/5/13; interview 95, 8/1/13; interview 78, 7/22/13; interview 103, 7/30/13; interview 88, 8/1/13; interview 73, 7/19/13.
128. Interview 88, 8/1/13.
129. Interview 76, 7/29/13; interview 103, 7/30/13. It is fair to note the independent evaluation of CMTP (Linkd 2009) notes the steering committee did not meet as frequently as

intended, with the "technical committee" becoming the de facto steering committee. The LGSP had a somewhat similar steering committee, but only one actor even made mention of the structure. Interview 85, 11/12/13.

130. Interview 81, 8/1/13.
131. Author interview with Layte, 2013.
132. Interview 85, 11/12/13.
133. The LGSP project and RTI did, in fact, consult frequently with DPLG, particularly as Project Consolidate—the South African Government's municipal capacity effort—became more prominent and RTI sought to keep LGSP aligned to, and supportive of, national government policy. Interview 97, 8/15/13; interview 85, 11/12/13. It was nonetheless further from DPLG than was CMTP.
134. That is, the component examined here; as noted above, what I call "LGSP" here is in fact LGSP phase 2, the part of LGSP run as an RTI project.
135. Creative Associates 2004, 28.
136. Interview 86, 7/30/13.
137. Creative Associates 2004.

## Chapter 8

1. Interview 82, 8/1/13. I examine this systematically in the South Africa data because of the much greater rate of full interview transcripts among South African case interviewees as compared to Liberian interviewees, as explained in chapter 5. There are no mentions of the "House of Commons," "House of Lords," "Senate," or "House"; in all cases the legislative body is mentioned as a whole. The U.K. Parliament and U.S. Congress exercise very different degrees of oversight, of course; what is true of this comparison also applies to references to USAID and DFID's respective Headquarters (HQ). The DFID's HQ is spoken about with much less foreboding, and much less sense that it casts a shadow over activities and decisions, than is USAID's HQ.
2. Interview 87, 9/20/13.
3. "It is all about the budget, right, the budget battle and the dream of federal agencies is that they could get, put together projects that year in and year out, programmes that year in and year out would have predictable funding, but every year the budget fight is a new adventure" (ibid.).
4. Interview 7a, 5/23/13.
5. Ibid.
6. Interview 49, 5/30/13.
7. Interview 44, 6/6/13.
8. Interview 81, 8/1/13.
9. Interview 12, 6/4/13.
10. Interview 109, 9/12/13.
11. In this ellipsis I asked the follow-up question: "Do you think that, in addition to being aggravating and frustrating to have that relationship, do you think it actually constrains the performance of projects?"
12. Interview 124, 8/5/13.
13. Interview 44, 6/6/13; interview 45, 6/10/13.
14. Interview 45, 6/10/13.
15. Interview 44, 6/6/13; interview 48, 6/12/13.
16. Interview 45, 6/10/13; interview 44, 6/6/13.
17. Interview 56, 6/4/13.
18. Leonardo Lawson 2009, 9.
19. Interview 45, 6/10/13; interview 44, 6/6/13; interview 48, 6/12/13.
20. The only dissatisfaction raised regarding DFID was that it has become increasingly constrained over time, lessening the judgments field staff can make and thus making the work less rewarding (interview 103, 7/30/13; interview 87, 9/20/13). The general impression was that DFID staff's autonomy has been reduced over time, though it is still much higher than that of USAID.
21. Interview 125, 7/31/13.
22. Author interview with Naidoo, 2013.

23. Interview 103, 7/30/13.
24. I only asked this question to those in a position to have been exposed to both organizations.
25. Cernea 1988.
26. Roberts 2014.
27. Natsios 2010.
28. Author interview with Sigrist, 2013. Sigrist was the head of DFID's Civil Service Capacity Building (CISCAB) project in its last phases, and thus is listed as an interviewee in the Liberia capacity-building section of Appendix I's interviewee tables.
29. Interview 7, 6/12/13. The two parts of this quote were not uttered in close temporal proximity to each other, but relate to the same concern and thus are connected via an ellipsis in the text.
30. Interview 21, 6/4/13. While this individual had collaborated with USAID on many occasions, he had never worked for USAID, and as such this quotation on its most natural reading ought not be read as directly comparing the two organizations.
31. While often attributed to George Bernard Shaw, there seems to be little evidence he is the actual source of these words.
32. One set of implications is how contracting to different IDOs changes contractors themselves. Schuller 2012's examination of two nongovernmental organizations (NGOs) operating in Haiti suggests that, for implementing partners, funding source not only affects navigation strategy but also long-term organizational trajectories. Both the Haitian NGOs Schuller follows receive substantial external funding, but from different sources. One NGO relies on external donor contracts, largely those of USAID; the other receives funding from European NGOs. Schuller finds that the NGO that relies on USAID funds sees its autonomy erode, and it is unable to truly incorporate beneficiary perspectives into its work given the need to meet targets and produce externally verifiable deliverables. Schuller links this explicitly to political authorizing environments, arguing that "results-oriented contracting" at USAID exists to "appease jittery Congress members"; this leads to a focus on "easily measurable things that can be explained to the taxpayer" (Schuller 2012, 148). The last quote ("easily measurable . . . ") is an interview quotation rather than Schuller's own words. By the end of the narrative, the USAID-dependent NGO is in clear decline while the other NGO is thriving. Schuller adds, then, evidence consistent with this book's suggestion that there may be long-term organizational learning and agent quality costs to reduced Navigation by Judgment. It also suggests that what is true of IDOs is true of the next stage of the principal-agent delegation chain— IDO relations with contractors.
33. See Grossman and Hart 1986; Hart and Moore 1988; Hart and Moore 1990.
34. While one Economics Nobel Laureate named Oliver seemed enough for this chapter, this could be framed as a "make vs. buy" problem, associated with Oliver Williamson. A key factor in making a make vs. buy choice is the degree to which task performance can be effectively measured. The more difficult the measurement, the greater the advantage of the firm choosing to "make" themselves rather than "buy" via contractors. See, e.g., Williamson 1999; Williamson 1983; Williamson 1981. Brown and Potoski 2005 provide an accessible summary of this strand of transaction cost economics.
35. Bush 2015.
36. Nicolls and Kupperstein 2007, 27.
37. Interview 48, 6/12/13; interview 60, 6/27/13; interview 47, 6/5/13.
38. Interview 52, 6/4/13; interview 47, 6/4/13; interview 41, 6/10/13; interview 64, 6/19/13.
39. Interview 45, 6/10/13; interview 41, 6/10/13.
40. Lawson 2009, 9.
41. While this would change the ability of contractors to use soft information relative to IDO field agents, it would not address the issues between field agents, headquarters, and political authorizers on which this book has mainly focused, however.
42. Dunning, Rose, and Mcgillem 2017, 3. The authors call this "external ownership." This paper interestingly stresses the high degree of commitment from USAID for country ownership. If true—if lower realized ownership persists in USAID projects despite the desire of USAID to have a high degree of ownership—this would further underscore that management practice (i.e., navigation strategy) is interfering with USAID's ability to achieve its desired results.

43. Interview 17, 5/28/13. USAID has recently made a number of changes to its operational guidance that aim to increase country ownership (e.g., USAID 2014a; USAID 2016a). Whether these changes actually alter realized country ownership is an open (empirical) question that will only be evaluable in a few years.
44. OECD 2016, 68.
45. Interview 107, 8/2/13.
46. See, e.g., Brinkerhoff 2000.
47. See, e.g., Eriksson 2001, annex 1 for a summary of statements about putting recipients "in the driver's seat."
48. Cingolani, Thomsson, and de Crombrugghe 2015.
49. Tendler 1997.
50. Fukuyama 2013.
51. Rasul and Rogger 2016.

## *Chapter 9*

1. This basic problem—that we can know much more about some of aid's impacts than others, with a strong bias toward the verifiable—also applies to the "macro" aid effectiveness literature. Our knowledge base is strongest regarding the effect of aid on highly observable outcomes like economic growth and the burden of disease (see, e.g., Clemens et al. 2011 on the aid-on-growth literature and Radelet 2015, chap. 9, for a readable overview of some of aid's clearest successes, including on disease burdens). We know much less about aid's long-term, systematic impact on social development, government effectiveness, etc. While the casual observer might assume that most aid has a link to economic growth, this proves not to be the case. Less than a quarter of foreign aid flows via projects that might plausibly affect economic growth in the short run. (This figure is my analysis of Table S4 of Clemens et al. 2011 in their online appendix, and excludes budget support and debt relief, neither of which would flow through a traditional project.)
2. Cameron, Mishra, and Brown 2016, 1. While randomized control trials are the "gold standard" for creating a comparison group, they are not the only method that allows such a comparison. The International Initiative for Impact Evaluation data includes all experimental, quasi-experimental, and observational studies that have a viable counterfactual.
3. Ibid., 9.
4. This argument echoes a more general external validity concern regarding rigorous impact evaluation in development, which is concerned that variation between contexts may make it difficult to apply findings from one context to another; see, e.g., Pritchett and Sandefur 2015. Woolcock 2013 argues that external validity falls as complexity rises; in this language I would argue that management is almost always a complex element of a project. Thus while we may be able to use rigorous evaluation to evaluate the performance of two different management strategies, evaluation is unlikely to provide a great deal of guidance to specific managers in how to address specific problems.
5. The allusion here is to Beckett's *Waiting for Godot*, in which the main characters, Vladimir and Estragon, wait for Godot, who never arrives. Beckett 1954.
6. OECD Development Assistance Committee 2013. The title itself suggests the aid sector's muddling of measurement as a management tool on the one hand and measurement as a means of rigorously evaluating impact on the other.
7. Ibid., 7.
8. Fifteen of the twenty-eight reported it was "often" a problem, ten "sometimes."
9. OECD Development Assistance Committee 2013, 7.
10. OECD 2016, 83.
11. Birdsall and Savedoff 2011; Gelb and Hashmi 2014. These models go even further than my suggestion of changing evaluation criteria, advocating not just that evaluation but also payments should be tied to outcomes. These payments are usually presumed to go to developing countries that would be responsible for these interventions. The underlying logic parallels that of pay-for-performance for IDO staff, with payments tied to verifiable outcomes.

12. Gelb and Hashmi 2014 suggest that the use of ex-post payments seems to be largely focused on outputs rather than long-term goals. Additionally where outcomes are indeed linked to disbursements, this is often in addition to, rather than a replacement for, output and process measures; see, e.g., Perakis and Savedoff 2015. Perakis and Savedoff helpfully distinguish between four different channels via which results-based aid might achieve better results; Navigation by Judgment has echoes in their recipient discretion channel. They find little evidence this channel is being given substantial attention, with programs instead designed to draw managerial and politicians' attention toward results.

13. DFID 2006, 5; see chapter 6, n. 98.

14. The subtitle of USAID's Evaluation policy is in fact "learning from experience." USAID 2016c.

15. Behn 2003 provides a particularly accessible overview and summary of these issues.

16. In international relations scholarship Grant and Keohane 2005 provide a broad overview of accountability mechanisms. From a public administration standpoint, the suggestion that professional accountability may prove superior to top-down monitoring dates back at least to Carl Friedrich's position in the 1940s in the Friedrich-Finer debates; Jackson 2009 provides an overview of the debate and Mulgan 2000 the connection between the debate and a more contemporary discussion of professional accountability. In more recent scholarship, Brehm and Gates 1999 cast doubt on the ability of supervisors to achieve hierarchical accountability, arguing that recruitment (selection) and professional peer communities are more responsible for the levels of "working, shirking, and sabotage" displayed by public employees than top-down controls.

17. Honig and Weaver 2017.

18. See, e.g., Romm 1998; DeHaven-Smith and Jenne II 2006.

19. As Patil, Veieder, and Tetlock 2014 put it, "It matters whether people think the answer "[to why monitoring occurs]" is 'because we lack confidence in your integrity or competence' or 'because we want to help you achieve objectives we all share'" (83). Moving away from a pure sanctions (reward and punishment) accountability approach is, arguably, likely to move agents away from the former and toward the latter.

20. E.g., DFID 2014; USAID 2014a; USAID 2016a. This paragraph draws on Honig and Gulrajani 2017.

21. The House of Commons International Development Committee suggested as much in its review of DFID's Smart Rules, noting its concern that merely changing the rules would be insufficient, given DFID's culture of rule-following. International Development Committee 2015.

22. This follows from what economists call "career concerns"; see, e.g., Holmstrom 1999; Tirole 1994; Dewatripont, Jewitt, and Tirole 1999.

23. Bain, Booth, and Wild 2016, 40.

24. Changes to IDO organizational practice could be plausibly, and relatively rigorously, studied as well. Such study might benefit both IDOs and the aid industry more broadly. While the number of observations, and the nature of the data, would make research of this kind less rigorous than a formal randomized control trial, candidate pilot sectors (or countries, or projects, as determined by the IDO) could be randomly assigned to pilot (treatment) or status quo management (control) status. A rigorous ex-post examination of outcomes (quantitative and qualitative) could be paired with ethnography and qualitative data collection, were IDOs willing to turn the research lens they often point "out" toward the developing the world on themselves. The World Bank social observatory has already begun to use qualitative ethnographic work to better understand project performance; see, e.g., Ananthpur, Malik, and Rao 2014; Majumdar, Rao, and Sandyal 2017. A long time horizon would allow for all project impacts to be considered, including those unforeseen at the outset. The view that many gains and costs to development projects are unanticipated at a project's beginning has a long history, dating at least to Hirschman 1967's theorizing of the "hiding hand."

25. While discussed in education as well, the United Kingdom's National Health System is where "earned autonomy" has been primarily employed. For discussion of impact see, e.g., Mannion, Goddard, and Bate 2007; Bevan and Hood 2006a; Hoque, Davis, and Humphreys 2004.

26. Ang 2014 argues that "experimental pockets" are critical to IDO organizational change.

27. From bureaucratic politics I have in mind, e.g., Carpenter 2001; Carpenter 2010; from public administration, e.g., Miller and Whitford 2016. Hawkins et al. 2006 certainly notes the need

to animate agents more fully in an IR context; it is not that the idea of doing so is novel, only that this book moves forward this existing agenda.

28. E.g., Huber and McCarty 2004; Huber and Shipan 2006; Huber and Shipan 2002; Carpenter 2001; Calvert, McCubbins, and Weingast 1989; Alesina and Tabellini 2008; Gailmard and Patty 2012; Brehm and Gates 1999; Barnett and Finnemore 2003; Miller and Whitford 2016; Nielson and Tierney 2003; Hawkins et al. 2006.

29. Beginning with agents is a feature of some classic works in bureaucratic politics—e.g., Wilson 1989 and Lipsky 1980—but seems not to have crossed over to international relations and the study of international organizations.

30. Gulrajani 2017, 375. See Yanguas and Hulme 2015 for an overview of this literature as it relates to politics and political economy.

31. Examples of moving beyond blueprints includes adaptive management, doing development differently, problem-driven iterative adaptation, and cash on delivery aid. Pritchett and Woolcock 2004; Andrews 2013; Bain, Booth, and Wild 2016; Faustino and Booth 2014; Israel 1989; Andrews, Pritchett, and Woolcock 2017; Birdsall and Savedoff 2011. For communities of practice see, e.g., the Doing Development Differently community (Doing Development Differently 2014; Bain, Booth, and Wild 2016; Wild, Booth, and Valters 2017; Booth, Harris, and Wild 2016), or Algoso and Hudson 2016 for an overview of such efforts.

32. Existing work with similar concerns include Vähämäki 2015; Gulrajani 2011; Clist 2016; Pritchett and Woolcock 2004; Andrews 2011.

33. This point builds on De Renzio 2016 and Easterly 2002. This is strictly true of bilateral aid donors such as USAID and DFID. For multilaterals such as the World Bank, developing-country aid recipients are in fact shareholders. They have only the faintest voice in these institutions, however, which tend to be dominated by large donor nations. See, e.g., Woods 2006; Fleck and Kilby 2006; Foot, MacFarlane, and Mastanduno 2003.

34. While Moynihan 2008 discusses the use and misuse of quantitative performance measurement, this analysis is still in the context of a government whose "clients" (citizens) can use soft, perceptual information to evaluate performance and perform at the ballot box.

35. Though this is not to suggest there are no general tendencies; that is, that some problems are not more common in public organizations than private. I believe each case needs an independent analysis, however. This broadly fits the thrust in the organizational economics and public administration "publicness" literatures of Rainey and Bozeman 2000; Williamson 1999; Dewatripont, Jewitt, and Tirole 1999; and Dixit 1997.

36. E.g., Ordóñez et al. 2009; Bernstein 2012.

37. E.g., Chandler 1977; Lawrence and Lorsch 1967; Simon 1947; Perrow 1967. This book's focus on the costs and benefits of principal control can also be framed as a tension between standardization and flexibility; as Canales puts it in a broader management context, "Bureaucratic rules both enhance and limit organizational performance." Canales 2013, 2. Canales further explicitly frames soft information gathered by agents as a critical benefit of flexibility.

38. E.g., Weick 1995.

39. As noted in chapters 1 and 5, this public version of the PPD excludes the EC data due to limitations in the data confidentiality agreement that was a condition of EC disclosure.

40. E.g., the PPD has enough observations to allow panel approaches (e.g., changes within country, or country-sector, over time), use of hierarchical models, fixed effects to account for some potential confounds, etc.

41. This variation would be absorbed by the fixed effects used in Part II's empirical models.

42. Collecting these data is far from trivial; the PPD alleviates merely one of the multiple barriers to such research. To be weighed against these difficulties are the potential benefits to both scholars and practitioners of work in this area. There are potentially rich avenues of research to scholars of bureaucratic politics, public administration and management, and organizational behavior in addition to scholars of foreign aid and international organizations. IDOs and the PPD offer the prospect of a relatively unexplored area where one might expect large effect sizes, novel contexts in which to generate theory or explore its boundaries, and substantively significant potential impacts for research findings.

43. As does the historic tension between agent judgment and central control. In his Trust in Numbers, historian Ted Porter provides what he describes as "stories of professions that, in

varying degrees, abandoned their open reliance on expert judgment in the name of public standards and objective rules." Porter notes that this "was never a voluntary process," and that these changes were prompted by a "climate of suspicion" which was "explicitly political." Porter 1995, 89.
44. Aghion et al. 2017.
45. Ibid., abstract.
46. For discussions and examples of these problems see Hasnain, Manning, and Pierskalla 2014; Hood 2006; Bevan and Hood 2006b; Cullen and Reback 2006; Smith 2002; Kerr 1975.
47. Bachman 2016.
48. Taylor 1911, p. 82 of the 2012 reprint from The Floating Press. While "traditional knowledge" is arguably slightly closer to Polanyi's tacit knowledge (Polanyi 1966) or Scott's metis (Scott 1998), traditional knowledge surely draws upon soft information.
49. Taylor 1911, 82.
50. Wilson 1989.
51. Ibid., 168.
52. Compstat is the formal name for the system in *The Wire's* Baltimore (introduced in chapter 4), operating in a number of major American cities and focusing on quantitative analysis of crime data. Gerrish 2016 has a nice description and meta-analysis of the impacts of Compstat and other performance-monitoring systems. For Compstat-specific discussions see, e.g., Behn 2008; Weisburd et al. 2003; Rosenfeld, Fornango, and Baumer 2005; Walsh 2001; Willis, Mastrofski, and Weisburd 2007.
53. *Planet Money* 2015.
54. Ibid.
55. On this last factory floor example, see, e.g., Bernstein 2012.
56. McChrystal et al. 2015.
57. Ibid., 218.
58. Ibid.
59. Both key phrases in this sentence are inspired by others. "Reductive seduction" from Martin 2016; "patina of objectivity" of numbers from Espeland and Sauder 2016.
60. They were named the Corps of Discovery because the land through which the team traveled, the challenges they would face, and the best way forward were unknown.
61. Technically, the very long prerace show; May 6, 2017. The winner was Always Dreaming, perhaps an appropriate name on which to close these notes given the bold, aspirational dreams of ending poverty and inclusive societies that drive so many development practitioners. Fast and Accurate, the horse whose name most evokes Navigation from the Top, finished 17th in a 20-horse field.

## Appendix II

1. The inclusion of time*recipient effects necessitates using five-year periods rather than individual years; at approximately 180 recipients*30 years, this generates nearly 5,000 dummy variables and thus would severely restrict degrees of freedom/analytic leverage, not to mention requiring advanced computing capacity to generate output. The models in Table II.6 do not include project size (though all findings are robust to its inclusion), as missing data on project size leads to significantly smaller samples when it is included and project size is of little substantive significance to the relationship between the key independent variables and project success.
2. This concern is also addressed by Table 6.2 in chapter 6.
3. The CDI is available at http://www.cgdev.org/cdi-2015; QuODA is available at http://www.cgdev.org/publication/quality-official-development-assistance-assessment-report. QuODA from Birdsall and Kharas 2010.
4. This is intuitively similar to a rank-based regression.
5. Credit to Chris Kilby, who as a discussant at NEUDC 2014 first generated this graph (that is, the graph below is generated by me, but is inspired by a similar graph generated by Chris).
6. Double-clustering is achieved via Cameron, Gelbach, and Miller 2006.

7. Note that the Paris Declaration monitoring surveys are, for bilateral donors, at the country level; thus KfW and GIZ share Germany's score. For the other bilateral donors in the sample I have added the IDO name to the country where appropriate.
8. Hallward-Driemeier and Pritchett 2015.
9. The ELF and WGI scales employed come from the Quality of Governance indicators developed by Teorell et al. 2013. The PRRG measure is reverse-coded, so higher numbers are associated with lower levels of rule-based governance. This is for ease of interpretation so that higher numbers indicate more difficult environments, consistent with all other scales used.
10. Andrews 2011; Andrews 2013; Buntaine, Parks, and Buch 2017.

# BIBLIOGRAPHY

Adam Smith International. 2007. *Liberia Civil Service Capacity Building Project (CISCAB) Final Inception Report.*

———. 2009. *Liberia Civil Service Capacity Building Project Progress Report March 2009–October 2009.*

Adams, Gordon, and Richard Sokolsky. 2017. Savaging State and USAID Budgets Could Do Wonders for Results. *Foreign Policy.* March 9, 2017. http://foreignpolicy.com/2017/03/09/savaging-state-and-usaid-budgets-could-do-wonders-for-results-tillerson-development-diplomacy-cuts/

Adler, Paul. 1993. Time-and-Motion Regained. *Harvard Business Review* 71 (1): 97–108.

Aghion, Philippe, Nicholas Bloom, Brian Lucking, Raffaella Sadun, and John Van Reenen. 2017. Turbulence, Firm Decentralization and Growth in Bad Times. Cambridge, MA: National Bureau of Economic Research Working Paper #23354.

Aghion, Philippe, and J. Tirole. 1997. Formal and Real Authority in Organizations. *Journal of Political Economy* 105 (1): 1–29.

Alesina, Alberto, and David Dollar. 2000. Who Gives Foreign Aid to Whom and Why? *Journal of Economic Growth* 5 (1): 33–63.

Alesina, Alberto, and Guido Tabellini. 2008. Bureaucrats or Politicians? Part II: Multiple Policy Tasks. *Journal of Public Economics* 92 (3–4): 426–447.

Algoso, Dave, and Alan Hudson. 2016. Where Have We Got to on Adaptive Learning, Thinking and Working Politically, Doing Development Differently etc.? Getting beyond the People's Front of Judea. In *From Poverty to Power* (blog). Available from http://oxfamblogs.org/fp2p/where-have-we-got-to-on-adaptive-learning-thinking-and-working-politically-doing-development-differently-etc-getting-beyond-the-peoples-front-of-judea/.

Ananthpur, Kripa, Kabir Malik, and Vijayendra Rao. 2014. The Anatomy of Failure: An Ethnography of a Randomized Trial to Deepen Democracy in Rural India. World Bank Policy Research Working Paper 6958.

Anderfuhren-Biget, Simon, Ursula Hafliger, and Simon Hug. 2013. The Values of Staff in International Organizations. In *Routledge Handbook of International Organization*, edited by Bob Reinalda, Chapter 20, 270–283. Abingdon, UK: Routledge.

Andersen, Simon Calmar, and Donald P. Moynihan. 2016. Bureaucratic Investments in Expertise: Evidence from a Randomized Controlled Field Trial. *Journal of Politics* 78 (4): 1032–1044.

Anderson, Mark. 2015. UK Passes Bill to Honour Pledge of 0.7% Foreign Aid Target. *The Guardian*, March 9. London. Available from https://www.theguardian.com/global-development/2015/mar/09/uk-passes-bill-law-aid-target-percentage-income

Anderson, Stephen E., and Shelom Nderithu. 2002. Decentralized Partnerships for School-Based Teacher Development in Mombasa, Kenya. In *Improving Schools through Teacher Development: Case Studies of the Aga Khan Foundation Projects in East Africa*, edited by Stephen E. Anderson, 137–184. Lisse, The Netherlands: Swets & Zeitlinger.

Andrews, Matt. 2011. Which Organizational Attributes Are Amenable to External Reform? An Empirical Study of African Public Financial Management. *International Public Management Journal* 14 (2): 131–156.

———. 2013. *The Limits of Institutional Reform in Development: Changing Rules for Realistic Solutions*. Cambridge, UK: Cambridge University Press.

Andrews, Matt, Lant Pritchett, and Michael Woolcock. 2013. Escaping Capability Traps through Problem Driven Iterative Adaptation (PDIA). *World Development* 51 (2): 234–244.

———. 2017. *Building State Capability*. New York: Oxford University Press.

Ang, Yuen Yuen. 2014. *Making Details Matter: How to Reform Aid Agencies to Generate Contextual Knowledge*. Winning Essay of the 2014 GDN Essay Competition on "The Future of Development Assistance", in partnership with the Gates Foundation. Available online at https://papers.ssrn.com/sol3/papers.cfm?abstract_id=2794434

Asian Development Bank. 2011. *Asian Development Bank Sustainability Report*.

Axelrod, Robert. 1984. *The Evolution of Cooperation*. New York: Basic Books.

Bachman, Rachel. 2016. Want to Cheat Your Fitbit? Try a Puppy or a Power Drill. *Wall Street Journal*. June 9. Available from https://www.wsj.com/articles/want-to-cheat-your-fitbit-try-using-a-puppy-or-a-power-drill-1465487106

Bain, Katherine, David Booth, and Leni Wild. 2016. *Doing Development Differently at the World Bank*. London: Overseas Development Institute.

Baker, George, Robert Gibbons, and Kevin J. Murphy. 1999. Informal Authority in Organizations. *Journal of Law, Economics, & Organization* 15 (1): 56–73.

Barh, Benson, Selam Kebrom, Cecelia Morris, Mbuyi Mutala, and Bruce Grogan. 2011. *Rebuilding Basic Health Services (RBHS): Year 2 Assessment*. USAID.

Barnett, Michael N., and Martha Finnemore. 2003. The Politics, Power, and Pathologies of International Organizations. *International Organization* 53 (4): 699–732.

Barron, Peter, Yogan Pillay, Tanya Doherty, Gayle Sherman, Debra Jackson, Sanjana Bhardwaj, Precious Robinson, and Ameena Goga. 2013. Eliminating Mother-to-Child HIV Transmission in South Africa. *Bulletin of the World Health Organization* 91 (1): 70–4.

Beckett, Samuel. 1954. *Waiting for Godot*. New York: Grove Press.

Behn, Robert. 2003. Why Measure Performance? Different Purposes Require Different Measures. *Public Administration Review* 63 (5): 586–606.

———. 2008. Designing Performancestat: Or What Are the Key Strategic Choices that a Jurisdiction or Agency Must Make When Adapting the CompStat/CitiStat Class of Performance Strategies? *Public Performance & Management Review* 32 (2): 206–235.

Belgian Technical Cooperation. 2008. *Annual Report 2008*.

Belle, N., and E. Ongaro. 2014. NPM, Administrative Reforms and Public Service Motivation: Improving the Dialogue between Research Agendas. *International Review of Administrative Sciences* 80 (2): 382–400.

Bermeo, Sarah Blodgett. 2016. Aid Is Not Oil: Donor Utility, Heterogeneous Aid, and the Aid-Democratization Relationship. *International Organization* 70 (1): 1–32.

Bernstein, E. S. 2012. The Transparency Paradox: A Role for Privacy in Organizational Learning and Operational Control. *Administrative Science Quarterly* 57 (2): 181–216.

Bertelli, Anthony M. 2006. Motivation Crowding and the Federal Civil Servant: Evidence from the U.S. Internal Revenue Service. *International Public Management Journal* 9 (1): 3–23.

Bertelli, Anthony M., and David E. Lewis. 2013. Policy Influence, Agency-Specific Expertise, and Exit in the Federal Service. *Journal of Public Administration Research and Theory* 23 (2): 223–245.

Bevan, Gwyn, and Christopher Hood. 2006a. Have Targets Improved Performance in the English NHS? *BMJ: British Medical Journal* 332: 419–422.

———. 2006b. What's Measured Is What Matters: Targets and Gaming in the English Public Health Care System. *Public Administration* 84 (3): 517–538.

Biddle, Stephen D. 2004. *Military Power*. Princeton, NJ: Princeton University Press.

Birdsall, Nancy, Homi J. Kharas, Ayah Mahgoub, and Rita Perakis. 2010. *Quality of Official Development Assistance Assessment*.Washington, DC: Center for Global Development.

Birdsall, Nancy, William D. Savedoff, Ayah Mahgoub, and Katherine Vyborny. 2012. *Cash on Delivery: A New Approach to Foreign Aid*. Washington, DC: Center for Global Development Books.

Blegen, M. A. 1993. Nurses' Job Satisfaction: A Meta-Analysis of Related Variables. *Nursing Research* 42 (1): 36–41.

Booth, David. 2012. Aid Effectiveness: Bringing Country Ownership (and Politics) Back In. *Conflict, Security & Development* 12 (5): 537–558.

Booth, David, Daniel Harris, and Leni Wild. 2016. *From Political Economy Analysis to Doing Development Differently: A Learning Experience*. London: ODI.

Bozeman, B., and G. Kingsley. 1998. Risk Culture in Public and Private Organizations. *Public Administration Review* 58 (2): 109–118.

BRDG. 2008. *BRDG Liberia Yearbook*. Self-published yearbook of USAID's BRDG project.

Brehm, John O., and Scott Gates. 1999. *Working, Shirking, and Sabotage: Bureaucratic Response to a Democratic Public*. Ann Arbor, MI: University of Michigan Press.

Brennan, Richard J., Deirdre Rogers, Shiril Sarcar, and Petra Vergeer. 2010. Identifying Indicators for Performance-Based Contracting (PBC) is Key: The Case of Liberia. World Bank.

Brinkerhoff, Derick W. 2000. Assessing Political Will for Anti-Corruption Efforts: An Analytic Framework. *Public Administration and Development* 20 (3): 239–252.

Brown, Trevor L., and Matthew Potoski. 2003. Managing Contract Performance: A Transaction Costs Approach. *Journal of Policy Analysis and Management* 22 (2): 275–297.

———. 2005. Transaction Costs and Contracting: The Practitioner Perspective. *Public Performance & Management Review* 28 (3): 326–351.

Buntaine, Mark T. 2016. *Giving Aid Effectively*. Oxford, UK: Oxford University Press.

Buntaine, Mark T., Bradley C. Parks, and Benjamin P. Buch. 2017. Aiming at the Wrong Targets: The Domestic Consequences of International Efforts to Build Institutions. *International Studies Quarterly*: 1–60.

Bush, Sarah Sunn. 2015. *The Taming of Democracy Assistance: Why Democracy Promotion Does Not Confront Dictators*. Cambridge, UK: Cambridge University Press.

Busuioc, E. Madalina, and Martin Lodge. 2015. The Reputational Basis of Public Accountability. *Governance* 29 (2): 247–263.

Calvert, R., M. McCubbins, and B. Weingast. 1989. A Theory of Political Control and Agency Discretion. *American Journal of Political Science* 33 (3): 588–611.

Cameron, A. C., J. Gelbach, and D. L. Miller. 2006. Robust Inference with Multi-Way Clustering. NBER Technical Working Paper #327. Cambridge, MA: National Bureau of Economic Research.

Cameron, Charles M., John M. De Figueiredo, and David E. Lewis. 2015. Quitting in Protest: A Theory of Presidential Policy Making and Agency Response. Working paper. Available from https://scholarship.law.duke.edu/cgi/viewcontent.cgi?article=6353&context=faculty_scholarship.

Cameron, Drew B., Anjini Mishra, and Annette N. Brown. 2016. The Growth of Impact Evaluation for International Development: How Much Have We Learned? *Journal of Development Effectiveness* 8 (1): 1–21.

Canales, Rodrigo. 2013. Weaving Straw into Gold: Managing Organizational Tensions between Standardization and Flexibility in Microfinance. *Organization Science* 25 (1): 1–28.

Carpenter, Daniel P. 2001. *The Forging of Bureaucratic Autonomy: Reputations, Networks, and Policy Innovation in Executive Agencies, 1862–1928*. Princeton, NJ: Princeton University Press.

———. 2010. *Reputation and Power: Organizational Image and Pharmaceutical Regulation at the FDA*. Princeton, NJ: Princeton University Press.

Celasun, Oya, and Jan Walliser. 2008. Predictability of Aid: Do Fickle Donors Undermine Aid Effectiveness? *Economic Policy* 23 (55): 545–594.

Center for Systemic Peace. 2014. State Fragility Index. Data set produced by Center for Systemic Peace, Vienna, VA, USA. Available from http://www.systemicpeace.org/inscrdata.html.

Cernea, Michael M. 1988. *Nongovernmental Organizations and Local Development*. World Bank Discussion Papers.

Challoner, Kathryn R., and Nicolas Forget. 2011. Effect of Civil War on Medical Education in Liberia. *International Journal of Emergency Medicine* 4 (6). doi:10.1186/1865-1380-4-6.

Chandler, Alfred D. 1977. *The Visible Hand: The Managerial Revolution in American Business*. Cambridge, MA: Belknap Press.

Chandy, Laurence, Brina Seidel, and Christine Zhang. 2016. *Aid Effectiveness in Fragile States How Bad Is It and How Can It Improve?* Brooke Shearer Series 5, Brookings Institution.

Chauvet, L., P. Collier, and M. Duponchel. 2010. What Explains Aid Project Success In Post-Conflict Situations? World Bank Policy Research Working Paper 5418.

Christensen, Tom, and Per Laegreid, eds. 2011. *The Ashgate Research Companion to New Public Management*. Burlington, VT: Ashgate.

Cingolani, Luciana, Kaj Thomsson, and Denis de Crombrugghe. 2015. Minding Weber More Than Ever? The Impacts of State Capacity and Bureaucratic Autonomy on Development Goals. *World Development* 72: 191–207.

Clemens, Michael, Steven Radelet, Rikhil Bhavnani, and Samuel Bazzi. 2011. Counting Chickens When They Hatch: Timing and the Effects of Aid on Growth. *Economic Journal* 122: 590–617.

Clist, Paul. 2016. Payment by Results in Development Aid: All That Glitters Is Not Gold. *World Bank Research Observer* 31 (2): 290–319.

Corder, Mike. 2012,. "Ex-Liberian President Charles Taylor sentended to 50 years in Prison." *The Globe and Mail (Canada)*. May 30. Available from https://web.archive.org/web/20120530103119/http://www.theglobeandmail.com/news/world/ex-liberian-president-charles-taylor-sentenced-to-50-years-in-prison/article2447255/

Creative Associates. 2004. *Grants Management and Technical Assistance (GMTA) Draft Final Report*. Prepared for USAID/SA/SO 1 under contract # 674-C-00-97-00091-00. Accessible via USAID's Development Experience Clearinghouse (DEC): http://pdf.usaid.gov/pdf_docs/pdacd117.pdf

Cruz, Cesi, and Christina J. Schneider. 2017. Foreign Aid and Undeserved Credit Claiming. *American Journal of Political Science* 61 (2): 396–408.

Cullen, Julie Berry, and Randall Reback. 2006. *Tinkering towards Accolades: School Gaming under a Performance Accountability System*. NBER Working Paper 12286. Cambridge, MA: National Bureau of Economic Research.

Dal Bo, E. 2006. Regulatory Capture: A Review. *Oxford Review of Economic Policy* 22 (2): 203–225.

Das, Jishnu, Clement Joubert, and Sander Florian Tordoir. 2017. Compensation, Diversity and Inclusion at the World Bank Group. World Bank Policy Research Working Paper 8058. Washington, DC: World Bank.

Deaton, Angus. 2013. *The Great Escape: Health, Wealth, and the Origins of Inequality*. Princeton, NJ: Princeton University Press.

Deci, E. L. 1971. Effects of Externally Mediated Rewards on Intrinsic Motivation. *Journal of Personality and Social Psychology* 18: 105–115.

DeHaven-Smith, Lance, and Kenneth C. Jenne II. 2006. Management by Inquiry: A Discursive Accountability System for Large Organizations. *Public Administration Review* 66 (1): 64–76.

De Mesquita, Bruce Bueno, and Alastair Smith. 2009. A Political Economy of Aid. *International Organization* 63 (2): 309.

Denizer, Cevdet, Daniel Kaufmann, and Aart Kraay. 2013. Good Countries or Good Projects? Macro and Micro Correlates of World Bank Project Performance. *Journal of Development Economics* 105: 288–302.

Derbyshire, Helen, and Elbereth Donovan. 2016. *Adaptive Programming in Practice: Shared Lessons from the DFID-Funded LASER and SAVI Programmes*. SAVI. Available from http://savi-nigeria.org/wp-content/uploads/2016/08/Laser_Savi_Report-online-version-final-120816pdf.pdf

De Renzio, Paolo. 2016. *Accountability Dilemmas in Foreign Aid*. Overseas Development Institute Working Paper. Available from https://www.odi.org/sites/odi.org.uk/files/resource-documents/10805.pdf

Desai, Raj, and Homi Kharas. 2010. *The Determinants of Aid Volatility*. Working Paper 42, Brookings Institution. Available from https://www.brookings.edu/wp-content/uploads/2016/06/09_aid_volatility.pdf

Development Alternatives Inc., and USAID. 2006. *BRDG—Liberia Grants Administration and Procurement Guide Handbook*. Available from https://www.dropbox.com/s/t1f3727l79uhz0i/BRDG%20Procurement%20Guide%20and%20Grants%20Manual%202006.pdf?dl=0

Dewatripont, Mathias, Ian Jewitt, and Jean Tirole. 1999. The Economics of Career Concerns, Part II: Application to Missions and Accountability of Government Agencies. *Review of Economic Studies* 66 (1): 199–217.

———. 2000. Multitask Agency Problems: Focus and Task Clustering. *European Economic Review* 44 (4–6): 869–877.

De Weijer, Frauke. 2012. Rethinking Approaches to Managing Change in Fragile States. Center for International Development Working Paper #58. Cambridge, MA: Harvard Kennedy School. Available from https://bsc.cid.harvard.edu/files/bsc/files/58_de_weijer_fragile_states.pdf

DFID. 2003. *CMTP Programme Memorandum*.

———. 2004. *Monitoring and Evaluation Framework for CMTP, October 2004*.

———. 2005. *CMTP Annual Review, November 2005*.

———. 2006. *CISCAB Project Memorandum and Framework, June 2006*.

———. 2007a. *OFM Project Logical Framework*.

———. 2007b. *CMTP Annual Review, March 2007*.

———. 2008. *HIV & AIDS MSP Annual Review—Aide-memoire*.

———. 2009a. *CMTP Project Completion Report*.

———. 2009b. *MSP Project Completion Report*.

———. 2009c. *OFM Annual Review 2009*.

———. 2010a. *OFM Project Completion Report*.

———. 2010b. *Working Effectively in Conflict-affected and Fragile Situations (Briefing Paper H: Risk Management)*.

———. 2013. *DFID Risk Management Guidance*, issued October 30, 2013.

———. 2014. *Smart Rules: Better Programme Delivery*.

Dietrich, Simone. 2013. Bypass or Engage? Explaining Donor Delivery Tactics in Foreign Aid Allocation. *International Studies Quarterly* 57: 698–712.

———. 2016. Donor Political Economies and the Pursuit of Aid Effectiveness. *International Organization* 70 (01): 65–102.

Dixit, Avinash. 1997. Power of Incentives in Private versus Public Organizations. *American Economic Review* 87 (2): 378–382.

Dixit, Avinash. 2002. Incentives and Organizations in the Public Sector: An Interpretative Review. *Journal of Human Resources* 37 (4): 696–727.

Dixit, Avinash, Gene M. Grossman, and Elhanan Helpman. 1997. Common Agency and Coordination: General Theory and Application to Government Policy Making. *Journal of Political Economy* 105 (4): 752–769.

Doing Development Differently. 2014. The Doing Development Differently Manifesto. *Statement of the October 2014 DDD Workshop*. Available from http://buildingstatecapability.com/the-ddd-manifesto/. Accessed April 18, 2015.

Dreher, Axel, Peter Nunnenkamp, and Maya Schmaljohann. 2015. The Allocation of German Aid: Self-Interest and Government Ideology. *Economics & Politics* 27 (1): 160–184.

Dunning, Casey, Sarah Rose, and Claire McGillem. 2017. Implementing Ownership at USAID and MCC: A US Agency-Level Perspective. CGD Policy Paper 99. Washington, DC: Center for Global Development. http://www.cgdev.org/publication/implementing-ownership-USAID-MCC

Dunleavy, P., and C. Hood. 1994. From Old Public Administration to New Public Management. *Public Money & Management* 14 (3): 9–16.

Easterly, William. 2002. The Cartel of Good Intentions: The Problem of Bureaucracy in Foreign Aid. *Journal of Policy Reform* 5 (4): 223–250.

———. 2006. *The White Man's Burden: Why the West's Efforts to Aid the Rest Have Done So Much Ill and So Little Good.* New York: Penguin Books.

Ekbladh, David. 2010. *The Great American Mission: Modernization and the Construction of an American World Order.* Princeton, NJ: Princeton University Press.

Elgot, Jessica, and Peter Walker. 2017. Foreign Aid 0.7% Pledge Will Remain, Says May. *The Guardian.* London.

Eriksson, John. 2001. *The Drive to Partnership: Aid Coordination and the World Bank.* World Bank Publications.

Espeland, Wendy, and Michael Sauder. 2016. *Engines of Anxiety: Academic Rankings, Reputation, and Accountability.* Russell Sage Foundation.

Eyben, Rosalind. 2010. Hiding Relations: The Irony of "Effective Aid." *European Journal of Development Research* 22 (3): 382–397.

Faustino, Jaime, and David Booth. 2014. Development Entrepreneurship: How Donors and Leaders Can Foster Institutional Change. Case Study #2, Working Politically in Practice Series. Asia Foundation and Overseas Development Institute: San Francisco, CA and London, UK.

Faye, Michael, and Paul Niehaus. 2012. Political Aid Cycles. *American Economic Review* 102 (7): 3516–3530.

Fleck, Robert K., and Christopher Kilby. 2006. World Bank Independence: A Model and Statistical Analysis of US Influence. *Review of Development Economics* 10 (2): 224–240.

Foot, Rosemary, S. Neil MacFarlane, and Michael Mastanduno. 2003. *US Hegemony and International Organizations: The United States and Multilateral Institutions.* Oxford University Press.

Foucault, M. 1978. *Discipline and Punish: The Birth of the Prison.* Penguin.

Frey, Bruno. 1994. How Intrinsic Motivation Is Crowded Out and In. *Rationality and Society* 6 (3): 334–352.

Frey, Bruno, and R. Jegen. 1999. Motivation Crowding Theory: A Survey of Empirical Evidence. *Journal of Economic Surveys* 15 (5): 589–611.

Fuchs, Andreas, Axel Dreher, and Peter Nunnenkamp. 2014. Determinants of Donor Generosity: A Survey of the Aid Budget Literature. *World Development* 56: 172–199.

Fukuyama, Francis. 2013. What Is Governance? *Governance* 26 (3): 347–368.

Gailmard, Sean, and John W. Patty. 2007. Slackers and Zealots: Civil Service, Policy Discretion, and Bureaucratic Expertise. *American Journal of Political Science* 51 (4): 873–889.

———. 2012. *Learning While Governing: Expertise and Accountability in the Executive Branch.* Chicago, IL: University of Chicago Press.

Garicano, Luis, and Luis Rayo. 2016. Why Organizations Fail: Models and Cases. *Journal of Economic Literature* 54 (1): 137–192.

Gelb, Alan, and Nabil Hashmi. 2014. The Anatomy of Program-for-Results: An Approach to Results-Based Aid. Working Paper.

Gerrish, Ed. 2016. The Impact of Performance Management on Performance in Public Organizations: A Meta-Analysis. *Public Administration Review* 76 (1): 48–66.

Ghani, Ashraf, Clare Lockhart, and M. Carnahan. 2005. *Closing the Sovereignty Gap: An Approach to State-Building.* London: Overseas Development Institute.

Giauque, David, Simon Anderfuhren-Biget, and Frédéric Varone. 2016. Stress and Turnover Intents in International Organizations: Social Support and Work-Life Balance as Resources. *International Journal of Human Resource Management*: 1–23.

Gibbons, Robert, and Rebecca Henderson. 2012. *What Do Managers Do? Exploring Persistent Performance Differences among Seemingly Similar Enterprises.* Harvard Business School.

Gibson, Clark, Krister Andersson, Elinor Ostrom, and Sujai Shivakumar. 2005. *The Samaritan's Dilemma: The Political Economy of Development Aid*. Oxford University Press.

Gigerenzer, Gerd. 2015. *Simply Rational*. Oxford University Press.

Gilardi, Fabrizio. 2002. Policy Credibility and Delegation to Independent Regulatory Agencies: A Comparative Empirical Analysis. *Journal of European Public Policy* 9 (6): 873–893.

Girod, Desha M., and Jennifer L. Tobin. 2016. Take the Money and Run: The Determinants of Compliance with Aid Agreements. *International Organization* 70 (1): 209–239.

GiveWell. Failure in International Aid. *Published on GiveWell*. http://www.givewell.org/ international/technical/criteria/impact/failure-stories#Harmful_aid_projects.

Gneezy, Uri, Stephan Meier, and P. Rey-Biel. 2011. When and Why Incentives (Don't) Work to Modify Behavior. *Journal of Economic Perspectives* 25 (4): 191–209.

Gneezy, Uri, and Aldo Rustichini. 2000. A Fine Is a Price. *Journal of Legal Studies* 29 (1): 1–17.

Goga, A. E., T. H. Dinh, and D. H. Jackson. 2010. *Evaluation of the Effectiveness of the National Prevention of Mother-to-Child Transmission (PMTCT) Programme Measured at Six Weeks Postpartum in South Africa*. South African Medical Research Council, National Departmetn of Health of South Africa and PEPFAR/US Centers for Disease Control and Prevention.

Goodhart, Charles. 1981. Problems of Monetary Management: The U.K. Experience. In *Inflation, Depression, and Economic Policy in the West*, edited by Anthoy Courkis, 111–144. Totowa, NJ: Barnes & Noble.

Gordon, Grant. 2016. Monitoring Conflict to Reduce Violence: Evidence from a Satellite Intervention in Darfur.

Gordon, J. E. 1968. *The New Science of Strong Materials: Or Why You Don't Fall through the Floor*. Penguin.

Government of Liberia. 2008. *Small Government, Better Service: Civil Service Reform Strategy*. Monrovia.

Government of the United Kingdom. 2002. *International Development Act 2002*.

———. 2006. *International Development (Reporting and Transparency) Act 2006*.

———. 2014. *International Development (Gender Equality) Act 2014*.

———. 2015. International Development (Official Development Assistance Target) Act 2015.

Graber, Mark L. 2013. The Incidence of Diagnostic Error in Medicine. *BMJ Quality & Safety* 22 (supp. 2): ii21–ii27.

Grant, Adam. 2013. *Give and Take: Why Helping Others Drives Our Success*. New York: Penguin.

Grant, Adam, and Justin Berg. 2010. Prosocial Motivation at Work: How Making a Difference Makes a Difference. In *Handbook of Positive Organizational Scholarship*, edited by K. Cameron and G. Spreitzer. Oxford University Press.

Grant, Robert M. 1996. Toward a Knowledge-Based Theory of the Firm. *Strategic Management Journal* 17 (S2): 109–122.

Grant, Ruth W., and Robert O. Keohane. 2005. Accountability and Abuses of Power in World Politics. *American Political Science Review* 99 (1): 29–43.

Green, Duncan. 2016. What Is Adaptive Aid? Useful Lessons from Six Case Studies. *OXFAM From Poverty to Power Blog*. Available from http://oxfamblogs.org/fp2p/what-is-adaptive-aid-useful-lessons-from-six-case-studies/.

Greene, Graham. 1936. *Journey without Maps*. Garden City, NY: Doubleday.

Griffiths, Simon, Samy Ahmar, John Seager, Leickness Simbayi, and Ntombizodwa Mbelle. 2014. *Mid-Term Evaluation of the SARRAH Programme*.

Groopman, Jerome. 2007. *How Doctors Think*. Houghton Mifflin.

Grossman, Sanford J., and Oliver D. Hart. 1986. The Costs and Benefits of Ownership: A Theory of Vertical and Lateral Integration. *Journal of Political Economy* 94 (4): 691.

Guerrero, Saul, Sophie Woodhead, and Marieke Hounjet. 2013. *On the Right Track? A Brief Review of Monitoring and Evaluation in the Humanitarian Sector*.

Gulrajani, Nilima. 2011. Transcending the Great Foreign Aid Debate: Managerialism, Radicalism and the Search for Aid Effectiveness. *Third World Quarterly* 32 (2): 199–216.

————. 2017. Bilateral Donors and the Age of the National Interest: What Prospects for Challenge by Development Agencies? *World Development* 96: 375–389.

Hackman, J. Richard, and Greg R. Oldham. 1980. *Work Redesign.* Addison-Wesley.

Hafliger, Ursula, and Simon Hug. 2015. *International Organizations, Their Empolyees and Volunteers, and Their Values.*

Hallward-driemeier, Mary, and Lant Pritchett. 2015. How Business Is Done in the Developing World: Deals versus Rules. *Journal of Economic Perspectives* 29 (3): 121–140.

Hannay, M., and M. Northam. 2000. Low-Cost Strategies for Employee Retention. *Compensation & Benefits Review* 32 (4): 65–72.

Harari, Michael B., David E. L. Herst, Heather R. Parola, and Bruce P. Carmona. 2017. Organizational Correlates of Public Service Motivation: A Meta-analysis of Two Decades of Empirical Research. *Journal of Public Administration Research and Theory* 27 (1): 68–84.

Harris, Bryant, Robbie Gramer, and Emily Tamkin. 2017. The End of Foreign Aid as We Know It. *Foreign Policy.* April 24. Available from http://foreignpolicy.com/2017/04/24/u-s-agency-for-international-development-foreign-aid-state-department-trump-slash-foreign-funding/

Hart, Oliver, and John Moore. 1988. Incomplete Contracts and Renegotiation. *Econometrica: Journal of the Econometric Society* 56 (4): 755–785.

————. 1990. Property Rights and the Nature of the Firm. *Journal of Political Economy* 98 (6): 1119–1158.

Hasnain, Z., N. Manning, and J. H. Pierskalla. 2014. The Promise of Performance Pay? Reasons for Caution in Policy Prescriptions in the Core Civil Service. *World Bank Research Observer* 29 (2): 235–264.

Hawes, Clarissa. 2016. "US DOT Wants Electronic Devices to Stop Trucks From Speeding." *Trucks.Com,* August 26. https://www.trucks.com/2016/08/26/transportation-department-speed-limiter-rule/

Hawkins, Darren G., and Wade Jacoby. 2006. How Agents Matter. In *Delegation and Agency in International Organizations,* edited by Darren G. Hawkins, David A. Lake, Daniel L. Nielson, and Michael J. Tierney, 199–228. Cambridge, UK: Cambridge University Press.

Hawkins, Darren G., David A. Lake, Daniel L. Nielson, and Michael J. Tierney. 2006a. *Delegation and Agency in International Organizations.* Cambridge University Press.

————. 2006b. Delegation under Anarchy: States, International Organizations, and Principal-Agent Theory. In *Delegation and Agency in International Organizations,* edited by Darren G. Hawkins, David A. Lake, Daniel L. Nielson, and Michael J. Tierney, 3–38.

Hirschman, Albert O. 1967. *Development Projects Observed.* Washington, DC: Brookings Institution.

Hoey, Lesli. 2015. 'Show Me the Numbers': Examining the Dynamics between Evaluation and Government Performance in Developing Countries. *World Development* 70: 1–12.

Hogarth, Robin M., Tomás Lejarraga, and Emre Soyer. 2015. The Two Settings of Kind and Wicked Learning Environments. *Current Directions in Psychological Science* 24 (5): 379–385.

Holmstrom, Bengt. 1979. Moral Hazard and Observability. *Bell Journal of Economics* 10 (1): 74–91.

————. 1999. Managerial Incentive Problems: A Dynamic Perspective. *Review of Economic Studies* 66 (1): 169–182.

Holmstrom, B., and P. Milgrom. 1991. Multitask Principal-Agent Analyses: Incentive Contracts, Asset Ownership, and Job Design. *Journal of Law, Economics, & Organization* 7: 24.

Honig, Dan, and Nilima Gulrajani. 2017. Making Good on Donors' Desire to Do Development Differently. *Third World Quarterly:* 1–17. doi:10.1080/01436597.2017.1369030.

Honig, Dan, and Catherine Weaver. 2017. A Race to the Top?: The Aid Transparency Index and the Normative Power of Global Performance Assessments. Unpublished working paper. Available from http://danhonig.info/sites/default/files/HonigWeaver_FINAL_22May2017.pdf

Hood, Christopher. 2004. The Middle Aging of New Public Management: Into the Age of Paradox? *Journal of Public Administration Research and Theory* 14 (3): 267–282.

———. 2006. Gaming in Targetworld: The Targets Approach to Managing British Public Services. *Public Administration Review* 66 (4): 515–521.

Hood, Christopher, and Ruth Dixon. 2015. What We Have to Show for 30 Years of New Public Management: Higher Costs, More Complaints. *Governance* 28 (3): 265–267.

Hoque, Kim, Simon Davis, and Michael Humphreys. 2004. Freedom to Do What You Are Told: Senior Management Team Autonomy in an NHS Acute Trust. *Public Administration* 82 (2): 355–375.

Huber, John D., and Nolan McCarty. 2004. Bureaucratic Capacity, Delegation, and Political Reform. *American Political Science Review* 98 (3): 481–494.

Huber, John D., and Charles R. Shipan. 2002. *Deliberate Discretion: The Institutional Foundations of Bureaucratic Autonomy.* Cambridge, UK: Cambridge University Press.

———. 2006. Politics, Delegation, and Bureaucracy. In *The Oxford Handbook of Political Economy,* edited by Robert E. Goodin, 256–272. Oxford University Press.

Hughes, Jacob, Amanda Glassman, and Walter Gwenigale. 2012. *Innovative Financing in Early Recovery: The Liberia Health Sector Pool Fund.* Center for Global Development Working Paper 288. Center for Global Development Working Paper 288. Washington, DC.

Independent Commission for Aid Impact (UK). 2014. *How DFID Learns (Report #34).*

Institute of Development Studies. 2014. Conflict and Fragility. Available from http://www.ids.ac.uk/idsresearch/conflict-and-fragility.

International Development Committee. 2015. *Department for International Development's Performance in 2013–2014: The Departmental Annual Report 2013–14.* HC 750: Thirteenth Report of Session 2014–15.

International Fund for Agricultural Development. 2009. *A Voluntary Separation Programme for IFAD 2009–2010 (Document #GC 32/L. 8).*

International Monetary Fund. 2003. *External Debt Statistics: Guide for Compilers and Users.*

———. 2013. *Liberia: Second Review under the Extended Credit Facility Arrangement and Request for Waiver of Nonobservance of Performance Criteria and Modification of a Performance Criterion. IMF Country Report #13/365.*

———. 2015. *Annual Report 2015 Statement on Diversity and Inclusion.*

Israel, Arturo. 1989. *Institutional Development: Incentives to Performance.* Baltimore, MD: Johns Hopkins University Press.

Jackson, Michael. 2009. Responsibility versus Accountability in the Friedrich-Finer Debate. *Journal of Management History* 15 (1): 66–77.

Jensen, Michael C., and William H. Meckling. 1990. Specific and General Knowledge, and Organizational Structure. In *Contract Economics,* edited by Lars Werin and Hans Wijkander, 251–274. Oxford: Blackwell.

John Snow International, Johns Hopkins University Center for Communication Programs, and Management Sciences for Health. 2010. *Rebuilding Basic Health Services Project Description.*

Johnson, Tana. 2016. Cooperation, Co-optation, Competition, Conflict: International Bureaucracies and Non-Governmental Organizations in an Interdependent World. *Review of International Political Economy* 23 (5): 737–767.

Kaiser Family Foundation. 2014. *The U.S. President's Emergency Plan for AIDS Relief Fact Sheet.*

Katz, Ingrid T., Ingrid V. Bassett, and Alexi A. Wright. 2013. PEPFAR in Transition—Implications for HIV Care in South Africa. *New England Journal of Medicine* 369 (15): 1385–1387.

Kay, Katty. 2014. Ebola Outbreak: Liberia "Close to Collapse." London: BBC World News.

Kerr, S. 1975. On the Folly of Rewarding A, While Hoping for B. *Academy of Management Journal* 18 (4): 769–783.

KfW Group. 2015. *KfW Sustainability Report 2015.*

King, Neil, Jr. 2015. Hillary Clinton Is Not the Only Critic of "Quarterly Capitalism." *Wall Street Journal.* Available from https://blogs.wsj.com/washwire/2015/07/31/hillary-clinton-joins-al-gore-prince-charles-and-etsy-in-criticizing-quarterly-capitalism/

Kuziemko, Ilyana, and Eric Werker. 2006. How Much Is a Seat on the Security Council Worth? Foreign Aid and Bribery at the United Nations. *Journal of Political Economy* 114 (5): 905–930.

Laffont, J. J., and Jean Tirole. 1991. Provision of Quality and Power of Incentive Schemes in Regulated Industries. In *Equilibrium Theory and Applications: Proceedings of the Sixth International Symposium in Economic Theory and Econometrics,* edited by W. Barnett, B. Cornet, C. D'Aspremont, J. J. Gabszewicz, and A. Mas-Colell, 161–196. Cambridge, UK: Cambridge University Press.

Lammers, Joris, Janka I. Stoker, Floor Rink, and Adam D. Galinsky. 2016. To Have Control over or to be Free from Others? The Desire for Power Reflects a Need for Autonomy. *Personality and Social Psychology Bulletin* 42 (4): 498–512.

Langworth, Richard M., ed. 2008. *Churchill by Himself: The Definitive Collection of Quotations.* New York: PublicAffairs.

Lawrence, Paul R., and Jay William Lorsch. 1967. *Organization and Environment: Managing Differentiation and Integration.* Harvard Business School Press.

Lawson, Marian Leonardo. 2009. *USAID's Office of Transition Initiatives after 15 Years: Issues for Congress.* Congressional Research Service.

Lepper, Mark R., David Greene, and Richard E. Nisbett. 1973. Undermining Children's Intrinsic Interest with Extrinsic Reward: A Test of the "Overjustification" Hypothesis. *Journal of Personality and Social Psychology* 28 (1): 129–137.

Leuffen, Dirk, S. Shikano, and S. Walter. 2013. Measurement and Data Aggregation in Small-n Social Scientific Research. *European Political Science* 12 (1): 40–51.

Levine, M. E., and J. L. Forrence. 1990. Regulatory Capture, Public Interest, and the Public Agenda: Toward a Synthesis. *Journal of Law, Economics, & Organization* 6: 167–198.

Levy, Brian. 2014. *Working with the Grain.* Oxford, UK: Oxford University Press.

Liberia Institute of Statistics and Geo-Information Services (LISGIS). 2008. *2008 National Population and Housing Census: Preliminary Results.*

Liebman, Jeffrey, and Alina Sellman. 2013. Social Impact Bonds: A Guide for State and Local Governments. Cambridge, MA: Harvard Kennedy School Social Impact Bond Technical Assistance Lab.

Lindblom, Charles E. 1959. The Science of "Muddling Through." *Public Administration Review* 19 (2): 79–88.

Linkd. 2009. *Review of Consolidation of Municipal Transformation Programme (CMTP).* Further identifying information redacted; provided by DFID pursuant to Freedom of Information Act request F2016-407. Disclosure 1.

Lipsky, Michael. 1980. *Street-Level Bureaucracy: Dilemmas of the Individual in Public Services.* Russell Sage Foundation.

Lopes, H., S. Lagoa, and T. Calapez. 2014. Work Autonomy, Work Pressure, and Job Satisfaction: An Analysis of European Union Countries. *Economic and Labour Relations Review* 25 (2): 306–326.

Lorenz, Chris. 2012. If You're So Smart, Why Are You under Surveillance? Universities, Neoliberalism, and New Public Management. *Critical Inquiry* 38 (3): 599–629.

Lynn, Laurence E., Jr. 1998. The New Public Management: How to Transform a Theme into a Legacy. *Public Administration Review* 58 (3): 231–237.

Majumdar, Shruti, Vijayendra Rao, and Paromita Sanyal. 2017. On the Frontlines of Scaling-Up: A Qualitative Analysis of Implementation Challenges in a CDD Project in Rural India. World Bank Policy Research Working Paper 8039.

Mannion, Russell, Maria Goddard, and Angela Bate. 2007. Aligning Incentives and Motivations in Health Care: The Case of Earned Autonomy. *Financial Accountability & Management* 23 (4): 401–420.

Mansbridge, Jane. 2014. A Contingency Theory of Accountability. In *The Oxford Handbook of Public Accountability,* edited by Mark Bovens, Robert E. Goodin, and Thomas Schillemans, 55–68. Oxford University Press.

March, James G., and Herbert Alexander Simon. 1958. *Organizations.* New York: Wiley.

Martin, Courtney. 2016. The Reductive Seduction of Other People's Problems. *Medium.com.*

Martinez, Jason. 2013. Two MLB General Managers Who Need Big Trade-Deadline Deals to Save Their Jobs. *Bleacher Report*, June 15.

Mays, Kelsey. 2016. The 2016 Cars.com American-Made Index. *Cars.Com*.

McChrystal, Stanley, Tantum Collins, David Silverman, and Chris Fussell. 2015. *Team of Teams*. New York: Penguin.

McGregor, Douglas. 1960. *The Human Side of Enterprise*. McGraw-Hill.

Melumad, Nahum, Dilip Mookherjee, and Stefan Reichelstein. 1992. A Theory of Responsibility Centers. *Journal of Accounting and Economics* 15 (4): 445–484.

Meyer, J. W., and Brian Rowan. 1977. Institutionalized Organizations: Formal Structure as Myth and Ceremony. *American Journal of Sociology* 83 (2): 340–363.

Millennium Challenge Corporation. n.d. The MCC Effect. Available from https://www.mcc.gov/news-and-events/feature/mcc-effect. Accessed December 5, 2017.

Miller, Gary J., and Andrew B. Whitford. 2016. *Above Politics: Bureaucratic Discretion and Credible Commitment*. Cambridge, UK: Cambridge University Press.

Mitchell, T. R., B. C. Holtom, T. W. Lee, and T. Graske. 2001. How to Keep Your Best Employees : Developing an Effective Retention Policy. *Academy of Management Executive* 15 (4): 96–109.

Modell, S. 2004. Performance Measurement Myths in the Public Sector: A Research Note. *Financial Accountability & Management* 20 (1): 39–56.

Moe, Terry M. 1989. The Politics of Bureaucratic Structure. In *Can the Government Govern?*, edited by John E. Chubb and Paul E. Peterson, 267–329. Washington, DC: Brookings Institution.

Mortimer, Jeylan T., and Jon Lorence. 1989. Satisfaction and Involvement: Disentangling a Deceptively Simple Relationship. *Social Psychology Quarterly* 52 (4): 249–265.

Moynihan, Donald P. 2008. *The Dynamics of Performance Management: Constructing Information and Reform*. Georgetown University Press.

Moynihan, Donald P., and Sanjay K. Pandey. 2007. The Role of Organizations in Fostering Public Service Motivation. *Public Administration Review* 67 (1): 40–53.

Mulgan, Richard. 2000. Accountability: An Ever-Expanding Concept? *Public Administration* 78 (3): 555–573.

Natsios, Andrew. 2010. The Clash of the Counter-bureaucracy and Development. *Center for Global Development Essay* (July).

Nguyen, A. N., Jim Taylor, and Steve Bradley. 2003. Job Autonomy and Job Satisfaction: New Evidence. *Lancaster University Management School, Working paper, 50*.

Nicolls, Martina, and Susan Kupperstein. 2007. *Final Evaluation: Building Recovery and Reform through Democratic Governance*.

Nielson, Daniel L., and Michael J. Tierney. 2003. Delegation to International Organizations: Agency Theory and World Bank Environmental Reform. *International Organization* 57 (2): 241–276.

Niskanen, William A. 1968. The Peculiar Economics of Bureaucracy. *American Economic Review* 58 (2): 293–305.

———. 1974. *Bureaucracy and Representative Government*. Transaction Publishers.

NZAid and Barbara Williams. 2012. NZAid Information Act Response to Ms. Joanna Spratt, June 5, 2012.

OECD. 1991. *The DAC Principles for the Evaluation of Development Assistance*.

———. 2000. DAC Criteria for Evaluating Development Assistance Factsheet: 2.

———. 2012. *Aid Effectiveness 2011: Progress in Implementing the Paris Declaration*. OECD Publishing.

———. 2014. *Development Assistance and Approaches to Risk in Fragile and Conflict Affected States*.

———. 2015. *Geographical Distribution of Financial Flows to Developing Countries 2015*.

———. 2016. *OECD Development Co-operation Peer Reviews: United States 2016*. Paris: OECD Publishing.

———. 2017. Net ODA (indicator). Available from https://data.oecd.org/oda/net-oda.htm. Accessed May 13, 2017.

OECD Development Assistance Committee. 2013. *Managing and Measuring for Results: Survey Highlights*. Paris: OECD.

Oliver, C. 1991. Strategic Responses to Institutional Processes. *Academy of Management Review* 16 (1): 145–179.

Olken, Benjamin A. 2007. Monitoring Corruption: Evidence from a Field Experiment in Indonesia. *Journal of Political Economy* 115 (2): 200–249.

Ordóñez, L. D., M. E. Schweitzer, A. D. Galinsky, and M. H. Bazerman. 2009. Goals Gone Wild: The Systematic Side Effects of Overprescribing Goal Setting. *Academy of Management Perspectives* 23 (1): 6–16.

Ostrom, Elinor, Clark Gibson, and Sujai Shivakumar. 2002. *Aid, Incentives, and Sustainability: An Institutional Analysis of Development Cooperation*. SIDA Studies in Evaluation.

The Paris Declaration on Aid Effectiveness. 2005. Available from http://www.oecd.org/dac/effectiveness/34428351.pdf

Patil, Sheftali V., Ferdinand Vieidier, and Philip E. Tetlock. 2014. Process versus Outcome Accountability. In *The Oxford Handbook of Public Accountability*, edited by Mark Bovens, Robert E. Goodin, and Thomas Schillemans, 69–89.

PEPFAR. 2004. *The President's Emergency Plan for AIDS Relief: U.S. Five Year Global HIV/AIDS Strategy*.

———. 2008a. *2008 Country Profile: South Africa*.

———. 2008b. Celebrating Life: Latest PEPFAR Results.

Perakis, Rita, and William Savedoff. 2015. Does Results-Based Aid Change Anything? Pecuniary Interests, Attention, Accountability and Discretion in Four Case Studies. *CGD Policy Paper 52*.

Perrow, Charles. 1967. A Framework for the Comparative Analysis of Organizations. *American Sociological Review* 32 (2): 194–208.

Perry, James L., and Lois R. Wise. 1990. Bases of The Motivational Public Service. *Public Administration Review* 50 (3): 367–373.

Pfeffer, Jeffrey, and Gerald R. Salancik. 1978. *The External Control of Organizations: A Resource Dependence Perspective*. Stanford, CA: Stanford University Press.

Pigni, Alessandra. 2016. *The Idealist's Survival Kit: 75 Simple Ways to Prevent Burnout*. Parallax Press.

Pilling, David. 2017. Liberia Is Outsourcing Education. Can It Work? *Financial Times*.

Pink, Daniel H. 2011. *Drive: The Surprising Truth about What Motivates Us*. Penguin Group US.

*Planet Money*. 2015. The Future of Work Looks Like a UPS Truck (Episode 563). National Public Radio.

Polanyi, Michael. 1966. *The Tacit Dimension*. Chicago, IL: University of Chicago Press.

Polgreen, Lydia. 2006. A Master Plan Drawn in Blood. *New York Times*.

Pollack, Kenneth M. 2002. *Arabs at War*. Lincoln: University of Nebraska Press.

Porter, Theodore. 1995. *Trust in Numbers*. Princeton, NJ: Princeton University Press.

Prendergast, C. 1999. The Provision of Incentives in Firms. *Journal of Economic Literature* 37 (1): 7–63.

———. 2001. *Selection and Oversight in the Public Sector, with the Los Angeles Police Department as an Example*. No. w8664. National Bureau of Economic Research.

———. 2007. The Motivation and Bias of Bureaucrats. *American Economic Review* 97 (1): 180–196.

Pritchett, Lant. 2013. *The Rebirth of Education: Schooling Ain't Learning*. Washington, DC: Center for Global Development.

Pritchett, Lant, and Justin Sandefur. 2015. Learning from Experiments When Context Matters. *American Economic Review* 105 (5): 471–475.

Pritchett, Lant, and Michael Woolcock. 2004. Solutions When the Solution Is the Problem: Arraying the Disarray in Development. *World Development* 32 (2): 191–212.

Radelet, Steven. 2007. Reviving Economic Growth in Liberia. Center for Global Development Working Paper Number 133.

———. 2015. *The Great Surge*. Simon & Schuster.

Radin, Anna K., Andrew A. Abutu, Margaret A. Okwero, Michelle R. Adler, Chukwuma Anyaike, Hilda T. Asiimwe, Prosper Behumbiize, et al. 2017. Confronting Challenges in Monitoring and Evaluation: Innovation in the Context of the Global Plan towards the Elimination of New HIV Infections among Children by 2015 and Keeping Their Mothers Alive. *Journal of Acquired Immune Deficiency Syndrome* 75 (1): 66–75.

Rainey, Hal G., and Barry Bozeman. 2000. Comparing Public and Private Organizations: Empirical Research and the Power of the A Priori. *Journal of Public Administration Research & Theory* 10 (2): 447–469.

Ramalingam, Ben. 2013. *Aid on the Edge of Chaos: Rethinking International Cooperation in a Complex World*. Oxford University Press.

Rasul, Imran, and Daniel Rogger. 2016. Management of Bureaucrats and Public Service Delivery: Evidence from the Nigerian Civil Service. *Economic Journal.*

Rasul, Imran, Daniel Rogger, and Martin J. Williams. 2017. Management and Bureaucratic Effectiveness: A Scientific Replication. Working Paper.

Republic of South Africa National Department of Health. 2011. *The National Integrated Prevention of Mother-To-Child Transmission (PMTCT) of HIV AcceleratedPlan.*

Roberts, Susan M. 2014. Development Capital: USAID and the Rise of Development Contractors. *Annals of the Association of American Geographers* 104 (5): 1030–1051.

Robinson, Linda, Paul D. Miller, John Gordon IV, Jeffrey Decker, Michael Schwille, and Raphael S. Cohen. 2014. *Improving Strategic Competence: Lessons from 13 Years of War*. Santa Monica, CA: RAND Corporation.

Romm, Norma R. A. 1998. Interdisciplinary Practice as Reflexivity. *Systemic Practice and Action Research* 11 (1): 63–77.

Romzek, Barbara S., and J. Stephen Hendricks. 1982. Organizational Involvement and Representative Bureaucracy: Can We Have It Both Ways? *American Political Science Review* 76 (1): 75–82.

Rose, Sarah. 2017. Should the Trump Administration Cut USAID to Expand MCC? Center for Global Development (blog post). Available from https://www.cgdev.org/blog/should-trump-administration-cut-usaid-expand-mcc.

Rosenfeld, Richard, Robert Fornango, and Eric Baumer. 2005. Did Ceasefire, Compstat, and Exile Reduce Homicide? *Criminology & Public Policy* 4 (3): 419–450.

Roser, Max. 2017. The Short History of Global Living Conditions and Why It Matters That We Know It. *Published online at OurWorldInData.org*. https://ourworldindata.org/a-history-of-global-living-conditions-in-5-charts/.

Ross, Terrance F. 2014. Is It Ever Okay to Make Teachers Read Scripted Lessons? *The Atlantic.*

RTI and LGSP. 2006. "LGSP Overview." http://lgsp.org.za/AboutUs/aboutUs.html, accessed March 17, 2015.

Rumsfeld, Donald. 2002. DoD News Briefing, February 2, 2002 11:30 AM EDT. Transcript via US Department of Defense, http://archive.defense.gov/Transcripts/Transcript.aspx?TranscriptID=2636

Russell, James A. 2011. *Innovation, Transformation, and War: Counterinsurgency Operations in Anbar and Ninewa Provinces, Iraq, 2005–2007*. Stanford, CA: Stanford University Press.

Ryan, R., and E. Deci. 2000. Self-Determination Theory and the Facilitation of Intrinsic Motivation. *American Psychologist* 55 (1): 68–78.

Samuel, M. O., and Crispen Chipunza. 2009. Employee Retention and Turnover: Using Motivational Variables as a Panacea. *African Journal of Business Management* 3 (8): 410–415.

Schuller, Mark. 2012. *Killing with Kindness*. Rutgers University Press.

Scott, James C. 1998. *Seeing Like a State: How Certain Schemes to Improve the Human Condition Have Failed*. Yale University Press.

Shavell, Steven. 1979. Risk sharing and Incentives in the Principal and Agent Relationship. *Bell Journal of Economics* 10 (1): 55–73.

Shook, John. 2010. How to Change a Culture: Lessons from NUMMI. *MIT Sloan Management Review* 51 (2): 63–68.

Simon, H. 1947. *Administrative Behavior: A Study of Decision-Making Processes in Administrative Organizations*. New York: Macmillan.

Singh, Hardeep, Ashley N. D. Meyer, and Eric J. Thomas. 2014. The Frequency of Diagnostic Errors in Outpatient Care: Estimations from Three Large Observational Studies Involving US adult populations. *BMJ Quality & Safety* 23: 727–731.

Singh, J. V. 1986. Peformance, Slack, and Risk Taking in Organizational Decision Making. *Academy of management Journal* 29 (3): 562–585.

Sirleaf, Ellen Johnson. 2009. Annual Message to the Fourth Session of the 52nd National Legislature of the Republic of Liberia.

Smalley, Megan. 2017. "Fleet-efficient Options". *Lawn and Landscape*. Available from http://www.lawnandlandscape.com/article/fleet-efficient-options/

Smith, Michael J. 2002. Gaming Nonfinancial Performance Measures. *Journal of Management Accounting Research* 14 (1): 119–133.

Snook, Steve. 1999. An Agency under Siege: USAID and Its Mission in Tanzania. In *Agencies in Foreign Aid*, edited by Goran Hyden and Rwekaza Mukandala, 68–115. New York: St. Martin's Press.

Sparks, Dinah, and Nat Malkus. 2015. *Public School Teacher Autonomy in the Classroom across School Years 2003–4, 2007–8, and 2011–12.*

Spector, P. E. 1986. Perceived Control by Employees: A Meta-Analysis of Studies Concerning Autonomy and Participation at Work. *Human Relations* 39 (11): 1005–1016.

Statistics South Africa. 2012. *Census 2011.*

Stein, J. C. 2002. Information Production and Capital Allocation: Decentralized versus Hierarchical Firms. *Journal of Finance* 57 (5): 1891–1921.

Stimson, Henry L. 1945. Memorandum on the Effects of Atomic Bomb.

Tarnoff, Curt. 2015. U.S. Agency for International Development (USAID): Background, Operations, and Issues. *CRS Report (Congressional Research Service).*

Taylor, Frederick. 1911. *The Principles of Scientific Management.* Harper & Brothers.

Tendler, Judith. 1975. *Inside Foreign Aid.* Baltimore, MD: Johns Hopkins University Press.

———. 1997. *Good Government in the Tropics.* Baltimore, MD: Johns Hopkins University Press.

Tendler, Judith, and Sara Freedheim. 1994. Trust in a Rent-seeking World: Health and Government Transformed in Northeast Brazil. *World Development* 22 (12): 1771–1791.

Teorell, Jan, Stefan Dahlberg, Soren Holmberg, Bo Rothstein, Anna Khomenko, and Richard Svensson. 2013. The Quality of Government Standard Dataset, version Dec13. University of Gothenburg: The Quality of Government Institute.

*This American Life.* 2010. Transcript 403: NUMMI.

Thompson, James D. 1967. *Organizations in Action: Social Science Bases of Administrative Theory.* Transaction Publishers.

Tingley, Dustin. 2010. Donors and Domestic Politics: Political Influences on Foreign Aid Effort. *Quarterly Review of Economics and Finance* 50 (1): 40–49.

Tiny Spark. 2017. An Idealist's Guide to Avoiding Burnout: Podcast Episode of March 17, 2017.

Tirole, Jean. 1994. The Internal Organization of Government. *Oxford Economic Papers* 46 (1): 1–29.

Ton, Zeynep. 2014. *The Good Jobs Strategy: How the Smartest Companies Invest in Employees to Lower Costs and Boost Profits.* New Harvest Houghton Mifflin Harcourt.

Tony Blair Africa Governance Initiative. 2011. *Annual Report.*

Ucko, David H. 2009. *The New Counterinsurgency Era: Transforming the U.S. Military for Modern Wars.* Washington, DC: Georgetown University Press.

UK Civil Service. 2016. *Civil Service People Survey: 2016 Results.*

UN General Assembly. 2015. Transforming Our World: The 2030 Agenda for Sustainable Development (Resolution A/Res/70/1, adopted 25 September 2015).

UN International Civil Service Commission. 2008. *Results of the Global Staff Survey on Recruitment and Retention.*

UNAIDS. 2013. *The Gap Report.*

UNICEF. 2012. *Options B and B+: Key Considerations for Countries to Implement an Equity-Focused Approach.*

US Congress Committee on International Relations, and US Congress Committee on Foreign Relations. 2003. *Legislation on Foreign Relations through 2002.*

US Department of State Office of Foreign Assistance Resources. 2016. Standard Foreign Assistance Master Indicator List (MIL). Available from http://www.state.gov/documents/organization/260455.xlsx. Accessed May 2, 2017.

US Government. 1993. *Government Performance and Results Act of 1993.*

US Office of Personnel Management. 2016. *Federal Employee Viewpoint Survey (FEVS).*

USAID. 2004. USAID Contract # 674-C-00-05-00001-00.

———. 2008. *Award Letter for USAID Cooperative Agreement No. 669-A-00-09-00001-00, November 5, 2008.*

———. 2011. *ADS Chapter 317: Procurement under Fixed Amount Reimbursement Activities.*

———. 2013. *Mid-Term Evaluation of the USAID/Liberia Health Sector Fixed Amount Reimbursement Agreement (FARA).*

———. 2014a. *Local Systems: A Framework for Supporting Sustained Development.*

———. 2014b. *Public Financial Management Risk Assessment Framework (PFMRAF) Manual: A Mandatory Reference for ADS Chapter 220.*

———. 2016a. ADS Chapter 201 Program Cycle Operational Policy. (Revised October 12, 2016).

———. 2016b. USAID Evaluation and Monitoring Terms Derived from Automated Directives System (ADS) Series 201.

———. 2016c. *Evaluation: Learning from Experience.*

———. 2017. USAID and US Department of State Performance Report. Available from *http://foreignassistance.gov/assets/Agency/Performance%20Report-%20USAID%20&%20DOS.csv.*

USAID and JSI. 2009. *Liberia Rebuilding Basic Health Services (RBHS).* Annual Report 5 November 2008–30 September 2009.

USAID Office of Inspector General. 2016. *Competing Priorities Have Complicated USAID/Pakistan's Efforts To Achieve Long-Term Development under EPPA.* Audit Report #G-391-16-003-P.

Vähämäki, Janet. 2015. The Results Agenda in Swedish Development Cooperation: Cycles of Failure or Reform Success? In *The Politics of Evidence and Results in International Development,* edited by Rosalind Eyben, Irene Guijt, Chris Roche, and Kathy Shutt, 135–154. Practical Action Publishing.

Verhoest, Koen, and Jan Wynen. 2016. Why Do Autonomous Public Agencies Use Performance Management Techniques? Revisiting the Role of Basic Organizational Characteristics. *International Public Management Journal:* 1–31.

Vigneau, E., and E. M. Qannari. 2003. Clustering of Variables around Latent Components. *Communications in Statistics—Simulation and Computation* 32 (14): 1131–1150.

Walsh, William F. 2001. Compstat: An Analysis of an Emerging Police Managerial Paradigm. *Policing: An International Journal of Police Strategies & Management* 24 (3): 347–362.

Weibel, Antoinette, Katja Rost, and Margit Osterloh. 2009. Pay for Performance in the Public Sector— Benefits and (Hidden) Costs. *Journal of Public Administration Research & Theory* 20 (2): 387–412.

Weick, Karl. 1995. *Sensemaking in Organizations.* Sage.

Weisburd, David, Stephen D. Mastrofski, Ann Marie Mcnally, Rosann Greenspan, and James J. Willis. 2003. Reforming to Preserve: Compstat and Strategic Problem Solving in American Policing. *Crimonology & Public Policy* 2 (3): 421–456.

Wild, Leni, David Booth, and Craig Valters. 2017. *Putting Theory into Practice: How DFID Is Doing Development Differently.*

Williamson, Oliver E. 1981. The Economics of Organization: The Transaction Cost Approach. *American Journal of Sociology* 87 (3): 548–577.

———. 1983. *Markets and Hierarchies.* Free Press.

———. 1999. Public and Private Bureaucracies: A Transaction Cost Economics Perspectives. *Journal of Law, Economics, and Organization* 15 (1): 306–342.

Willis, James J., Stephen D. Mastrofski, and David Weisburd. 2007. Making Sense of COMPSTAT: A Theory-Based Analysis of Organizational Change in Three Police Departments. *Law & Society Review* 41 (1): 147–188.

Wilson, James Q. 1989. *Bureaucracy: What Government Agencies Do and Why They Do It.* Basic Books.

Wood, Abby K., and David E. Lewis. 2017. Agency Performance Challenges and Agency Politicization. *Journal of Public Administration Research and Theory* 27 (4): 581–595.

Woods, Ngaire. 2007. *The Globalizers: The IMF, the World Bank, and Their Borrowers.* Cornell University Press.

Woolcock, Michael. 2013. Using Case Studies to Explore the External Validity of "Complex" Development Interventions. *Evaluation* 19 (3): 229–248.

World Bank. 2006. *Engaging with Fragile States: An IEG Review of World Bank Support to Low-income Countries under Stress.* World Bank Publications.

———. 2013. *Country Partnership Strategy for the Republic of South Africa 2014–2017.*

———. 2016. *2016 World Bank Global Reporting Initiative Index.*

———. 2017. World Bank Projects & Operations Database.

Wright, Joseph, and Matthew Winters. 2010. The Politics of Effective Foreign Aid. *Annual Review of Political Science* 13 (1): 61–80.

Wrzesniewski, A., B. Schwartz, X. Cong, M. Kane, A. Omar, and T. Kolditz. 2014. Multiple Types of Motives Don't Multiply the Motivation of West Point Cadets. *Proceedings of the National Academy of Sciences* 111 (30): 10990–10995.

Yanguas, Pablo, and David Hulme. 2015. Barriers to Political Analysis in Aid Bureaucracies: From Principle to Practice in DFID and the World Bank. *World Development* 74: 209–219.

# INDEX

Page numbers in italics indicate tables and figures.